Making Sense

A Student's Guide to Research and Writing

Making Sense

Religious Studies

MARGOT NORTHEY
BRADFORD A. ANDERSON
JOEL N. LOHR

OXFORD
UNIVERSITY PRESS

OXFORD
UNIVERSITY PRESS

Oxford University Press is a department of the University of Oxford.
It furthers the University's objective of excellence in research, scholarship, and education by
publishing worldwide. Oxford is a registered trade mark of Oxford University Press in the UK
and in certain other countries.

Published in Canada by
Oxford University Press
8 Sampson Mews, Suite 204,
Don Mills, Ontario M3C 0H5 Canada

www.oupcanada.com

Copyright © Oxford University Press Canada 2012

The moral rights of the author have been asserted

Database right Oxford University Press (maker)

First Edition published 2012

Library and Archives Canada Cataloguing in Publication

Northey, Margot, 1940–
Making sense : a student's guide to research and writing :
religious studies / Margot Northey, Bradford A. Anderson and Joel N. Lohr.

Includes bibliographical references and index.
ISBN 978-0-19-543952-6

1. Religion—Research. 2. Report writing. 3. English language—Rhetoric.
I. Anderson, Bradford A. II. Lohr, Joel N. III. Title.

BL41.N67 2011   808'.0662   C2011-902434-9

Front cover images: Hands: ©iStockphoto.com/VikramRaghuvanshi;
Statue: ©iStockphoto.com/pasmatic-t2; Praying: ©iStockphoto.com/mammuth;
Cathedral: Buena Vista Images/Getty Images
Back cover image: Dome of Imam Mosque: javarman/Veer Images

Oxford University Press is committed to our environment. The pages of this book have been printed
on Forest Stewardship Council ® certified paper.

Printed and bound in Canada.

3 4 — 15 14 13 12

CONTENTS

ACKNOWLEDGEMENTS

As with any writing endeavour, this book bears the influence of many people who are unacknowledged in its pages.

Special thanks are due to Dr. Andrew Davies, who encouraged an early version of this project and was very supportive throughout its subsequent development. Several people gave us much-needed guidance on this project in its various stages. Among these we would like to thank Dr. Craig Allert, Professor Brian Bocking, Professor Tony Cummins, Professor Douglas Davies, Professor Irving Hexham, and Professor Joel Kaminsky. We would also like to thank the anonymous reviewers for their valuable feedback.

We are grateful to Tamara Capar, Suzanne Clark, Mark Thompson, and Dana Hopkins of Oxford University Press, who offered valuable editorial guidance and encouragement along the way.

Finally, this project developed out of our own teaching and learning experiences, and we would like to thank the students who have allowed us to test out many of our ideas on them over the past several years. You will find traces of your influence in these pages as well.

A NOTE TO THE STUDENT

Religion in its various forms is one of the most enduring features of humanity. Not surprisingly, it has become a popular and crucial field of critical enquiry. This is particularly the case in higher education, where religious studies is flourishing. This book is meant to serve as a practical guide for those who find themselves joining this conversation.

This volume retains the core elements that mark the *Making Sense* series: clear, concise, and readable guidelines that will help you do well in all aspects of your studies. Practical guides for students of religious studies are hard to find, and until recently one of the only books available was Nancy Vyhmeister's *Quality Research Papers for Students of Religion and Theology*. In 2008, another guide was published titled, *A Guide to Writing Academic Essays in Religious Studies*, by Scott Brown. Both of these volumes have strengths particular to their respective topics, and you may wish to consult them as you progress in your studies; as will become apparent, we are indebted to them in certain respects. However, it was clear to us that more was needed to address a broader range of topics related to your education in general, and religious studies in particular.

Our book is different, therefore, in that our aim is to offer guidance on how you can succeed in *all* aspects of your *religious studies* education. As such, we've included a variety of topics that we feel are important dimensions of your education, including learning time management, studying for and taking examinations, giving oral presentations, processing feedback from your courses, and, of course, researching and writing various types of essays. We've also focused on several areas that are vital to religious studies in particular: using religious and sacred texts, doing comparative research, and learning foreign languages, to name a few. Our hope is that this guide will help you in both the big-picture aspects of higher education, as well as the subject-specific issues related to religious studies.

This book need not be read front to back, as it was purposely designed so that you can consult the chapter you need, when you need it. However, we do recommend that you read the first three chapters before anything else, as these introduce religious studies and higher education more generally. Further, because we build upon it later in the book, we recommend reading Chapter 5, on general essay writing, before reading those that follow.

A recurring marginal icon will alert you to passages that discuss ways you can use technology to enhance your work.

A NOTE TO THE INSTRUCTOR

Depending on the needs of your course, you may find it useful to assign students to read the chapters in this book in sequence, or you may wish to assign the chapters in an order of your own choosing. As we mentioned in our Note to the Student, the first three chapters are designed to introduce religious studies and higher education in a general way, so you may find that these chapters are most beneficial to students near the beginning of the course. Also, throughout this book you will find various sample documents such as grading rubrics and essay proposal forms (see, for example, pages 52 and 60). Should you wish to use these or adapt them for your classroom, they can be downloaded in Word document or PDF format from the OUP website (www.oupcanada.com/NortheyReligion). Finally, we value your suggestions to make future editions of this book stronger. Please send these to **makingsense .religion@gmail.com.**

CHAPTER 1

Introduction to Higher Education and Religious Studies

Objectives

- Understanding post-secondary education
- Comprehending research in the humanities
- Getting to know religious studies

POST-SECONDARY EDUCATION

Going to university or college can be an amazing and sometimes challenging experience. In many ways, higher education has become a rite of passage in our culture, a step into adulthood and a move toward independence. Your time here will bring about enduring friendships, vocational training for the future, and a host of other life-changing experiences. These are all worthwhile and important dimensions of your university years. However, we believe that one of the most significant aspects of your time at university (and one that is perhaps undervalued in our current culture) is the way in which your thinking will be shaped and challenged. This is one of the most noticeable differences between high school and post-secondary education; thus, we will begin our exploration by looking at critical thinking at the post-secondary level. In Chapter 2, we will look at how you can make the most of your university experience.

To begin, let's do some "thinking about thinking."[1] It is useful to recognize that "thinking" happens in a variety of ways. For example, there are lower-level thinking skills, such as knowledge and comprehension, which simply involve remembering and understanding information. This is the kind of thinking that is often expected in high school education. There are also higher levels of thinking that entail *making use* of the information you have acquired. These thinking processes include analysis, synthesis, evaluation, and application. Here our thinking requires more from us, as we are asked to interact with the information we have obtained. You will need to engage these "critical" thinking skills in your post-secondary studies. *Critical thinking* is a term widely used at the university level to mean persistent, analytical, "thoughtful" thinking about issues; it doesn't mean just criticizing or dismissing ideas.

These two different modes of thinking have been helpfully described as "having" versus "being" modes of study:

> The "having" mode of study is evident whenever we see study as something permanent to "have." All we need to discover is how to "have" and own it. Our view of degree study is that whoever designed the course has set aside a fixed amount of knowledge and once we have this knowledge we are awarded a qualification. . . . To a certain extent, we all want to hold on to knowledge as statements and information. The trouble with this is that new ideas can be particularly threatening. If we see our lecture notes as fixed statements or information to be memorized, the last thing we want to happen is that someone comes along to change them. A further difficulty in the having mode is that ideas which cannot easily be written down as statements can be rather frightening because they are out of our control.[2]

This stands in contrast to the "being" mode of study:

> In the being mode, what we hear stimulates our own thought processes, giving rise to new ideas and change. We are active participants in learning because we are trying to understand concepts and issues, rather than to possess knowledge. . . . If we are only collecting information, it is unlikely that our thought processes are working to build a better understanding of the material to hand. We are not asking ourselves questions. In the being mode, our concern is rather different from this. We are trying to penetrate statements and information to raise issues, analyze and test assumptions for ourselves. We are trying to dwell in ideas and understand them.[3]

This is not to suggest that the "having" mode of learning is not important in higher education; we all need to remember information for exams and find ways of organizing our thought processes so that we can write effective essays. But what happens when exams call for more than merely remembering information? What if you are asked to interact with material and analyze or evaluate it? This calls for an entirely different set of skills, what we like to call *engaged learning*. When using these skills, you are doing more than simply recalling information. You are engaging with it. For many people this seems daunting, and you may feel that you have never learned this way in the past. However, we want to make clear that engaged learning is not something you need to fear. In fact, that is this book's aim: to assist you as you begin your academic journey by helping you learn how to tackle various challenges in higher education. For example, one area where you can be an engaged learner is in doing *research*.

WHAT IS RESEARCH?

One way that post-secondary education will encourage you to be an engaged learner is through research. What exactly is research? At its most basic level, research is the collecting, organizing, and presenting of data. In the sciences, research often follows the scientific method, where experiments are undertaken, results collected, and conclusions drawn. In religious studies, and the humanities more generally, research may appear more conceptual or abstract, as it often includes interpreting texts, investigating historical developments, or examining the history of ideas within an established tradition. For example, in religious studies you may be asked to *research* the historical development of Hinduism, *analyze* the practices of an established community, *make sense of* a particular Jewish scriptural text, *interpret* a religious concept in film or literature, or *examine* a contemporary religious conflict.

All of these require research on your part, whether it's through the collection of historical data; first-hand observation of, or interaction with, a group of people; the study of a language or written text; or reflection on the relationship between culture and religion. As you can imagine, answers to questions like these will not appear out of thin air; this type of research requires an active and engaged mind and an openness to learning. This includes, among other things, a willingness to approach these various topics as objectively as possible, an awareness of your presuppositions, and a good dose of intellectual curiosity. These characteristics have an obvious relationship to your experience as an engaged learner. When you investigate a problem, interact with material, and come to a conclusion on your own, you are more likely to remember, assimilate, and apply that information at a later time than if you are simply given the conclusion up front. So the mindset with which you approach your studies in general, and your research in particular, will go a long way toward determining how engaged your learning experience is. (We will explore some of the more practical aspects of research, such as finding and using sources, in the chapters that follow.)

At this point, we will examine how engaged learning relates to the field of religious studies.

GETTING TO KNOW RELIGIOUS STUDIES

The shape and scope of religious studies differ everywhere the discipline is taught. However, there are three important aspects of religious studies that, if understood, will aid your transition into the subject area:

1. the importance and pervasiveness of religion in everyday life;
2. the diverse nature of religious studies; and
3. the issue of religious presuppositions.

The importance and pervasiveness of religion

Religion affects all of our lives in significant ways, regardless of our religious views. Consider the following examples:

- the influence of the "religious right" on North American politics;
- the banning of headscarves and other symbols of Muslim religious expression in some European countries;
- debates over gay marriage;
- immigration policies in the European Union; and
- ongoing peace talks in the Middle East.

In one way or another, these are all related to religion. But religion goes much deeper. It affects more than just these larger, at times external, issues; it saturates the fabric of everyday life in our world— from the way economies function, to the way justice is understood and administered, to the very days of the week that most people work. And these facets of life are often linked to the religious worldviews of the people who founded our countries. Is it hard to believe that women could not vote in Quebec until 1940 or that African-Americans did not have equal rights in the US until as late as the mid-1960s? Does it matter that much of the debate surrounding these issues is related to religious viewpoints? It may also surprise you that the governing structure of most countries is based on particular religious views, whether the system is democratic, monarchical, communist, or theocratic. Even in democratic countries where the separation of religion and politics is a vital tenet, many people vote based upon deeply held religious views and a candidate's congruence with them.

But this is not the place to survey religion, or even to define it. Many excellent textbooks do just that, and you will undoubtedly engage with this issue in your journey into religious studies. We simply encourage you to look at the world around you and observe how pervasive religion is. To engage with religious studies is to recognize both how religion has shaped the world in the past as well as how it continues to influence the world in which we now live. In this respect alone, religious studies is as important as any subject being taught in colleges and universities today.

The diverse nature of religious studies

Perhaps you are only taking one course in religion, or maybe you are a religious studies major. Perhaps you are only really interested in one topic related to a specific religion, such as religious ethics, Sharia Law, or archaeology and the ancient Near East. You might wonder how and why these issues are related. Let's start by answering the seemingly simple question: What do we mean by the term "religious studies"?

DIVERSITY IN CONTENT AND APPROACHES

The field of religious studies is vast, and when we say "religious studies," it can mean a lot of things to different people. Broadly speaking, religious studies is an academic field that falls into the humanities (sometimes called the arts) and social sciences. Many people think of religious studies as the study of contemporary, mainstream religions—that upon finishing a degree in religious studies they will have learned a lot of facts about religions like Hinduism, Islam, Judaism, and Christianity. While partly true, this definition is too limited. Of course, all subjects within this field relate to religion in one way or another, but courses in religious studies can also cover a broad and seemingly disparate range of topics, from nature spirituality, to the psychology of belief, to film and religion. Religious studies can also cover so-called dead religions, those that no longer have adherents; by no means, therefore, are topics limited only to those religions that have practising members today. Your religious studies education will likely include forays into history, literature, linguistics, philosophy, psychology, art, sociology, and other disciplines. This is why a professor in your religious studies department might be an expert in Egyptian hieroglyphs or Hittite inscriptions while another might be an expert in Pacific Christianity or Buddhism, religious art and icons, or even death rituals and funerary rites. Others might teach in more than one department, perhaps philosophy, classics, anthropology, art, or even English. Thus, probably more than any other subject taught at colleges and universities, religious studies is a diverse and interdisciplinary enterprise. By "interdisciplinary," we mean that it draws from a wide variety of academic fields and subject areas to investigate the many and varied aspects of religion.

Approaches and Methods in Religious Studies

There are numerous approaches to the academic study of religion in religious studies departments today. Some of these approaches overlap with one another, and some may be considered subsections within broader fields of study. Below are some of the approaches you may encounter. Companion volumes on religious studies are a good place to start if you are interested in more detail on any of these subjects. See, for instance, Robert A. Segal (ed.), *The Blackwell Companion to the Study of Religion* (Oxford: Blackwell, 2006).

- *Comparative studies*: the analysis of similarities and differences, most often in relation to two or more religious traditions, practices, or ideas
- *Cultural and media studies*: the impact and intersection of religion and culture in general, or more specifically religion and particular types of media (such as literature, film, or television)
- *Environmental studies*: the relationship between the environment, ecology, and ethics and religion and religious traditions
- *Ethnic studies*: the investigation of religion and religious traditions from the vantage point of specific races or ethnicities
- *Ethnography*: the study of particular peoples or communities in relation to their religious beliefs and practices based on fieldwork; common in anthropology
- *Gender and sexuality studies*: the exploration of religion and particular religious traditions from the perspective of gender and sexuality; investigates how gender and sexuality are shaped by religion, as well as how religion in turn shapes these dimensions of life; examples include feminist studies, women's studies, and queer theory
- *Historical studies*: the study of events, people, and processes that have shaped particular ideas and traditions
- *New literary criticism*: the practice of close readings of texts as they now stand, apart from their historical development

or the original intention of the author; commonly used with poetry and sacred texts
- *Post-colonialism*: the analysis of religious ideas, traditions, and texts in light of colonialism and its effects
- *Psychology*: the attempt to understand religion and belief through the science of psychology
- *Textual and linguistic studies*: the close study of particular written texts and the original languages in which they were written, as well as the history of their development; often used in relation to ancient or sacred texts

DIVERSITY IN COMMITMENTS AND MOTIVES

As you can see, religious studies is diverse in its content as well as in the approaches you can take to study its many aspects. The people studying and teaching religious studies are just as diverse, because they have a variety of commitments and reasons for engaging in their studies. This can be seen quite readily in looking at your own university or college. For instance, many institutions have religious studies departments that stand on their own with no religious affiliations or obligations. Yet other institutions have theological departments, religious colleges, or seminaries that are linked to religious groups or denominations. The aim of these programs is to train people in specific religious practices. To make matters more complicated, these theologically oriented schools can sometimes operate in conjunction with, or as a subsection of, religious studies departments, and some faculty members may teach in both. What is one to make of all this?

To begin with, theological departments or seminaries and religious studies departments often offer similar courses of study. For example, you'll often find courses on historical examinations of traditions, philosophical investigations of religious concepts, and ancient languages needed to better understand sacred texts in both settings. So there is bound to be some overlap in what is studied, and in fact much of this handbook will apply to both. Broadly speaking, however, theological departments and seminaries are confessional in their approach. The term *confessional* derives from the Christian idea of someone publicly "confessing to" or declaring their faith (not the confession of sins!). Here, it implies that those involved are *insiders* or adherents to a particular faith, and they are investigating issues related to religion from this perspective. Religious studies, meanwhile, is generally concerned with describing and understanding all things related to religion from a *consciously neutral perspective* (as far as that is possible, as we will discuss below). The relationship between religious studies and confessional approaches is a complex one, and we are not able to deal with every aspect of it here. However, you should be aware that it is a key issue, and if you continue in religious studies you will deal with this relationship in more detail. The most relevant issue for you at this stage is to understand the philosophy and perspective of your particular institution or department, and to approach your studies accordingly. If you are unsure on these matters, it might be wise to schedule an appointment with the head of your department or a faculty member in order to gain a better understanding of what your department is all about.

Taken together, we can see that religious studies is indeed a diverse field. This diversity ranges from the content studied, to the methods and approaches used, to the religious commitments and motivations of those involved. Understanding that this diversity exists will help you acclimate to your studies and to engage with your classes more fully.

Religious presuppositions

This leads us to one final issue related to religious studies: the question of religious presuppositions and objectivity. Some 80 per cent of Americans self-identify as religious (with over 76 per cent of that total identifying as Christian), and in other countries religions such as Christianity, Islam, and Buddhism likewise condition the outlook of the vast majority of the student population. Canadian percentages are generally lower, though not so much so that the challenges discussed here are irrelevant. An estimated 5 billion people are directly involved in the world's major religions, thus North American figures are not out of step with those of the rest of the world.[4]

Given this, we often face difficulties in pursuing the subject of religion objectively, that is, from a critical distance, with self-awareness of biases, and without religious partiality. At the same time, it is also misleading to think that "non-religious" persons will automatically be objective in their study of religion, for at times those who identify as non-religious or atheist have strong views about religion as well.

In some ways the problem is not entirely unique, as other fields (political science, anthropology, and psychology, to name a few) face similar difficulties when students come to their studies with strong, already formed views about the subject matter. However, problems of partiality are particularly accentuated in religious studies. It is unlikely that someone will come to geography, biology, nursing, or English with views about the subject as strong as a student might have about religion. It is also true that a person's views or opinions about religion are often long-held ones, ones identified with family, religious adherence, and personal or community identity. As such, religious views are not easily negotiated or reconfigured, and often people feel threatened when others disagree with or challenge their views about God, Allah, the Buddha, or whatever is significant in their religion. The challenges here are great and many, and they confront not only students, but instructors as well. How do students ensure that their study and writing in this subject will not be inappropriately influenced by preconceived ideas about religion, a divine being, or what is right and wrong?

It is impossible to "bracket off" one's personal beliefs completely in the study of religion. Postmodern thinking has reminded us that perfect objectivity, or purely neutral approaches to any subject, is not possible. This is undoubtedly true and we need to acknowledge that any positions or views that we hold, including religious, economic, ethnic, and political, will contribute to how we think about and approach a subject. However, even if we cannot fully remove these points of bias in our studies, it is important to recognize them and to attempt to limit their influence in order to engage with a subject more fully.

This does not mean that you must cease to be religious or give up your faith if you have one in order to partake in religious studies; it does mean that it is necessary to be aware of your presuppositions. You will need to learn not to allow preconceived views or opinions about religion to influence your studies without due reflection. As Cunningham and Kelsay observe, "If we begin with the premise that we possess all religious truth and everything that cannot fit in our worldview is wrong, sympathetic understanding will be impossible."[5] Someone who constantly refutes or dismisses each religious idea he or she encounters is less likely to learn about a particular religion to the fullest or be balanced in describing and analyzing a subject. For you, the issue of objectivity may not be a great problem. However, our experience as teachers has taught us that for many students these matters present recurring problems, and they do need to be addressed.

You may be wondering if meeting the goal of objectivity means that you can never express a strong opinion. This question is especially important in light of what we said earlier in this chapter, where we described university as a place that moves you beyond a high school–level education (primarily concerned with information) to one that gives you the tools to analyze and evaluate material (engaged learning). David Ford, a professor at Cambridge University, offers some excellent insight on this subject. He agrees that students need to move beyond description or simple data collection, arguing that students and researchers need to be engaged with their content in such a way that, in time, constructive analysis, respectful assessment, and demonstration of preferable theories takes place too. He likens it to an economics department at a university. While departments of economics would naturally study economic history, econometrics, and various ways of describing, analyzing, and theorizing about economies, departments at the forefront of their field are also concerned with thinking about and putting forward constructive theories to better our nations' economies. In other words, they want to take part in and add to the discussion, not simply present the facts that are being discussed. The ability to contribute at the leading edge of economics only comes as a result of steadily increasing knowledge, understanding, and engagement with the material: that is, through repeated practice. The same might be said for any academic program in religious studies. One would hope that those in religious studies departments would have something constructive to add to the discussion of the world's religions, present and past, through constructive analysis and respectful assessment. However, the problem comes when we theorize and argue straightaway for certain ideas without understanding the religious landscape, or when we do so with unrecognized biases or disregard for objectivity and balance.[6] As with economics, we can develop our understanding and knowledge of the subject only through repeated study, research, and discussion; there are no shortcuts. Thus, it is particularly important at the beginning of your studies that you actively seek to recognize biases you may hold, and to strive for objectivity as you begin to understand the complexity of religion and religious studies.

Clearly, the religious views people hold affect our world, whether they influence arguments for or against human rights, for the endorsement or rejection of a particular war, for engaging in or abstaining from certain medical practices, or for the oppression or emancipation of a minority group. In your studies, you will be asked to reflect on these and other issues. Such reflection should take into account the many complex facets an issue may have. It would be unwise to pursue religious studies without carefully exercising judgment or evaluation at some level, some of the time. Like a scientist who needs to readjust a long-held theory based on newly discovered evidence, we may need to adjust our judgments in the light of new evidence. For this reason, our judgments should be held loosely, or at least with openness to further learning and renewed processes of evaluation. And, there may be times when we would do well to withhold judgment altogether. Decisions regarding when to do this are part of a complex but important process in your development as a student.

CONCLUSION: TAKING RESPONSIBILITY FOR YOUR EDUCATION

Without doubt, your time at college or university will be a life-changing experience. However, the extent to which it affects you depends in large part on how you invest yourself in it. We have suggested that adopting a mindset of "engaged learning" will help in this regard. Instead of seeing your education simply as a means to an end—an exercise that will result in a degree—we hope you will view the entire process as a chance to be an active learner who is engaging with subjects that matter and making a difference in the world. As an engaged learner, you will have the opportunity not only to understand the subjects you are studying, but also to contribute in new and meaningful ways to the world around you.

You may have already noticed that if you are going to be an engaged learner, it will require that you take responsibility for and ownership of your education. This is true, and there is no getting around it: *you* are the determining factor in how rewarding your education will be. As the Chinese proverb states, "Teachers open the door, but you must enter by yourself."

ENDNOTES

1. Benjamin Bloom was a pioneer in this field, and this section roughly follows his findings. See B.S. Bloom, *Taxonomy of Educational Objectives, Handbook I: The Cognitive Domain* (New York: David McKay, 1956).
2. Rob Barnes, *Successful Study for Degrees*, 2nd ed. (London: Routledge, 1995), pp. 10–11. Barnes' work is based on the earlier study by E. Fromm, *To Have or To Be?*, 2nd ed. (London: Sphere Books, 1979).
3. Barnes, *Successful Study*, pp. 11–12.
4. For more on the 2001 figures used here, see Timothy Beal, *Religion in America: A Very Short Introduction* (Oxford: Oxford University Press, 2008).
5. Lawrence S. Cunningham and John Kelsay, *The Sacred Quest: An Invitation to the Study of Religion*, 5th ed. (Boston: Prentice Hall, 2010), p. 7.
6. See David F. Ford, *Theology: A Very Short Introduction* (Oxford: Oxford University Press, 1999), pp. 16–18.

CHAPTER 2

Making the Most of Your Time in Higher Education

Objectives

- Getting to know and making the most of various learning environments
- Thinking about time management and the need to plan ahead
- Reflecting on long-distance and part-time studies

During your first few weeks at university or college, you may feel like you are doing more surviving than thriving. It probably seems hard enough to find all of your classes and to show up on time, let alone to take in and analyze everything being presented in class. What you should remember, however, is that your post-secondary education is truly a unique experience, and it is something you will want to capitalize on as much as possible. Right now you are surrounded by amazing resources, expert teachers, and thoughtful peers who can significantly add to your learning experience, if you allow them to do so. Here are a few tips for being "engaged" with your new learning environments.

LEARNING ENVIRONMENTS

Let's start with the classroom, which is what many of us first picture when we think about education. Your time in the classroom is indeed one of the most important aspects of your post-secondary experience. The classroom dynamics will vary depending on the number of students in your classes; there may be small group discussion as well as interaction between the instructor and the students. The form most associated with classroom delivery, however, is the lecture, where the instructor spends most of his or her time addressing the class.

The lecture is especially prominent in lower-level courses that tend to have larger numbers of students. How can you make the most of lectures?

To begin with, it is vitally important that you attend lectures. After all, your instructor is the one who will assess your work, or who will set the guidelines for graders to follow; if you want to know what your instructor wants you to learn, as well as why it is important, the lectures will give you the best idea. Moreover, you need to know whether your instructor or institution has an attendance policy. If your class attendance and participation contribute to your overall grade, showing up can be an easy way to bolster your marks, while skipping class may mean needlessly losing valuable percentage points.

You should also think about a few things that might seem trivial at first, starting with where you sit in the classroom. It may be helpful to avoid sitting near the door, where you might be distracted by outside noises or by students slipping in late, or close to peers who talk during the lecture. Where you sit in your first few classes can set a pattern for the rest of the semester, so choose your seat carefully. Also, in today's world of wireless Internet access and mobile communication devices, it is easy to be distracted by email, instant messaging, social networking websites, or online games. Some instructors encourage students to turn off all wireless devices or wireless access to their computers to ensure they get the most out of the lecture. Both out of respect for your instructor and to optimize your own learning experiences, you should consider turning off distractions during your lectures.

What about in the lecture itself? Whether you make the most of lectures will depend on how you interact with the information being delivered. Perhaps the most obvious thing to do is to take notes. There are, however, many different ways to take notes, some more beneficial than others. For instance, you have probably been in class with a fellow student who is feverishly attempting to write down every word the instructor utters, or every detail that appears onscreen. We don't believe this is helpful, as note-taking is more than simply recording every piece of information presented to you. In fact, it may be that trying to record every word is actually counterproductive to your overall learning experience. Instead of thinking about and interacting with the information being delivered, you are focusing on many small details that may not be relevant. Word-for-word note-taking does not lead to engaged learning. An easy and more effective way of interacting with your lectures is to put your notes in your own words. Summarize what is being said, and focus on the big picture.[1] More and more instructors are providing notes for their students, whether in class or via electronic formats. Rather than taking too many notes, you might be tempted in these cases to do the opposite: because you are being given the information in written form, you may think you can sit back and listen to the information, without making any of your own notes. Notes from instructors are indeed a valuable resource; however, if you are trying to be an engaged learner, then you will want to interact with the material so that you are truly absorbing and understanding the information being given. We suggest taking your own notes alongside those provided or adding additional comments to those provided by your instructor. This might include making summary statements or highlighting key words, as well as noting any questions for further reflection that might arise.

Inevitably there will be times in the classroom when something is unclear, or when you are unable to follow what is being discussed. How should you respond in this situation? It is important to remember that your instructors really do want to be understood, and want you to engage with the subject they are teaching you. So, if there are things that you feel need clarification or further explanation, feel free to ask your instructor. There are various contexts where this may be most appropriate (see Chapter 14 for more on this). Sometimes there is room for this during or at the end of the class itself, depending on how much time your instructor allows for interaction. Other times it may be more appropriate to talk to your instructor after class or to set up an appointment with him or her during office hours. Regardless, remember that your instructors are here to help you, so make the most of this valuable resource.

Outside of class, there are other ways to ensure that you are fully engaging with your course's material. For instance, some students find it helpful to look over and summarize their class notes within twenty-four to forty-eight hours of the lecture. Others highlight key words and phrases, creating a list of important terms and topics that they need to keep in mind. You may also find it helpful to compare notes with other students and, if possible, discuss what they understood as the key points of the lecture (for example by outlining the three main ideas from the lecture). All of these are simple ways of helping you to engage with the material in an active way. Several of these issues will be dealt with again in Chapter 11, on examinations.

But there is more to your post-secondary experience than just the classroom. Another learning environment you will find yourself in is the seminar, or small group discussion (also referred to as a tutorial). These gatherings allow students a more intimate setting within which they can talk about their subject matter. (This is also the case for small class or lecture settings, which often allow for or even demand greater interaction on the part of the student than the larger lecture format. In these cases, the class often functions as both the place for information delivery and for student discussion.) Smaller group settings are very important, especially if your lectures are not geared toward interaction. Again, be aware that you will take from these sessions what you invest in them. With this in mind, it is important that you take discussion times seriously, and adequately prepare for them. This might entail reading, taking notes, or engaging with class material online. Whatever the case may be, your preparation is important as it allows you to engage in and contribute to your seminar discussions. We understand that some people will thrive in these settings, while others will find them difficult. If you are an extrovert, your input can be very helpful in this context. However, be aware of the group as a whole, and do your best not to dominate the conversation. For those who are more introverted, you should see your seminar as a safe place to interact, ask for clarification, and so on. You may need to push yourself to take part, but the rewards will be well worth the risk.

Finally, there are a host of other learning environments at your institution of which you can take advantage. Libraries, for instance, hold more than just books on shelves; there are journals, electronic documents and databases, computer facilities, and knowledgeable staff who want to help you succeed (we will discuss the library in more detail in Chapter 4). In the same way, your religious studies department will often hold guest lectures, seminars, and tutorials that you can attend; it is also home to expert faculty members more than willing to give you guidance. In summary, your college or university is an amazing resource. But it is up to you to take advantage of the opportunities that are put before you, whether in the classroom, in seminars, or at the library. We encourage you to dive in and make the most of these opportunities.

TIME MANAGEMENT

Attending and making the most of lectures, seminars, and other university resources is a big part of your education. However, you will find that another key to success in your post-secondary experience is how you use your time outside of the classroom. Balancing work, family, and other obligations is difficult at the best of times. Now you have to add your academic life to the equation: finishing required reading, planning written projects, researching and writing essays, and studying for exams all require your attention and forethought. In this sense, engaged learning will require you to become an expert time manager.

In their *Student Skills Guide*, authors Drew and Bingham offer some excellent tips and strategies for organizing your life as a student. For starters, in order to manage your time well, you have to understand how you currently use your time. To get a better picture of this, you could try filling out a schedule that outlines how you currently spend your waking hours.[2] You may wonder if this is really worth the time. However, we have found this to be a surprisingly fruitful exercise in our own lives. In analyzing how we spend our time, it became apparent that we were not as efficient with our own time as we had once thought. Once you have a better idea of where you are spending your time and energy, you can plan for your studies more effectively and realistically.

The next step is to prioritize the various aspects of your life. It is common to speak of tasks in the following ways:

1. Urgent and important—do it now.
2. Urgent but not important—do it if you can.
3. Important but not urgent—start it before it gets urgent.
4. Not important and not urgent—don't do it.

Once you have identified how urgent your various tasks may be, it is also important that you decide how much time you will dedicate to these different tasks. Phil Race, for example, suggests the following balance within this system:

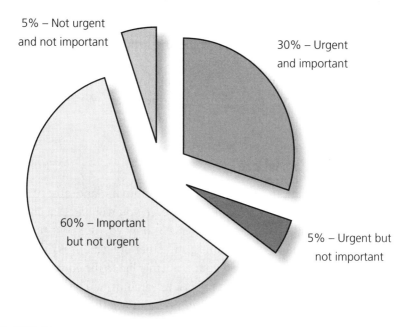

Figure 2.1   Prioritizing your time as a student

Source: Adapted from Phil Race, *How to Get a Good Degree: Making the Most of Your Time at University* (Buckingham: Open University Press, 1999), pp. 45–47.

The key is to avoid the "tyranny of the urgent," that is, not to allow the most urgent tasks to dominate your schedule. Race suggests that more than half your time should be spent on things that are important (those things that *need* to be done and may be a big part of your assessment) without letting them become urgent.[3] This approach allows you to feel in control of your studies because dealing with last-minute deadlines is not your only concern.

After you have analyzed how you currently use your time and have attempted to prioritize your commitments, you need to create a realistic schedule for yourself. To begin, keep in mind that you want to avoid the "tyranny of the urgent." We suggest making both an extended calendar that outlines your entire semester or term, as well as a more detailed, week-by-week calendar. Good scheduling requires the identification of targets and deadlines. This involves sitting down with all of your syllabi and making careful judgments about how much time you need to allot for each assignment. It is important that you identify what you need to get done (targets) and when it needs to be done (deadlines). Consider the sample chart below. Try to develop something similar for yourself and see how much it helps you organize your time:[4]

Table 2.1   General assignment targets and deadlines

Main target	Deadline	Time needed
Reading for Islam	September 12	3 hours
Buddhism essay	October 28	6 weeks
Philosophy examination	December 18	4 weeks

Source: Adapted from Sue Drew and Rosie Bingham, *The Student Skills Guide*, 2nd ed. (Hampshire: Gower Publishing, 2001), pp. 26–28.

Within a plan like this, you may have sub-tasks for each main target:

Table 2.2   Specific assignment targets and deadlines

Main target	Deadline	Time needed
Buddhism essay	October 28	6 weeks
Sub-tasks		
Essay proposal	September 23	1 week
Research for essay	October 14	3 weeks
First draft	October 21	1 week
Final editing	October 26	1 week

Source: Adapted from Sue Drew and Rosie Bingham, *The Student Skills Guide*, 2nd ed. (Hampshire: Gower Publishing, 2001), pp. 26–28.

For each main target or task it is also helpful to identify what tools you will need and work these into your plan. For instance, how many books and articles will you need to do research for your essay? What resources will you need when studying for an exam? The more detail you put in when planning, the better off you will be in the end. (If this seems overwhelming at this stage, be aware that we will deal with specific issues regarding research, essay writing, and exams later in the book.)

Next, it is important to monitor and revise your targets and plans. When you are doing this, keep in mind that things can go wrong, and they inevitably will. A resource will be unavailable, your computer will crash, or an unforeseen emergency will eat into your time (hopefully not all in the same week!). If you are not keeping up with your tasks, try to readjust your schedule instead of becoming frustrated or despondent. This may mean re-prioritizing some of your work as you go along.

Finally, good time management requires that you avoid time wasters. First, you have to identify things that distract you from your work. Perhaps turning off your phone or not checking your email during your study time would be helpful. Or, you may need to work in a location where you know your family or friends won't interrupt you, or in a place away from a television or Internet connection. It can also be beneficial to identify what helps you study effectively. What time of day are you most alert for study? How long can you go before you need a break? What circumstances help you study? Effective study also includes looking after yourself: if you are losing concentration, take a short coffee break or a walk, or perhaps reward yourself for reaching certain goals. These issues may seem small, but taking time to think about them can greatly increase your productivity and, in turn, your ability to succeed in higher education.

PART-TIME AND DISTANCE-EDUCATION STUDENTS

Managing your time as a student is always a challenge. For those who are studying as part-time or distance-education students, this issue is even more acute. For instance, when should you study? Some people opt for evenings; however, this can be difficult after the strain of a long day at work and is complicated by the many familial, social, or other obligations you may have. Others choose weekends as their time of study; yet this can often lead to bitterness at having to give up precious free time. There are other issues as well. Studying can cause a financial strain: the cost of courses may be quite high, yet many part-time students must cut down on their work hours to concentrate on their studies. Motivation is another issue, as you do not always have lecturers or fellow students by your side pushing and prodding you to work hard. There are no easy answers in these situations, but it is best to be aware of them so that you can deal with them in an effective manner. Here are some helpful guidelines for part-time and distance-education students.[5]

First, try to connect your studies with your interests and non-academic life. Perhaps you have a personal interest in how Buddhists view life after death, or perhaps you would like to know what Christians of various denominations think about capital punishment. If you can connect your study to your interests, the valuable time you spend in study will not simply be for the degree given at the end (though this is a benefit), but will enrich your vocation and personal life along the way. Moreover, it is important to realize that you bring a unique perspective to your classes, as you may be approaching your studies from a different vantage point than many traditional students. In fact, instructors often value the input of part-time, mature, and other non-traditional students precisely because of this input.

Second, make a contract with yourself regarding the time you will spend on your studies—then try your best to stay on track. This cannot be stated strongly enough: you rarely feel motivated to study in your free time. Further, it is important that you protect your leisure time to maintain a balanced life. It is therefore vital that you carefully timetable your academic obligations and frequently revise your schedule as circumstances change. It may help you to share your personal contract with a family member or friend, and have them keep you accountable.

Finally, make use of the learning environments available to you. This is as important an issue for part-time or distance-education students as it is for traditional students—if not more so. Stay in contact with your instructors, and do not be afraid to ask them for direction in your work. If possible, connect with others in your geographical area who may be studying similar disciplines, so you can study together or talk about the subjects you're studying, just as you would if you were attending class in person.

In summary, whether you are a full-time, part-time, or distance-education student, how you manage your time is vital to your ability to make the most of your educational experience. Good time management will help you lay the groundwork to become a truly engaged learner.

ENDNOTES

1. Further guidance on note-taking can be found in Sue Drew and Rosie Bingham, *The Student Skills Guide*, 2nd ed. (Hampshire: Gower Publishing, 2001), pp. 33–47.
2. Drew and Bingham (*Student Skills*, pp. 24–25) offer an example; there are also many such timetables available online.
3. Phil Race, *How to Get a Good Degree: Making the Most of Your Time at University* (Buckingham: Open University Press, 1999), pp. 45–47.
4. Adapted from Drew and Bingham, *Student Skills*, pp. 26–28.
5. Drawn from Estelle M. Phillips and D.S. Pugh, *How to Get a PhD: A Handbook for Students and Their Supervisors*, 2nd ed. (Buckingham: Open University Press, 1994), pp. 114–115.

CHAPTER 3

Writing and Thinking

Objectives

- Thinking about initial strategies in writing
- Considering general guidelines for writing
- Learning to find the right tone and style in writing
- Reflecting on bias-free language

In Chapter 1 we outlined several issues you need to be aware of as you delve into religious studies at the post-secondary level. We stressed the importance of "thinking" throughout the chapter, and we encouraged you to be an engaged learner in your studies. Before we explore some of the more practical aspects of writing essays, we want to spend a little more time looking at the relationship between how you think and what you write.

To begin with, you are not likely to produce clear writing unless you have first done some clear thinking, and thinking can't be hurried. It follows that the most important step you can take before beginning to write is to leave yourself enough time to think. Psychologists have shown that you can't always solve a difficult problem by "putting your mind to it"—by determined reasoning alone. Sometimes when you're stuck it's best to take a break, sleep on it, and let the subconscious or creative part of your brain take over for a while. Very often a period of relaxation will produce a new approach or solution (starting an essay a day or two before it's due will not allow you this chance to relax). Just remember that leaving time for creative reflection is not the same thing as sitting around listening to music, hoping inspiration will strike out of the blue.

INITIAL STRATEGIES

Writing is about making choices: choices about what ideas you want to present and how you want to present them. Practice makes this kind of decision-making easier, but no matter how fluent you become, with each piece of writing you will still have to make choices. You can narrow the field of choice from the start if you realize that you are not writing for just anybody, anywhere, for no particular reason. With any writing you do, it's always a sound strategy to ask yourself two basic questions:

- What is the purpose of this piece of writing?
- Who is the reader or audience?

Your first reaction may be, "Well, I'm writing for my instructor to satisfy a course requirement," but that's not specific enough in an academic sense. To be useful, your answers have to be precise.

Think about the purpose

Depending on the assignment, your purpose in writing an essay may be any one (or more) of the following:

- to demonstrate your knowledge of a topic or text;
- to show that you understand certain terms or theories;
- to show that you can do independent research;
- to demonstrate that you can apply a specific theory to new material;
- to demonstrate your ability to evaluate secondary sources; and
- to show that you can think critically or creatively.

An assignment designed to see if you have read and understood specific material requires a different approach from one that is meant to test your critical thinking. In the first case, your approach will tend to be *descriptive*, with the emphasis on presenting facts. In the second case, you will probably want to structure your essay around a particular argument or assertion that other people might dispute. Your aim in this kind of *argumentative* or *persuasive* essay is to bring your reader around to your point of view.

Think about the reader

Thinking about the reader does *not* mean playing up to the instructor. To convince a particular person that your own views are sound means that you have to consider his or her way of thinking. If you are writing a paper on the effects of immigration on the religious landscape of Canada for your religious studies professor, your analysis will be different than it would be if you were writing about immigration in Canada for an economics professor. You will have to make specific decisions about the terms you should use or explain, the background information you should supply, the sources you should use, and the details you will need in order to convince that particular reader. In the same way, if you plan to write a paper defending the use of Sharia Law in modern society, you will have to anticipate any arguments that your reader or audience may raise so that you can address them. If you do not know who will be reading your paper—your professor, your tutorial leader, or a grader—just imagine someone intelligent and interested, skeptical enough to question your ideas but flexible enough to accept them if your evidence is convincing.

Think about the length

Before you start writing (or researching), you will also need to think about the length of your assignment in relation to the time you can spend on it. If your professor has assigned a particular topic and a particular length, it should be fairly easy for you to assess the level of detail required and the amount of research you will need to do. If only the length is prescribed, that restriction will help you decide how broad or how narrow the topic you choose should be. You should also keep in mind how much the assignment is worth. A paper that is worth 50 per cent of your final grade will merit more of your time and effort than one that is worth only 10 per cent.

Think about the tone

In everyday writing to friends, including emails and texts, you probably adopt a casual tone, but academic writing is usually more formal. Just how formal you need to be will depend on the kind of assignment and the instructions you have been given. In some cases—for example, if your professor asks you to visit a religious service and report back on your impressions of it—you may be able to use an informal style. Essays and reports, however, usually require a more formal tone. What kind of style is too informal for most academic work? Here are the main pitfalls to avoid:

USE OF SLANG

Although the occasional slang word or phrase may be useful for special effect, in general the use of slang is not acceptable in academic writing because slang expressions are usually regional and short-lived. They may mean different things to different groups at different times. (Just think of how widely the meanings of *hot* and *cool* can vary, depending on the circumstances.) In a formal essay, where clarity of expression is important, it is better to use words with well-established meanings that will be understood by the greatest number of readers.

EXCESSIVE USE OF FIRST-PERSON PRONOUNS

Since a formal essay is not a personal outpouring, you want to keep it from becoming *I*-centred. There is no need to begin every sentence with "I think" or "In my view" when the facts or arguments speak for themselves. In fact, starting a sentence with "I think" makes what follows seem like an opinion and not a fact that can stand up on its own. It is certainly acceptable to use the occasional first-person pronoun if the assignment calls for your point of view—as long as your opinions are backed by evidence. Also, if the choice is between using *I* and creating a tangle of passive constructions (for example, "It is hoped that it can reasonably be concluded, based on the evidence that has been presented, that . . ."), it is almost always better to choose *I*. (A hint: when you do use *I*, it will be less noticeable if you place it in the middle of the sentence rather than at the beginning. This advice is especially useful when writing resumés as well as essays.) Here are some examples of ways to avoid both *I*-centred and unnecessarily passive sentences:

- ✗ Having analyzed the new doctrinal statement, I believe it is illogical.
- ✗ The new doctrinal statement, having been analyzed, appears to me to be illogical.
- ✓ When analyzed, the new doctrinal statement seems illogical.

- ✗ In this essay, Smart's views on phenomenology will be set out, and they will be examined in light of several recent critiques of this approach.
- ✓ In this essay, I will investigate Smart's views on phenomenology and examine them in light of several recent critiques of this approach.
- ✓ This essay will investigate Smart's views on phenomenology and examine them in light of several recent critiques of this approach.

Many departments in colleges and universities have developed their own policies regarding use of the first person, so make sure you know what your institution or individual instructors expect.

USE OF CONTRACTIONS

Generally speaking, contractions (such as *can't*, *isn't*, and *it's*) are not suitable for academic writing, although they may be fine for letters or other informal kinds of writing—for example, this handbook. While avoiding contractions may initially make you feel that your writing has become stilted or unnatural, virtually all formal academic writings in religious studies avoid contractions, and students are encouraged to adopt this practice. If you feel that you must use a few contractions, use them very sparingly, since excessive use of contractions makes formal writing sound chatty and informal. Further, using contractions may result in the loss of valuable marks from your grader.

Also be aware of going too far in the other direction. Finding a suitable tone for academic writing can be a challenge. The problem with trying to avoid excessive informality is that you may be tempted to go to the other extreme. If your writing sounds stiff or pompous, you may be using too many inflated phrases, long words, or passive constructions. For example, it is more fitting to write about "religious practices" than "contextualized ritualistic manifestations." When in doubt, however, remember that a more formal style is the best option.

GUIDELINES FOR WRITING

Whenever you embark on a writing project, try to keep the following guidelines in mind:

- Think about your audience, the reader or readers of your writing.
- Be clear about your subject and your purpose, what it is you hope to achieve.
- Define your terms, especially those prone to ambiguity or used in a particular way in religious studies.
- Include only relevant material; don't pad your writing to achieve a certain number of words.
- Strive for consistency of expression throughout the work.
- Make sure you are accurate in all of your statements, in your analysis and presentation of data, and in your documentation of sources.
- Order your information logically.
- Be simple and clear in expressing your ideas.
- Make sure that your argument is coherent.
- Draw conclusions that are clearly based on your evidence. Do not introduce new or unsupported ideas in your conclusion.
- Allow yourself lots of time to work on drafts before completing the final copy.
- Make sure to edit and proofread your work carefully.

In the chapters that follow we will consider these guidelines in greater detail.

USING BIAS-FREE LANGUAGE

It is more important than ever to avoid bias in the language we use—both spoken and written. Just as you give thought to your reader(s) and to the kind of tone you wish to create, you will also want to take pains to use language that steers clear of any suggestion of bias, no matter how unintentional it may be. The potential for bias is far-reaching, involving gender, race, culture, age, disability, occupation, religion, and socio-economic status. Although our society has not come up with ideal solutions in every case, developing an awareness of sensitive issues will help you to avoid using biased language.

Religion

As noted in Chapter 1, the issue of bias is extremely important in religious studies. It can be difficult to speak objectively about one's own beliefs and convictions, not to mention those of others. However, it is vital that any beliefs we may hold—religious or otherwise—do not colour our writing on these issues.

It is important to recognize that assumptions in the area of religion can be far-reaching, and you may not even know you have them. Even those who would not consider themselves religious may use terms of reference that are not value-free or neutral. In North America and Europe, where academic and general discourses have been heavily influenced by Christianity, the terms we use often reflect a Christian point of view. Consider, for instance, the chronological designations BC and AD. These terms are linked to a Christian perspective in which all years before the time of Jesus of Nazareth (the "Christ" of Christianity) are "Before Christ," and all years after are "Anno Domini" ("in the year of our Lord"). While a better alternative is to use the terms BCE ("Before the Common Era") and CE ("Common Era"), it should be recognized that other cultures and societies have their own dating systems as well. For example, 2011 CE is the year 5771 in the Jewish calendar. Likewise, a term like "Old Testament" implies that this body of literature exists in relationship to a *New* Testament: it is a specifically Christian way of looking at this collection. Yet, others who do not regard the New Testament to be sacred, such as the Jewish people, would call the "Old Testament" the Tanakh, or the Hebrew Bible, or simply the Bible. Likewise, referring to the figure Jesus as "Jesus Christ" or "Jesus the Messiah" suggests a pre-conceived judgment about him. These are only a few examples. Students are encouraged to determine if the terms they use imply a point of reference or privileging of any one religion. Calling something unorthodox, a "false religion," heretical, or a sect—without explanation, or as a value judgment—are further symptoms of this problem.

Gender

At one time, it would have been acceptable to refer to a person of either sex as "he," a practice still preferred by some traditionalists:

If an adherent converts, he will face alienation.

But as sensitivity to sexist language has increased, we have become more careful about this use of a generic pronoun. Here are some options for avoiding the problem:

- Use the passive voice:

  Alienation will be faced by an adherent who converts.

- Restructure the sentence:

  An adherent who converts will face alienation.

- Use he or she, although this is cumbersome and should be used sparingly:

  If an adherent converts, he or she will face alienation.

- Use the plural form:

  If adherents convert, they will face alienation.

Another option is to alternate, using the masculine form in one instance and the feminine form in the next.

Recently, some writers have used the neutral "they" to refer to a singular antecedent:

When a writer aims for simplicity, they will occasionally break with grammatical convention.

Be careful, however. This may still raise the hackles of a traditional reader. Another trouble spot involves gender-specific nouns, such as stewardess, waitress, or fireman. The best solution in these cases is to look for gender-free words, for example, flight attendant, server, and firefighter. There are also problems related to pronouns and how we refer to religious communities, persons, and deities. It is not uncommon to use feminine personal pronouns (she or her) to refer to certain religious ideas or groups (like the Church or ancient Israel) and masculine pronouns (he and him) to refer to God, Allah, Brahman, or other deities. Some traditional religious adherents may insist on gendered language while others would suggest that God, Allah, and other deities transcend gender. This highlights the need for students to be sensitive and to exercise caution.

Our recommendation is to avoid gendered language when possible or to use it sparingly. Though seemingly cumbersome initially, an alternative is simply to repeat the specific name of the deity (or the term *God*) instead of using a personal pronoun.

Race and culture

The names used to describe someone's racial or cultural identity often carry negative connotations for some readers although they might be acceptable to others. For example, consider the term *Negro*. The search for neutral language has produced alternatives such as *black* or *African Canadian*. We have similar problems with the term *Indian*, with alternatives such as *Aboriginal*, *Native*, and *First Nations*. The best approach is to find out what the racial or cultural group in question prefers. Even if there isn't an easy answer, being aware of a potential problem is already part of the solution.

CONCLUSION

As you begin your studies, academic writing may seem strange and difficult. However, academic writing is less threatening when you begin by thinking through the appropriate issues: What is the purpose of this piece? Who is the reader, and what kind of tone should I employ? What language is appropriate for academic writing in general, and for this topic in particular? What assumptions am I making? If you think through these issues carefully, you will go a long way toward making the writing process a more manageable and enjoyable one.

CHAPTER 4

Finding and Using Academic Resources

Objectives

- Using a research library
- Identifying and evaluating academic sources
- Learning to read and use academic sources
- Understanding plagiarism and academic honesty

One thing in particular will become clear to you as you begin to write essays: apart from personal reflection assignments, it is impossible to write essays without researching other people's writings and thoughts. With this in mind, we will begin to explore how to find and appropriately use resources for your work.

USING A RESEARCH LIBRARY

The first port of call when locating resources is, not surprisingly, the library. Using the library at your college or university can seem like a daunting task. Not only are university libraries much larger than the average public or secondary school library, but there may also be more than one on your campus. Without some help, you may find yourself lost and frustrated, and you might end up leaving empty-handed. If you take a little time to learn about your library and how it functions, however, you will save valuable time when you need it most—when the crunch is on.

Many post-secondary institutions offer tours of the library and seminars on how to use library resources for students. We highly recommend taking advantage of these if they are available. Don't be afraid to ask a librarian when such tours or seminars might be offered. If none are available, take some time to acquaint yourself with how your library runs: what type of cataloguing system it uses, where any special collections or archives may be, how to access journals and periodicals, and who you may approach should you need assistance. Knowing this information will make your trips to the library fruitful and much less frustrating.

Locating sources in the library

Thanks to advances in technology, finding suitable material for your research has never been easier. The first place to begin is your library's catalogue. A catalogue is the way in which a library organizes its materials. Catalogues contain bibliographic information (including author's name, title, publication details, and key words) about each resource in the library's collection so that the material can be located. In the past, libraries used "card catalogues," in which each resource was detailed on a small note card. Today, the majority of catalogues are electronic, which means you can search much of the available content at a library computer terminal (and in many cases the catalogue is available to students online, so you can search from home) by simply typing in a key word, author name, or title. However, technology also has its disadvantages. For instance, a basic search of the word "Judaism" may call up hundreds or even thousands of results. You will need to refine your search to a more specific topic so that you have manageable results. You may choose to do a search on several key words at one time, such as "medieval Judaism" or "Judaism, Canada." Both of these searches would offer you more refined results and a better starting place for your research.

Another way to locate resources is through indexes and databases. Not all the material you can use will be found in your library's catalogue. For instance, specific journal articles and other periodical information will not be found in the catalogue system. This does not mean, however, that you need to look through countless back issues of journals to find a relevant article. Rather, you need to consult indexes and databases to find these sources. Indexes and databases contain information on periodicals and articles, sorted by author, title, and subject. They will often contain abstracts, or short summaries of articles, which will give you a good idea whether they will be relevant for your work. While your library may have printed indexes available in book form, there are also an ever-increasing number of online databases available that make this task easier. For example, JSTOR (short for Journal Storage) is an online archive of journal articles that allows you to search for authors, titles, and keywords in a variety of journals and fields of study. An index commonly used in religious studies is ATLA (American Theological Library Association).

If your library has such databases, you will be able to search for articles, and often even access them, electronically. As you progress to higher levels of study, the use of journals and periodicals will become increasingly important in your research; as such, it is vital that you learn how to access and use these resources.

One further way that you might find help locating resources is by checking reference material. Reference material includes dictionaries, encyclopedias, and other resources that helpfully summarize and collate information on a larger subject. Often, these types of sources will offer a short bibliography at the end of a particular entry, and these may help point you in the direction of other appropriate sources. For instance, if you are writing an essay on the concept of karma in Jainism, the article on "Karma, kamma" in the *Oxford Dictionary of World Religions* identifies some of the seminal works on the subject. You can then check your library catalogue to see if the library has these works available.

Locating sources outside of the post-secondary library

If you are a distance-education or part-time student with limited access to a university library, you may think that you are at a distinct disadvantage when it comes to finding and using resources. However, you may have more resources at your disposal than you realize. First of all, check to see if your institution's library catalogue is online. If it is accessible online, you can search and some-times reserve material right from home. Moreover, post-secondary libraries are hosting more and more electronic materials that you can access online and sometimes download, including journals and ebooks.

Second, local public libraries usually carry religious materials, so take the time to see what they have to offer. On top of this, many libraries (post-secondary and public) are willing to track down resources for you and may offer inter-library loans that can greatly assist you. Inter-library loans are a great resource. If this is a service your library offers, they may be able to gain access to an article or book through another lending institution, whether it is across town, on the other side of the country, or even in another country. As you progress in your studies, this service can be crucial as you seek to find that one source that is vital to your work. Be sure to ask at your library about these services.

Third, if you have a college or university near you—even one at which you are not enrolled—they may grant you access as a *reader*, which means you can use and photocopy their material. You will have to contact the institution in question to find out how to become a reader there.

Finally, the used book industry is thriving, in large part due to increased Internet sales. Many sources that may be integral to your work can be found at very reasonable prices online. Used book stores are often worth perusing at regular intervals as well, particularly those located near post-secondary institutions. So, even if your university library is not at your doorstep, there are other ways to hunt down sources; be creative and use what is available to you.

IDENTIFYING AND EVALUATING ACADEMIC SOURCES

Locating resources for your research is important, but this is only one step in the process. The next thing you need to do is identify the types of sources you have found, evaluate the appropriateness of these resources, and then decide which will be most helpful for your particular assignment.

Types of sources

There are different types of resources, and as you begin to research and write essays, it will be helpful to classify which types you are dealing with. In general, there are three main categories of sources used in academic work: primary, secondary, and reference (or tertiary) materials. *Primary* sources contain original, non-interpreted, or non-evaluated information. These can be almost anything, depending on your field of research. *Secondary* sources analyze, evaluate, or interpret the information contained within primary sources. This broad category includes most books, articles, and other writings by scholars and researchers. Finally, *reference* or tertiary materials are works that compile, analyze, and digest secondary sources. As such, they offer helpful summaries on what are often complex subjects. These tend to be factual, and include encyclopedias and dictionaries. These three classifications are not set in stone, and not all sources are easy to classify within this framework. In fact, some works will cross over into more than one category. When you are starting out, however, these categories may help you think through the nature and scope of your sources.

Let's look at some examples of these types of materials. If you are studying a sacred text within a religion, that text will function as a primary source for your work. Let's say that you are writing on the topic of Karma Yoga in Hinduism. In this case, the Bhagavad Gita, as one of the sacred texts of Hinduism, will be a primary source for your research. Books and articles that analyze the Bhagavad Gita's use of this theme, such as Robert N. Minor's *Bhagavad-Gita: An Exegetical Commentary*, will be secondary sources. Articles in dictionaries and encyclopedias, for instance the "Karma-Yoga" entry in the *Concise Oxford Dictionary of World Religions*, will serve as reference material. To take another example, you may be writing on a historical event or period, say the separation of the Eastern and Western churches in the eleventh century. In this case, your primary sources will be the surviving writings that document this period. Secondary sources will be writings that comment on these events, for instance Henry Chadwick's *East and West: The Making of a Rift in the Church: From Apostolic Times until the Council of Florence*. Entries in dictionaries and encyclopedias, such as the article on "The Great Schism" in the *Oxford Dictionary of the Christian Church*, will serve as reference material.

The further you go in religious studies, the more you will find yourself working with primary sources. While you will be asked to evaluate and analyze, rather than simply *read about*, primary sources when you reach upper-level classes, we suggest that you use all three types of sources in your research from day one. This will assure your instructor that you are doing thorough research and covering all your bases in the quest for appropriate sources.

Evaluating sources

There is one more important factor in your selection of resources, and that is the *quality* of the sources available. We are told from a young age not to judge a book by its cover, but knowing who has published a particular source and how old that source is may indeed tell you if it is worth your time.

Generally, scholars ask themselves a series of questions when evaluating a source's usefulness for their study. As a student you can do the same.[1]

- Who wrote it? Are they qualified to write on this topic? Are they employed in an academic (or related) context? (Browse the book's jacket, or look the author up on the Internet.)
- Who published it? Are they reputable? Is it an academic publisher?
- Is it academic (especially regarding journals) or is it popular in nature?
- What topics are in the table of contents? Are these topics important to your research?
- When was it written? To your knowledge, has scholarship advanced on the topic since its publication?
- What style is the writing? Is it generally objective and formal?
- What books are in the bibliography? With which sources is the author interacting?
- Are there footnotes (or endnotes)?

These questions should help you weed out those sources that are not necessarily suitable for your research (even though they may be good books).

With regard to secondary sources, while "new" is not always better than "old," a recent publication date is (hopefully) an indicator that the author of the work is interacting with the most recent data or ideas on a particular subject. As such, while older materials may be valuable resources, and you might choose to consult them to see what they have to say, it may not be appropriate to use them without consulting more recent material. It is important to remember the distinction made earlier between types of sources. For example, if you are researching the Spanish Inquisition, an older resource that is a primary source is obviously good and indeed may be crucial for your research. If, however, you are researching current trends in dealing with religious conflict, then you will want to make sure you are consulting up-to-date sources that can give you the fullest picture of the issue as it stands today.

As we will discuss in Chapter 5, try to find out as much as you can about a source before you spend time reading it thoroughly. If needed, it may help to skim the first chapter or two, as well as the conclusion, before giving the book your undivided attention. As you do this keep in mind that, as one writer has quipped, "Skimming is not what it used to be."[2] While you may have found skimming a useful technique in the past, it becomes more difficult at the post-secondary level because the material you are dealing with contains concepts that can be complicated or difficult to grasp at first. As always, leave yourself a good amount of time when doing research.

Another aspect of research to bear in mind is the number of sources you should cite. Having a vast quantity of sources is not necessarily as important as making sure the sources you do use are relevant and helpful. We suggest asking your instructor about the number of sources she or he expects you to use, and perhaps you might ask him or her to take a look at your preliminary bibliography to see if you are on the right track. Alternatively, as we will discuss in the next chapter, you might want to submit an essay proposal form, which would include this information.

Finding quality academic sources online

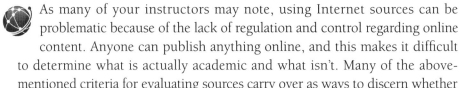 As many of your instructors may note, using Internet sources can be problematic because of the lack of regulation and control regarding online content. Anyone can publish anything online, and this makes it difficult to determine what is actually academic and what isn't. Many of the above-mentioned criteria for evaluating sources carry over as ways to discern whether an Internet source is valuable for research. It is important to distinguish here between sources you retrieve online through your institution's databases and indexes (as discussed earlier), and sources you find in your own Internet

searching. For example, an article from an academic journal that you retrieve using JSTOR will be considered reliable, assuming you use the criteria for evaluating sources outlined above. However, a website such as Wikipedia, which is freely available online, would be considered an Internet source. Here are a few further issues to note for such Internet sources:

- *Check the source of the site.* If it is a university webpage, or a site devoted to academic matters, it may be suitable for research. If it is someone's personal webpage or blog, it should probably be avoided (unless the nature of the assignment calls for a survey of people's thoughts and opinions).
- *Check the author's background.* As with books, it is vital to determine whether the author is a reputable scholar or specialist. (Do they have a PhD or other relevant terminal degree? Do they teach at an academic institution?)
- *Check whether the source has a print counterpart.* Many academic sources available online today are reproduced from print—whether an online version of a journal, magazine, book, or dictionary. If a source has been in print before going online, this usually adds to its pedigree.
- *Check for endnotes, bibliographies, and other citations.* If an article or source is truly academic, it should have notes (usually endnotes when published online), or at least a bibliography to bolster its claims.
- *Be wary of online encyclopedia articles that can be edited by anyone, such as those found in Wikipedia.* Although sources such as these can be helpful, they can just as often contain errors, unsubstantiated claims, or ideological slants particular to the author. The information might also be modified (or tampered with) on a day-to-day basis.
- *Use extreme caution and discernment.* Before using something as a source for your essay that could drastically affect your marks, think it through. You may even want to consult your course instructor as to whether it would be advisable to use a particular source.

READING ACADEMIC SOURCES

Once you have located appropriate sources, you are ready to apply the principles of engaged learning to your reading and note-taking. As you dig into academic sources, you may notice that some can be quite difficult to read. This is true for a number of reasons: they use a good deal of jargon (terminology particular to the subject in question, which you might not be familiar with), there are many references and notes, and the ideas discussed are often abstract and complicated.[3] In light of this, you may need to read a particular chapter, article, or section once, twice, or even three times to take in fully what is being said. You will also need to record your thoughts and reactions (i.e. take notes) as you go along, as there will be too much information for you simply to recall at a later time. Because of these issues, a few pointers on note-taking in your research might be helpful.[4]

- *There are various ways to approach note-taking.* Some people use note cards, others use a notebook or loose-leaf paper in a folder, and still others take their notes with a computer. One method is not better than the others; it is simply a matter of choice and comfort. Find a method that works best for you.
- *Make sure you take down all the source's bibliographic information.* You must provide all relevant information, including author(s) or editor(s), title, series or volume, name of publisher, and date and place published. Having all of the relevant information will be important later as you craft your bibliography or works cited. For example, if you are taking notes from Hallaq's book on Islamic law, you would need all of the following information: Wael B. Hallaq, *The Origins and Evolution of Islamic Law*, Themes in Islamic Law (Cambridge: Cambridge University Press, 2005). There is nothing more frustrating than having to track down a book again to find bibliographic information you failed to write down the first time.
- *Subsequent references within your own notes should be clear.* Provide enough information to give you clarity at a later point (for instance, Hallaq, *Origins and Evolution*, 75).
- *Don't write down everything.* Keep notes short. Be judicious in your note-taking, deciding which information is relevant for your research. Also, many students and researchers choose to keep each note to one idea or thought. It is better to have many short notes than a few convoluted paragraphs of notes. This will help later on as you attempt to organize your notes for the writing process. This is also true for taking notes on a computer; keep notes short and make sure you provide bibliographic information with each note, in case you move or copy-and-paste your notes into different sections at a later time.

- *Each note will be either a paraphrase or a quotation from your source.* Make sure you distinguish these so you can identify which type each note is later.
- *Be accurate with quotations.* Copy verbatim what the author has said if you are quoting someone, and be sure to note the exact page number(s) where the quote is located.
- *Highlight key words.* To stay organized, highlight important words or phrases, or make use of titles in your notes to aid in the process of sorting and organizing. Many people find colour-coding their notes to be a useful way of organizing their ideas.

Remember, there is no formula for reading constructively and taking quality notes. Much depends on your personality and learning style. Try to find a system that works well for you and see how things go in your first few essays.

PLAGIARISM AND ACADEMIC HONESTY

While we will focus on appropriately documenting and acknowledging your sources in Chapter 15, it is worth highlighting now the importance of academic honesty. Two of the primary functions of documenting your sources are to show academic honesty and to acknowledge what has influenced your research and writing. If you fail to acknowledge your sources, you are essentially allowing your reader to assume that the words and ideas you present are entirely your own; in other words, you are plagiarizing, and the penalties can be severe.

Plagiarism is a form of stealing; as with other offences against the law, ignorance is no excuse. Penalties for plagiarism range from a grade of zero to outright expulsion. You can avoid plagiarism by giving credit where credit is due. If you are using someone else's idea, acknowledge it, even if you have changed the wording or just summarized the main points. You should not think your work will seem weaker because you have acknowledged the ideas of others. On the contrary, it will be all the more convincing; serious academic studies are almost always built on the work of preceding scholars, with credit duly given to earlier works.

When beginning to do research, you might find it hard to decide when to acknowledge others and when it's not necessary to do so. In general, you should provide a notation when you have quoted, paraphrased, or alluded to an entire work or to a specific passage in that work.[5] That said, you may feel like you need to give a notation after every sentence as you begin your writing. You will soon settle into a pattern of recognizing when to offer a citation, however. In the early stages of essay writing, err on the side of caution and document your sources consistently, even when in doubt.

The following examples highlight similarities and differences between quotations, paraphrases, and allusions:

Quotation:

As William James remarks, "Were one asked to characterize the life of religion in the broadest and most general terms possible, one might say that it consists of the belief that there is an unseen order, and that our supreme good lies in harmoniously adjusting ourselves thereto."

(The proper use of quotation marks will be dealt with in greater detail in Chapter 17.)

Paraphrase:

Religious life, as William James notes, can be understood as a belief in an unseen order, and living in response to that reality.

Allusion:

Some understand religious life as living in response to the belief in an unseen order.

In all of these cases a notation would be required because we are referencing William James, *The Varieties of Religious Experience: A Study in Human Nature* [1902] (New York: Simon & Schuster, 1997), p. 41. James is being quoted, paraphrased, or is the source of an allusion, even if not named. Remember that *plagiarism involves not only using someone else's words but also expressing ideas that you found elsewhere without making it clear that they were taken from another source.*

Where should you draw the line on acknowledgements? As a rule, you do not need to give credit for things that are common knowledge. For instance, you do not need to cite that Gandhi was assassinated in 1948 or that Muhammad is considered the founder of Islam. However, you should acknowledge any clever turn of phrase that is neither well known nor your own. And always document any fact or claim—statistical or otherwise—that is unfamiliar or open to question.

For students in a hurry, online material can be a particular hazard and can cause a lot of grief. Even though websites are instantly accessible, the material is not common property. In fact, it is the property of the individual or organization that publishes it and is protected by copyright in the same way that printed material is. It is crucial that you properly acknowledge the information you find on a website, even if you are summarizing or building upon it, just as you would acknowledge any other source.

In summary, knowing when to acknowledge your sources is a learning process that will take some time. When in doubt, be overly cautious and offer plenty of citations. Giving credit where credit is due is not only a hallmark of academic research, but it's your legal responsibility as a student.

WRITING CHECKLIST: FINDING AND USING ACADEMIC RESOURCES

- ☐ Have I familiarized myself with my institution's library (or libraries)? Do I know the "lay of the land" in order to find what I need?
- ☐ Have I utilized the full gamut of databases, library search tools, journal searches, dictionary articles, and indexes available to me?
- ☐ Have I ensured that my selected sources are appropriate by checking their date, publisher, author, academic writing level, and so on?
- ☐ Have I been careful and selective in using the Internet for online searches, and have I ensured that my sources are reputable?
- ☐ Have I kept notes that are useful to the writing process? That is, are my notes legible, clear, appropriately referenced, and organized, and do they contain enough information?
- ☐ Do I understand when to reference a source in my paper or when I am relying on another person's ideas? Do I understand plagiarism? Do my notes reflect this information?

CONCLUSION

Learning to locate and use appropriate sources efficiently is key to writing good research papers and succeeding in your post-secondary education. In fact, finding the right sources and using them well is often what distinguishes an average student from an excellent one. In this chapter, we looked at the various ways you might find, read, and keep track of the sources you will use in your research, including those found in libraries, on the Internet, or through online databases. We also raised the issue of plagiarism. Next we turn to some of the nuts and bolts of writing essays.

ENDNOTES

1. The following questions are adapted from Nancy J. Vyhmeister, *Quality Research Papers: For Students of Religion and Theology,* 2nd ed. (Grand Rapids, MI: Zondervan, 2008), pp. 69–72. We also draw from her work on evaluating sources more generally.

2. Rob Barnes, *Successful Study for Degrees*, 2nd ed. (London: Routledge, 1995), p. 51.

3. These and other issues are helpfully raised in Barnes, *Successful Study*, p. 56.

4. We here draw from Vyhmeister, *Quality Research Papers*, pp. 76–77.

5. The following guidelines can be found in many university handbooks on essay writing. We draw here from the terminology found in Durham University's "Taught MA Handbook, 2009–2010," pp. 58–59; available online at www.dur.ac.uk/resources/theology.religion/postgrad/TaughtMAHandbook.pdf.

CHAPTER 5

Writing Essays

Objectives

- Distinguishing between different types of essays
- Planning your research
  - Defining the problem
  - Identifying the approach
  - Recognizing academic jargon
  - Gathering sources
  - Drafting a working outline and thesis
- Writing drafts of the essay
  - Drafting different sections of your essay
  - Editing your essay
  - Formatting your essay

We noted in Chapter 1 that research is a way of helping students engage with their studies in a meaningful way, allowing them to interact critically with the subject matter. One of the primary ways that such research takes place in religious studies is through writing essays. This chapter will focus on some of the steps you can follow in that process.

If you are one of the many students who dread writing academic essays, you will find that following a few simple steps in planning and organizing will make the task easier—and the result better. You will probably develop your own steps for writing essays over time. We would like to offer some practical suggestions to get you going on this process. This is not a one-size-fits-all process, and the amount of time you spend on each stage will depend on the nature of the assignment. For a short, straightforward essay requiring little research, you will likely spend most of the time drafting and editing. For a more complex essay, when you must take into account what others before you have said, it's likely that over half of your time will be spent on research and planning. Understanding the total process of completing a written assignment will serve you well no matter the nature of the assignment.

DISTINGUISHING BETWEEN DIFFERENT TYPES OF ESSAYS

The first step in the process is to determine what type of essay you are writing. There are a number of different types of essays that you may be required to write in your religious studies courses, and the type should be easy to discern based on the description given in your syllabus. In this chapter we tackle general essay writing, both descriptive and argumentative. Later in the book we will address book reviews and short assignments (chapters 6 and 7), as well as interpretive and comparative essays (chapters 8 and 9).

PLANNING YOUR RESEARCH

Once you have determined what type of essay you are going to be writing, the next step is to plan your research. Some students claim they can write essays without any planning at all. On the rare occasions when they succeed, their writing usually is not as spontaneous as they might think; in fact, they have thought or talked a good deal about the subject in advance and have come to the task with some ready-made ideas. More often, students who try to write a lengthy essay without planning just end up frustrated. They get stuck in the middle and don't know how to finish, or they suddenly realize that they're rambling.

In contrast, most writers say that the planning stage is the most important part of the whole process. Certainly the evidence shows that poor planning usually leads to disorganized writing. In the majority of students' essays, the single greatest improvement would not be better research or better grammar but better organization.

This insistence on planning does not rule out exploratory writing. Many people find that the act of writing itself is the best way to generate ideas or to overcome writer's block; the hard decisions about organization come after they've put something down on the page. Whether you organize before or after you begin to write, at some point you need to plan. In Chapter 2 we noted several issues related to time management, both in general and in relation to specific assignments. Good time-management skills are especially important when it comes to writing research essays. You may want to revisit the suggestions we gave in Chapter 2 as you work through this chapter.

We suggest a four-step process that will allow you to plan your research in an effective manner, in order to begin writing your essay. The steps are as follows:

1. define the problem;
2. identify your approach;
3. gather introductory sources and do some preliminary research; and
4. draft a working outline.

Define the problem

Research essays deal with a specific issue or problem. As one author notes, good essays will deal with "a gap in knowledge, an unclear situation, an unresolved question, a lack of information, an unknown, a specific question to be investigated and answered, or a problem to be researched and solved."[1] Even descriptive essays that trace ideas or compare histories can be written around a problem or issue. You will find that structuring an essay around a problem or issue, rather than simply an idea, will make for a more engaging final product.

Many guides for writing essays begin with a section on how to choose your topic. In some cases, you will need to pick a topic, narrow your topic down to a particular theme, and then find a problem within that theme to research. For other assignments, your topic is chosen for you, or a specific question is posed, or you may even be given a predetermined title, which will define the scope of your essay before you begin. Whichever of these situations you find yourself in, you will need to define the underlying problem that you will be investigating in your essay.

Let's begin with picking a topic or issue on your own. In this case, you will need to start with a broad topic and then narrow it down to a manageable theme for your given assignment. How do you go about doing this? The best way of analyzing a topic is to ask questions that will lead to useful answers. Journalists often approach their stories through a six-question formula: *who*? *what*? *where*? *when*? *why*? and *how*? For example, let's say you are taking a course on Islam, and you would like to research the Hajj, the annual Muslim pilgrimage. Consider this topic in terms of the six-question formula:

- *What* is the history of the Hajj? How did it become one of the Five Pillars of Islam?
- *Where* does the Hajj take place? What is the significance of this location?

- *Who* is expected to participate in the Hajj, and how often?
- *When* does the Hajj take place?
- *Why* is the Hajj undertaken? What role does in play in Muslim life?
- *How* do Muslims prepare for the Hajj?

Most often, the questions you ask initially—and their answers—will be general, but they will stimulate more specific questions that will help you refine your topic and locate a specific problem or question you would like to investigate.

If your instructor supplies you with essay topics or titles, it may be that the problem or question is *implicit* in what you have been assigned. Keep in mind that if a topic or essay title has been set, it has been set for a reason. Usually the instructor has chosen this topic because she or he feels it will benefit you and your understanding of the subject. Figuring out why this is so, then, becomes very important.

For example, consider the following hypothetical essay title, which has been set by your instructor: "Discuss the authorship of the Dasam Granth." Implicit in this title are various questions and problems that could be addressed. The obvious question is straightforward: Who wrote the Dasam Granth (a Sikh religious text)? But behind this might be larger questions and disagreements over the authorship of the various parts of this collection, and your instructor wants you to know, and be able to explain, why.

Here, then, are a few tips on defining the problem of an essay. First, though there may be various ways you can approach a topic or an essay title, you will probably need to pick one question or problem and stick with it. Second, it may be helpful to get in touch with your instructor early in the semester in order to make sure you are approaching your essay from a constructive perspective and that you have truly understood the title or topic. Third, state the question or problem as clearly as possible, and keep coming back to it. This is what you will be researching, and it will guide your work. Try to formulate your essay question as succinctly as possible.

Identify the approach

Once you have defined the main problem or issue, your next step is to identify the approach you will take to answer the question. Here the terminology of the essay question or title becomes crucial. What are you asked to do with the problem? Analyze? Compare? Discuss? Explain? Each of these terms requires that you approach the problem in a different way. If the approach is specified by your instructor, you simply need to make sure you understand the term and what is being asked of you. If you haven't been given this kind of instruction, you may want to consult your instructor to make sure you are taking the right approach. Here are a few examples:

Academic Jargon and Terms

Outline   State simply, without much development of each point (unless asked).

Trace   Review by looking back—on stages or steps in a process, or on causes of an occurrence.

Explain   Show how or why something happens.

Discuss   Examine or analyze in an orderly way. This instruction allows you considerable freedom, as long as you take into account contrary evidence or ideas.

Compare   Examine and show how two things are similar. However, note that this term can also mean 'compare and contrast'; that is, examine differences as well as similarities. Ask your professor if you are uncertain which you should do.

Contrast   Examine and show how two things differ.

Evaluate   Analyze strengths and weaknesses, providing an overall assessment of worth.

Take, for example, the following essay topic: "Trace the spread of Buddhism in China." The approach we are asked to take is to *trace*. As stated above, to trace means to "review by looking back—on stages or steps in a process, or on causes of an occurrence." The key here is to make sure you are doing specifically what the question asks. If you are asked to trace, outline, or explain an issue, you need to stay away from comparing and contrasting, evaluating, proving, or justifying. Conversely, if you are asked to evaluate or discuss a problem, mere explanation or description will not suffice.

Our experience as professors indicates that this is one of the greatest obstacles students face in achieving a good grade for an essay. A student is asked to *compare* and *contrast* the writings of two religious thinkers (for example) but the student never moves beyond a basic description of each. Or, conversely, the student is asked to *trace* the development of a religious teaching but instead writes an essay plagued by judgments or hypotheses that are irrelevant to the task at hand. Identifying the correct approach may well be the most important thing you do in producing an effective essay. The next step is to start collecting resources that will help you begin your research.

Gather sources and begin research

In order to move on to the next stage, outlining your essay, it is often necessary to gather a few resources to get you going. Wherever possible, it is wise to start with primary sources (that is, original, non-interpreted, or non-evaluated source material on which others comment or build). As we discussed in Chapter 4, primary material—usually in the form of books, articles, or historical texts—is what you will base your essay on. Surprising as it may seem, the best way to begin working with this material is to give it a quick initial skim. Don't just dive in and read from cover to cover; first look at the table of contents, scan the index, and read the preface or introduction to get a sense of the author's purpose and plan. Getting an overview will allow you to focus your questions for a more purposeful and analytic second reading. *Make no mistake:* a superficial reading is *not* all you need. You still have to work through the material carefully a second (or even third) time. But an initial skim followed by a focused second reading will give you a much more thorough understanding than one slow plod ever will.

After looking at the primary sources, you may also want to consult some secondary sources and reference material. However, always be sure you have a firm grasp of the primary sources before you turn to secondary sources (analyses of the primary material). Sometimes instructors discourage secondary reading in introductory courses. They know that students who turn to commentaries may be so overwhelmed by the weight of authority that they will rely too heavily on them. For more on how to identify and use proper resources, including online data, see Chapter 4.

Draft a working outline

At this point in your preparation you should have a fairly good idea of what you will be doing in your essay. You have defined the problem you will be addressing, as well as the approach you will be taking. You also will have done some preliminary research to better understand your topic. It is now time to start thinking about which particular issues need to be addressed, how you will structure your essay, and what you would like to say (or argue) in it. This process will result in an *essay outline*.

COMPONENTS

First, it is helpful to think about the various *components* that make up your subject. How can you divide the subject into parts or categories? Can the main divisions be further subdivided? In other words, how might the topic be broken down into smaller elements? This question forces you to take a close look at the subject and helps you to avoid oversimplification or easy generalization.

Suppose that your assignment is to discuss the circumstances surrounding the Protestant Reformation of the sixteenth century. After thinking about the various components involved in this topic, you might decide that you can break the topic down into

1. religious issues;
2. political issues; and
3. social issues that brought about the Reformation.

Alternatively, you might divide it into

1. important people;
2. important places; and
3. important events.

Then, since these components are too broad, you might break them down further, perhaps deciding to focus on point 1, important people:

a. those who remained in the Roman Catholic Church; and
b. those involved in the Reformation, separating early reformers and late reformers.

Approaching your subject this way will help you appreciate its complexity and avoid making wide-sweeping generalizations that do not apply to all areas of the subject. In addition, asking questions about the components of your subject will help you to find one aspect of it that is not too large for you to explore in detail.

THESIS

As you work through possible components and issues related to your essay, you should also start thinking about a thesis. As noted above, not all essays centre on arguments. Yet every essay, even the descriptive kind, needs a controlling idea around which all the material can be organized. This central idea is usually known as a thesis, though in the case of a descriptive essay you may prefer to think of it as a theme. Consider these statements:

THEME: Tolkien's *The Lord of the Rings* employs many religious and spiritual themes.

THESIS: Religious struggle is the most appropriate category for understanding Tolkien's *The Lord of the Rings*.

The first is a rather straightforward statement of fact; an essay centred on such a theme would probably focus on describing religious and spiritual tropes found in Tolkien's work. By contrast, the second statement is one with which other people might well disagree; an essay based on this thesis would have to present a convincing argument. The descriptive form can produce an informative and interesting essay, but many students prefer the argumentative approach because it is easier to organize and is more likely to produce strong writing.

If you have decided to present an argument, you will probably want to create a *working thesis* as the focal point around which you can start organizing your material. This thesis should incorporate the various aspects of your subject matter. Bear in mind that this working thesis does not have to be final: you are free to change it later in your planning. It simply serves as a linchpin, holding together your information and ideas as you organize. It will help you define your intentions, make your research more selective, and focus your essay.

Later in the writing process you will probably want to make your working thesis into an explicit thesis statement that can appear in your introduction. It is worth taking the time to work this statement out carefully. Use a complete sentence to express it, and above all make sure that it is *restricted*, *unified*, and *precise*.[2]

A restricted thesis

A restricted thesis is one that is narrow enough for you to examine thoroughly in the space you have available. For example, you may wish to restrict your thesis to a particular location and/or time: "New religious movements in North America grew exponentially in the twentieth century." Or, it may be important to restrict your thesis to one aspect of a religion, perhaps a particular branch or denomination: "The teachings of Svetambara Jainism promote the liberation of women and gender equality." Whatever the discipline or subject, make sure that your topic is restricted enough that you can explore it in depth.

A unified thesis

A unified thesis must have one controlling idea. Beware of the double-headed thesis: "The teachings of Confucius are universal and they have drastically shaped modern China." What is the controlling idea here? The universality of Confucianism or how these teachings have shaped modern China? It is possible to have two or more related ideas in a thesis, but only if one of them is clearly in control, with all the other ideas subordinated to it: "Although the teachings of Confucius are generally regarded to be universal in nature, their impact can be seen most clearly in modern China."

A precise thesis

A precise thesis should *not* contain vague terms such as *interesting* and *significant*, as in "The fourteenth Dalai Lama, Tenzin Gyatso, is one of the most interesting religious leaders of the twentieth century." Does *interesting* mean "wise or forward-thinking in his teaching," "controversial," or "intriguing"? Do not say simply, "Sheila Watson's use of symbols is an important feature of her writing" when you can be more precise about the work you are discussing, the kind of symbols you've found there, and exactly what they do: "In *The Double Hook*, Sheila Watson adapts traditional symbols from Christian and Indian mythology to underscore the theme of spiritual death and regeneration."

Remember to be as specific as possible when creating a thesis in order to focus your essay. Do not just make an assertion—give the main reason for it. Instead of saying "Wiccans often practice their religion in private" and leave it at that, add an explanation: ". . . because many outsiders associate witchcraft with Satanism and its practitioners are thus liable to persecution." If these details make your thesis sound awkward, don't worry; a working thesis is only a planning device, something to guide the organization of your ideas. You can change the wording in your final essay.

ESSAY OUTLINE

With these notes on theses in mind, we return to the matter of constructing an outline. If you tend to have problems organizing your writing, your outline should be formal, meaning you have written out your thesis statement, a topic sentence for each paragraph, and the main points of each paragraph in complete sentences. On the other hand, if your mind is naturally logical, you may find it is enough just to jot down a few words on a scrap of paper. For most students, an informal but well-organized outline in point form is the most useful model. If you have used index cards to organize your research materials, these can provide a simple way to begin your outline. Rearranging the cards in different orders will give you an idea of how topics fit together before you put the outline down on paper. If you prefer to work on a computer, your word processor offers a range of outline styles.

At this stage, the work you did previously in defining the problem, identifying your approach, researching the topic, isolating components, and developing a thesis becomes the basis for your outline. Here, for example, is a sample outline for the essay topic noted above, "Discuss the circumstances surrounding the Protestant Reformation of the sixteenth century."

THEME: The Protestant Reformation occurred because of several important factors, including religious issues, political changes, and social upheaval.

Introduction

    I. Religious issues

        A. The Roman Church in Europe

        B. Early dissidents

            1. John Wycliffe

            2. Jan Hus

        C. Internal strife

            1. Theological controversies—indulgences

            2. The rise of Martin Luther and John Calvin

    II. Political changes

        A. Shifting alliances and political structures

        B. Changing economic systems

    III. Social upheaval

        A. The Renaissance

        B. Peasant unrest

        C. The printing press and the rise of literacy

Conclusion

Here are some further guidelines for developing outlines:

- **Code your categories**. Use different sets of markings to establish the relative importance of your entries. The example here moves from Roman numerals to uppercase letters to

Arabic numerals, but you could use another system. Computer programs have a default format but also offer alternatives.

- **Categorize according to importance**. Make sure that only items of equal value are put in equivalent categories. Give major points more weight than minor ones.
- **Check lines of connection.** Make sure that each of the main categories is directly linked to the central thesis; then see that each subcategory is directly linked to the larger category that contains it. Checking these lines of connection is the best way of preventing essay muddle.
- **Be consistent.** In arranging your points, use the same order every time. You may choose to move from the most important point to the least important, or vice versa, as long as you are consistent.
- **Be logical**. In addition to checking for lines of connection and organizational consistency, make sure that the overall development of your work is logical. Does each heading/idea/discussion flow into the next, leading your reader through the material in the most logical manner?
- **Use parallel wording**. Phrasing each entry in a similar way makes it easier for your reader to follow your line of thinking.

Be prepared to change your outline at any time in the writing process. Your initial outline is not meant to put an iron clamp on your thinking but to relieve anxiety about where you're heading. A careful outline prevents frustration and dead ends—that "I'm stuck. Where do I go from here?" feeling. But since the very act of writing will usually generate new ideas, you should be ready to modify your original plan. As you work with the material and your interests in the subject evolve, you may decide that you want to focus on only one of your three main points, perhaps in this case religious issues or even just key figures like Wycliffe and Hus. Just remember that any new outline must have the consistency and clear connections required for a unified essay.

When you have completed an outline, you've come to the end of your planning and you're ready to begin writing. You have defined the problem, identified your approach, gathered resources and begun your research, and drafted an outline based on your carefully thought-out theme or thesis statement. Next, you may find it helpful to work through an essay proposal form, to ensure that all the above information is complete. We recommend this practice (especially as you begin writing essays) and your instructor may require you to submit one. An example might look like this:

Essay Proposal Form

Instructor: _____ Course ID: _____

Student Name: _____ Student ID: _____

Essay Due Date: _____

1. Essay Will Be:

    ☐   Thematic

    ☐   Interpretive (of a sacred or religious text)

    ☐   Comparative

    ☐   As prescribed in the syllabus or by the instructor

    ☐   Other _____

2. Provisional Essay Title:

    _____

3. Primary Essay Problem or Question:
    (What is the main question or problem that I am dealing with in this essay?)

    _____

    _____

    _____

4. Methodology and Approach:
    (What exactly does the course assignment ask me to do? Trace? Compare? Outline? How will I approach my problem?)

    _____

    _____

    _____

5. Provisional Thesis:
    (What do I hope to argue, however provisional my thesis may be?)

    _____

    _____

    _____

6. Personal Objectives:
    (What do I hope learn through this paper? What are my objectives as a student?)

    _____

    _____

    _____

7. Preliminary Bibliography:
    (You have gathered sources to begin your research; give their details here.)

    _____

    _____

    _____

    _____

    _____

    _____

    _____

8. Brief Essay Outline:

    _____

    _____

    _____

    _____

You are now ready to start doing further research, and to begin writing drafts of your essay.

WRITING DRAFTS OF THE ESSAY

Writing is a process, and good writers understand that writing happens in various stages over time. In this section we will explore what it means to write drafts of essays and what should happen at each stage of writing. Our suggestion is that your essay should go through at least three stages of drafts and revisions.

First draft

Now that you've collected and collated all of your research and notes, you can begin your first draft. The first draft is essentially a quick rough copy to get your ideas down on paper. Don't spend too much time worrying about style or grammar. Instead, follow your outline and begin to move through the various points of your argument.

In general, essays have the following elements: 1) title page/preliminary pages; 2) introduction; 3) main body; 4) conclusion; and 5) bibliography/appendixes. The three middle parts—introduction, body, and conclusion—need to form one flowing piece of writing. The length and number of points or paragraphs in your essay will eventually need to be determined, something usually controlled by the page (or word count) limit set by your instructor.

Many people think that an essay is simply written from beginning to end. Though many essays have been written this way, it is probably not the most effective approach. In fact, we find that students have an easier time if they skip the introduction at first and get right into the meat of the essay. If you feel you must write a quick introduction to get going, do so but don't spend too much time on it. It's best to let this wait until the end, when you have written the bulk of the paper and even the conclusion. Here is what needs to be included in each of the three main sections, in the order that we recommend you write them.

Main body: Here you report the findings of your research. This is the longest part of the essay, and it is divided into sections, based on the components you have already outlined. These components now become the points in your main body. Your main points will often have sub-points that further your argument (see the sample outline on page 50). Most teachers allow the use of headings if they help you organize your material. We encourage you to use these where possible (check with your instructor about their use if in doubt; for more on headings, see Chapter 10). Start with your weakest arguments, and build up to your strongest. Be sure to *demonstrate* and *illustrate* your points rather than simply assert them or appeal to an authority who agrees with you. Be especially careful not to plagiarize ideas (see Chapter 4 for more on this topic). Use lively and vivid language throughout.

Conclusion: This section of your essay summarizes your findings and draws conclusions. It may be beneficial to revisit or restate the problem you are addressing and how you went about dealing with it. Your conclusions should again be made clear. You may want to address larger implications of your conclusion by addressing more general issues (but do so carefully and do not overstate things). To take the example essay above, you might conclude that the Reformation paved the way for the multitude of Christian denominations that have emerged over the past few centuries. Remember that no new evidence is brought in at this time. It is tempting to add just a few more arguments in your conclusion—don't do it! Sum up what you have said and reiterate your argument. You will want to craft this section with care: what you say must match the problem or question addressed at the beginning, and you must state how you have gone about dealing with the problem. End this paragraph on a strong point, or what we might call the *clincher*, a strong statement that leaves the reader in agreement with your argument.

Introduction: Now you can write your introduction. Your outline and crafted thesis statement will be the basis for this section. Your introduction is the reader's guide to your essay, and should include the following:

1. The question or problem being studied. This may include more general or background information on the problem to give the reader a good understanding of the issue that is being researched.
2. The main points or components of the subject you will explore and the approach you will take in examining them.
3. Your desired result. It is helpful to include your thesis as the last sentence of your introduction, as a statement that succinctly clarifies the results of your research and will serve as the controlling idea of the essay.

(For further tips on writing effective introductions and conclusions, see Chapter 10.)

One way to summarize this method of essay writing is through what Sheridan Baker calls the "funnel approach."[3] In your introduction, you capture the reader's attention through an interesting fact or general statement about your topic and then funnel things down, showing how your specific thesis applies

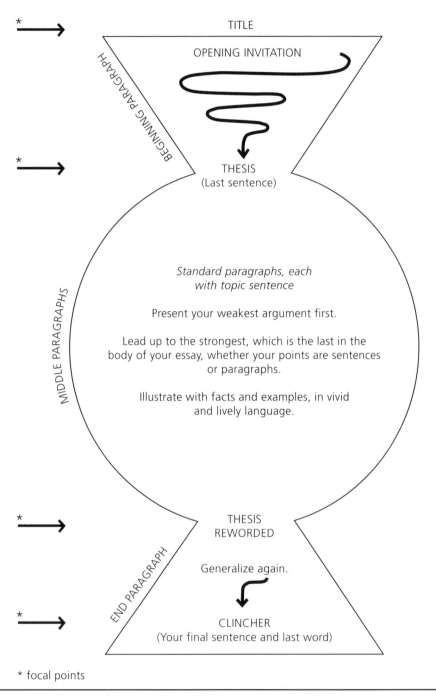

TITLE

OPENING INVITATION

BEGINNING PARAGRAPH

THESIS
(Last sentence)

MIDDLE PARAGRAPHS

*Standard paragraphs, each
with topic sentence*

Present your weakest argument first.

Lead up to the strongest, which is the last in the
body of your essay, whether your points are sentences
or paragraphs.

Illustrate with facts and examples, in vivid
and lively language.

THESIS
REWORDED

END PARAGRAPH

Generalize again.

CLINCHER
(Your final sentence and last word)

* focal points

Figure 5.1   The funnel approach

Source: Sheridan Baker and Laurence B. Gamache, *The Canadian Practical Stylist*, 4th ed. (Don Mills, ON: Addison-Wesley, 1998), pp. 55–6. Reprinted by permission of Pearson Canada Inc.

to it. Your middle paragraphs work one after another, building up your case before your conclusion, where you reword your (hopefully proven) thesis and show how your work affects broader issues related to your topic. You conclude the essay with your clincher statement.

A Note on Writer's Block

Anyone who writes will experience "writer's block," an inability to know what to write or how to proceed with your work, at some point in their writing careers. Here are some helpful suggestions for getting past this crisis:[4]

- Scribble or "free write" any ideas that come to mind for 2–3 minutes. Worry about rearranging it all later.
- Remind yourself that this first step is only a draft, and nobody needs to see it but you. Just start writing, even if you end up deleting large portions of what you have initially written.
- Verbalize your thoughts—get your thoughts flowing by speaking your ideas out loud.
- Brainstorm and make diagrams; write down everything you know on a topic, or use a diagram to organize your thoughts.

These are a few ideas to get your writing going when it stalls. Remember that this happens to all of us, but the key is to keep pressing ahead and working on a consistent basis. Slowly, but surely, your work will get done.

Second draft

When you have finished a rough first draft of your essay, let your work sit for a day or two in order to give yourself some critical distance and clarity on the subject. This will let you notice things that you may not see if you reread immediately after finishing your draft. Then reread your work and start to make corrections (it may be helpful to print a hard copy at this stage so that you can easily mark up your writing). Editing doesn't just mean checking your work for errors in grammar or spelling. It means looking at the piece as a whole to see if the ideas are *well organized*, *well documented*, and *well expressed*. It may mean making changes to the structure of your essay by adding some paragraphs or sentences, deleting others, and moving others around. Experienced writers may be able to check several aspects of their work at the same time, but if you are inexperienced or in doubt about your writing, it is best to look at the organization of the ideas before you tackle sentence structure, diction, style, and documentation.

What follows is a checklist of questions to ask yourself as you begin editing. This list will help you focus on the first step of the editing process: examining the organization of your work. Since you probably will not want to check through your work separately for each question, you can group some together and overlook others, depending on your own strengths and weaknesses as a writer.

Checklist for organization:
- ☐ Is my title concise and informative?
- ☐ Are the purpose and approach of this essay evident from the beginning?
- ☐ Are all sections of the paper relevant to the topic?
- ☐ Is the organization logical?
- ☐ Are the ideas sufficiently developed? Is there enough evidence, explanation, and illustration?
- ☐ Would a person who has not read the primary material understand everything I am saying? Should I clarify some parts or add any explanatory material?
- ☐ In presenting my argument, do I take into account opposing arguments or evidence?
- ☐ Do my paragraph divisions make my ideas more coherent? Have I used them to keep similar ideas together and signal movement from one idea to another?
- ☐ Do any parts of the essay seem disjointed? Should I add more transitional words or logical indicators to make the sequence of ideas easier to follow?
- ☐ Do my conclusions accurately reflect my argument in the body of the work?

Another approach would be to devise your own checklist based on comments you have received on previous assignments. This is particularly useful when you move from the overview of your paper to the close focus on sentence structure, diction, punctuation, spelling, and style. If you have a particular weak area—for example, irrelevant evidence or run-on sentences—you should give it special attention. Keeping a personal checklist will save you from repeating the same old mistakes.

Do not be alarmed if you end up making a lot of marks and scribbles on your essay at this stage—this is the purpose of draft writing. In completing these corrections, you should have fine-tuned the structure, transitions, use of language, and references. When you've made your corrections, you will have your second draft. It may be helpful, once again, to leave your work for a day or two (or at least a few hours) in order to clear your mind. At this stage it may also be a good idea to ask an outside reader to look over your work, as you will have become overly familiar with it. A fresh pair of eyes may catch things that have slipped past your radar.

Third draft

Editing the second draft to produce a third entails looking for the same problems mentioned in draft one, and it is here that you can begin to finesse or polish your writing. The corrections and revisions you make here should put you very close to the finish line. Your word-processing program will catch typos and spelling errors, but remember that it may not point out actual words that are wrongly used (such as "there" when you mean "their"; see Chapter 16 for more on fixing your own grammar mistakes). Think of a computer spell checker as a useful first check rather than a final one. Similarly, grammar checkers, though helpful, are not completely reliable. They will pick up common grammar errors and stylistic problems, but they do make mistakes and will likely never equal the judgment of a good human editor.

FORMATTING YOUR ESSAY

We've all been told not to judge a book by its cover, but the very warning suggests that we have a natural tendency to do so. Readers of essays tend to do the same thing. A well-formatted, attractive essay makes the reader more receptive and, fairly or unfairly, often gets a higher mark than a sloppy paper that is more difficult to read. Good looks will not substitute for good thinking, but they will certainly enhance it.

Always double-space your work and use one-inch margins to frame the text in white space and allow room for your reader to write comments. Number each page and (unless you are instructed not to) provide a neat, well-spaced cover page that includes the essay title, your name, the date, the name of your instructor, and the course number or title. Make good use of formatting features such as italics for emphasis and bold for the title and headings, and choose appropriate font faces. One rule of thumb is to use a serif font such as Times New Roman, usually 12-point, for the body of the essay and a sans serif font such as Arial for the title and headings. However, most instructors will provide you with guidelines specifying their particular preferences for presentation and formatting.

Keep in mind that while a computer can make your work look good, fancy graphics and a slick presentation will not replace intelligent thinking. Having made your final changes, read over your work one last time (if you can stand it!) with a critical eye. Take the time to change anything that is unsatisfactory. In this last read, ask yourself the following questions:[5]

- Is my content strong and my argument sound?
- Is my research material sufficient and appropriately cited? (See Chapter 15.)
- Is my structure logical and are my ideas suitably linked?
- Is my writing clear and concise?
- Is my formatting sharp?

If you can answer "yes" to these questions, you are ready to submit a quality essay.

GRADING RUBRICS

Before you submit your essay, it is always helpful to know what criteria your instructor will use in grading your essay. What is she or he looking for? How do the various aspects of your essay affect its overall grade? What follows is an example of an essay-grading rubric, outlining the sorts of things that may play a part in the grading process. Not all instructors will provide you with a sheet like this, but you should feel comfortable asking your instructor what they're

Essay-Grading Rubric

Student Name: _____ Student ID: _____

Assessment Criteria:
Understanding and explanation of the topic or subject (10 marks possible)

10 _____ Excellent understanding and explanation

8–9 _____ Very good . . .

7 _____ Good . . .

6 _____ Satisfactory . . .

5 _____ Marginal . . .

3 _____ Inadequate . . .

Critical engagement with and evaluation of the topic (7 marks possible)

7 _____ Excellent engagement and exceptionally perceptive evaluation

6 _____ Very good engagement and perceptive evaluation

5 _____ Good engagement and evaluation

3 _____ Little engagement or evaluation

1 _____ No engagement or evaluation

Organization and argument structure (5 marks possible)

5 _____ Outstanding, creative, and original; very well-constructed argument

4 _____ Competent and effective; well-constructed argument

3 _____ Adequate, reasonably clear, and logical

1 _____ Unsatisfactory, lack of organization, unclear in various places

The mechanics of the paper: grammar, punctuation, spelling, etc. (4 marks possible)

4 _____ Very clear and fluent; correct grammar, punctuation, and spelling; no, or almost no, errors

3 _____ Clear and fluent; few errors in grammar, punctuation, or spelling

2 _____ Relatively clear and fluent; some errors in grammar, punctuation, or spelling; areas too informal in tone

1 _____ Lack of clarity; poor grammar, punctuation, and spelling; too informal in tone

Selection and use of sources (4 marks possible)

4 _____ Excellent use of sources, correct referencing, consistent style

3 _____ Very good use of sources, correct referencing, consistent style

2 _____ Satisfactory use of sources, satisfactory referencing, mostly consistent style; source selection too limited

1 _____ Adequate or poor use of sources, unsatisfactory referencing, inconsistent style; source selection poor or incomplete

Total _____/30

Grade Scale:
(A) 25.5–30; (B) 22.5–25; (C) 19.5–22; (D) 15–19; (F) below 15

Comments:

_____

_____

_____

_____

_____

looking for. Keeping your teacher's grading rubric in mind as you write and finish your essay will help you ensure that you don't lose unnecessary marks.

PROTECTING YOUR WORK

Lost files are the nightmare of the computer age. Keeping adequate copies of your work will protect you from losing it as a result of a technological problem. The following practices will ensure that your work is adequately protected:

- Save regularly to protect against a computer failure.
- Create a backup so that you have copies on both your hard drive and on a USB flash drive or a server. Perhaps send yourself a copy of the assignment as an email attachment.
- Keep a copy of your file at least until you receive your grade for the course.
- Print an extra copy to be on the safe side.

Following these simple steps doesn't take much time at all and will give you valuable peace of mind.

PRE-WRITING AND POST-WRITING CHECKLISTS

As you prepare for and write your essays, checklists can be helpful tools. Below are some pre-writing and post-writing questions, all drawn from material in this chapter, that you can use as a guide during the writing process.

Pre-writing checklist:
- ☐ Have I given myself enough time to fully engage with this essay?
- ☐ Have I put together a timetable, with goals and deadlines for finishing various aspects of this essay, from proposal to research to drafts?
- ☐ Have I clearly understood the title or question being asked in this essay?
- ☐ Have I identified the main question or problem that I will address in this essay?
- ☐ Have I understood the approach I will take, based on the essay question given (e.g., explain, trace, compare)?
- ☐ Do I have the appropriate sources to do preliminary research?
- ☐ In my preliminary research, have I identified key themes, components, and ideas to serve as main points for my outline?
- ☐ Have I established a thesis statement, to serve as a controlling idea for the essay?
- ☐ Is this thesis restricted, unified, and precise?

Post-writing checklist:
- ☐ Have I checked and re-checked spelling and grammar?
- ☐ Is my title concise and informative?
- ☐ Are the purpose and approach of this essay evident from the beginning?
- ☐ Are all sections of the paper relevant to the topic? Does every sentence matter?
- ☐ Is the organization logical?
- ☐ Are the ideas sufficiently developed? Is there enough evidence, explanation, and illustration?
- ☐ Would an educated person who has not read the primary material understand everything I am saying? Should I clarify some parts or add any explanatory material?

☐ In presenting my argument, do I take into account opposing arguments or evidence?

☐ Do my paragraph divisions make my ideas more coherent? Have I used them to keep similar ideas together and signal movement from one idea to the next?

☐ Do any parts of the essay seem disjointed? Should I add more transitional words or logical indicators to make the sequence of ideas easier to follow?

☐ Do my conclusions accurately reflect my argument in the body of the work?

☐ Do my introduction and conclusion do their jobs adequately?

☐ Is my research material sufficient and appropriately cited?

☐ Is my structure logical and are my ideas suitably linked?

☐ Is my writing clear and concise?

☐ Is my formatting sharp?

☐ Have I backed up my work, both electronically and on paper?

CONCLUSION

You may think that this sounds like a lot of work for one essay. But keep in mind that a good portion of your final grade will be based on research essays, so it's worth investing the time necessary to produce good ones. Moreover, the people marking your essays have undoubtedly graded hundreds of essays on similar topics. These experts can easily spot an essay that has not gone through proper revision or has not been given adequate time for preparation. The time you invest in both the planning and writing stages will be well worth it in the end.

With this in mind, give yourself plenty of time for the process of planning and writing your essays. Your essay will not (and should not!) be completed in a mere hour or two. Give it a couple of weeks in order to ponder the subject and your proposed thesis thoroughly. Also, consider using an essay proposal form, or come up with a proposal plan that you think will work for you. It is vital that your planning is well thought out and organized. Furthermore, be realistic about these issues and how they might change: your outline, your thesis, and even your approach may develop over the course of your research. Finally, realize that this is a learning process and you will not write fantastic essays in your first attempts. However, as you continue to develop as a researcher and writer, your essays will become more focused, clearly articulated, and well written.

As noted at the beginning of this chapter, the purpose of writing essays is to help you engage with the subjects you are studying in a meaningful and productive way. We encourage you to think of your essays as an invitation to discover whole areas of religious studies that you might not have known existed. Embrace the challenges they pose, and soak in what you discover in the process. Not only will the time you invest in preparing for and writing your essays lead to better grades, but you will also find yourself being enriched by this important aspect of engaged learning.

ENDNOTES

1. Nancy J. Vyhmeister, *Quality Research Papers: For Students of Religion and Theology*, 2nd ed. (Grand Rapids, MI: Zondervan, 2008), p. 36. Although we modify various aspects, in what follows we draw from Chapter 5 of this work.
2. Joseph F. Trimmer, *Writing with a Purpose*, 12th ed. (Boston: Houghton Mifflin, 1998), pp. 62–63.
3. Sheridan Baker and Laurence B. Gamache, *The Canadian Practical Stylist*, 4th ed. (Don Mills, ON: Addison-Wesley, 1998), pp. 55–56.
4. Adapted from Stella Cottrell, *The Study Skills Handbook*, Palgrave Study Guides, 3rd ed. (Houndmills: Palgrave, 2008), p. 172.
5. Adapted from Cottrell, *Study Skills Handbook*, p. 162.

CHAPTER 6

Writing Book Reviews and Book Reports

Objectives

- Distinguishing between book reports and book reviews
- Reading for a review
- Reviewing fiction and film
- Understanding the structure and content of a review

Book reports and reviews are a common component of religious studies, particularly in upper-level undergraduate classes. While such assignments may sound fairly easy and may be something you have done in the past, you should be familiar with what is expected in an academic college- or university-level book review. (An example of a short book review can be seen in Appendix 1.)

BOOK REPORTS AND BOOK REVIEWS

First of all, it is helpful to distinguish between book reports and book reviews. While your aim in a book report is to summarize a book's structure and content as objectively as possible, you are not usually asked to offer any critical or evaluative comments. When you write a book review, on the other hand, you do both: you are writing a descriptive element but you are also using an analytical approach to the text. So instead of simply stating what a book says (as in a report), your review will look at *how* it is said, *why* it is said, and *how effectively* the author's case is made.

OBJECTIVE: CONVINCE YOUR READER

In a book review, the student is usually expected to present his or her own argument in order to convince the review's reader of something about the book (or aspects of the book): whether the book is or is not persuasive, well written, or important to the discipline; whether or not it makes a unique contribution to the academy (or church, synagogue, particular faith community, etc.). Here, you will want to read the course assignment carefully and, if in doubt, ask your instructor exactly what she or he is looking for in your evaluation. You may also want to determine if your instructor will be using a grading guide, or rubric, in assessing your review (we provide a sample rubric below). Whatever the case, it is especially important in constructing your argument that you engage the content of the book in a fair and even-handed way, using an approach that demonstrates critical awareness and openness to perspectives other than your own. As well, you must guard against making *ad hominem* attacks, that is, making personal attacks against the author rather than critiquing the content of the book itself. Often instructors will be looking to see how well you can engage with arguments or ideas that are different from your own.

READING FOR A REVIEW

It's only natural that the books you find engaging and readable will be the ones you'll most enjoy reviewing. That said, the books you find easiest to read may not lend themselves well to a critical review. While some courses may give you a pre-assigned text to review, others may offer you an option. If this option is given, choose your book carefully. If possible, do some exploratory research beforehand so that you know what kind of book you are getting into.

Once you've chosen your book, the next step is to begin reading carefully and critically. Because you will use few, if any, outside sources for your book review, your reading of the book is central and vital. With this in mind, it is important that you engage in active and critical reading.

Begin by looking at the book's table of contents, which will show you what the author considers to be most important and what kind of material will be presented in the book; then quickly skim through the book itself. The information inside will be much more understandable once you know where the book as a whole is going. Getting a "big picture" view is important, especially because demonstrating comprehension of what the author is saying, and why she or he is saying it, is one of the main goals in book reports and reviews.

The second step is a more thorough reading. At this stage you should be taking the bulk of your notes. Since you have already determined, in your first, quick reading, the relative importance that the author gives to various ideas, you can be selective and avoid getting bogged down in less important details in this second, more thorough reading. Just be sure that you do not neglect any crucial passages or controversial claims. As we discussed in Chapter 2, try to condense ideas when you're taking notes. Don't take them down word for word, and don't simply paraphrase them. You will have a much firmer grasp of the material if you resist the temptation to quote; force yourself to *interpret* and *summarize*, even at this early stage. This approach will also help you make your review concise. Remember: you want to be brief as well as clear. Condensing the material as you take notes will ensure that your review is a true summary, not just a string of quotations or paraphrases.

When structuring your review, move from first *explaining* the book's content, to *evaluating* its effectiveness in its stated purposes, to *expressing* your personal perspectives and reactions to the book, if this is asked for. This may require at least two readings of your book; regardless of how many times you do read the text, you need to ask different sets of questions each time so that you cover both the explanation and evaluation of it.

Explanation ("what") questions: These questions focus on summary and description.

- What does the title say about the book?
- What is the author's viewpoint and main purpose?
- Is there a main thesis the author is arguing for?
- What kind of evidence is used to back up the author's argument?
- How is the book structured?
- Do the chapters and sections flow into one another?

Evaluation ("why" and "how") questions: These questions focus on analyzing the above-mentioned descriptions.

- Does the book fulfill its stated purpose? Why and how?
- Do the author's argument(s) and evidence hold up to scrutiny?
- Does the structure of the book further its argument? Is it logical and easy to follow?

This type of reading takes time and requires that you pay extremely close attention to the text. We suggest that you read a chapter at a time, underlining or highlighting (assuming you own the book!) and taking notes as you go. If you are doing more than one reading, take the first time around to focus on explanation and the second on evaluation. It may help to divide your notes into two columns on a sheet of paper; state your explanatory comments in the left column (summary of content, argument and main points), and begin making your evaluative comments in the right hand column. If you are working on a computer, you could separate your notes into two separate files—one for explanatory notes, and one for evaluative notes.

Reviewing Other Forms of Communication and Media

While subject-specific academic books are probably the most common medium you will be asked to review, students in religious studies are increasingly being asked to review other forms of literature and media, such as fiction and film, for their coursework. We suggest that the principles outlined above are helpful no matter what it is that you are asked to review, with a few adjustments. Here are a few tips that should help if you are asked to do a review of film or written fiction:

Reviewing Works of Fiction and Film

- As with reviews of academic works, reviews of fiction and film need to include a summary of the content, an evaluation of the work, and a personal response (if assigned). As such, fiction needs to be read and films need to be watched with an eye to the questions noted above. However, your response to these questions will be slightly different in that films and works of fiction rarely state their methods, aims, and purposes explicitly.
- Begin with a summary of the book or film, which will serve as your explanation of its content. While some reviewers insist on not giving away all of the plot points or the climax of a story, particularly when reviewing for the general public, this is less an issue when submitting a review to an instructor who has assigned (and thus most likely read or seen!) the book or film.
- When offering evaluation of fiction and film, it may be helpful to ask literary, narrative, and style-oriented questions.
  - How developed were the characters, and how so?
  - How was the plot structured, and how well did this serve the story?
  - Was there a theme or message to the book or film? If so, was it presented thoughtfully or was it forceful?

– What are the stylistic qualities of the work? Is the book well written? What literary devices (irony, foreshadowing) does it employ? Is the film aesthetically pleasing? How do the cinematography and music add or detract from the film?

• Finally, remember to address how the work in question relates to the topic you are studying. This is essential. Your instructors will be interested to know not only how you responded to the work in question, but what connections you see between the novel or film and your subject of study.

STRUCTURE AND CONTENT OF A REVIEW

The structure of a book review will vary but often contains the following elements: *bibliographic information, background information, explanation, evaluation*, and *expression of your personal response*.

First, if you have not already done so on the title page, give the complete bibliographic information of the book before your introductory paragraph. This information includes the names of the author(s) and/or editor(s), the full title and subtitle, the place of publication, the name of the publisher, the date of publication, the edition number (if applicable), and the number of pages. An example might look like this:

Campbell, Heidi A. *When Religion Meets New Media*. Media, Religion, and Culture Series. New York: Routledge, 2010, pp. 232.

As in a regular essay, it is appropriate to begin with a small *introduction* to let the reader know what the review will include. Though not strictly required, it is also helpful to include some background information on the author to suggest why he or she is qualified to write in this particular field; for example, you might mention work experience and previous publications. This exercise may also help you identify any influences or authorial presuppositions that could underlie the book's content and message.

Your *explanation* of the text comes next (if you are writing a book report and not a review, this section will represent the bulk of your assignment). This section answers the "what" questions you asked during your reading. Thus, your explanation section will include the author's viewpoint and main purpose in writing, a summary of the book's overall content, and the main thesis and argument made. At a more specific level, you should highlight the structure of the book (how it flows and how the chapters relate to one another), as well as the evidence that is given in support of the argument (how each chapter fits into the bigger picture). It is important to give a balanced review of all of the book's content; offering a detailed analysis of one or two chapters at the expense of the rest of the book will give your instructor the impression that you have not fully read or understood the book. Also keep in mind that most book reviews have a very limited word count, so it is vital that you highlight the most significant aspects of the book's content. Your review needs to be both concise and balanced, not always an easy task.

If you are writing a review, you will now move from explanation to an *evaluation* of the text. Here you answer the "how" and "why" questions from your reading. You should note whether the book fulfills its stated purpose, how effective the author's arguments are, and how the book's methodology and structure play into the overall thesis. You should also point out the book's strengths and weaknesses, as well as how persuasive the given evidence and arguments are. There are other modes of evaluation as well. For instance, if you are familiar with other literature in the same field, it may be helpful to compare arguments and conclusions with the book under review in order to highlight what is new and insightful or perhaps falls short of the mark. Comparing the book you are reviewing to other literature in the field may be what separates a good review from a great one. Such comparison will not always be appropriate, however. Be sure to ask your instructor before interacting with other sources in a review.

Following the evaluation, you may be asked for an *expression* of your personal response. Depending on the course and its intent, this section takes on greater or lesser importance. In cases where this is asked for, you should feel free to express your own reaction to the book; however, it is important to maintain a position of professionalism and a degree of objectivity, even within your own personal reflections. Though you can't simply say "this book is awful," you can say that it felt weak for specific reasons, listing these in a clear and concise fashion in order to provide a rationale for your negative reaction.

Finally, as in all essays, it is helpful to finish your review with a *conclusion* that reiterates your comments and the overall assessment of the book. As discussed in chapters 5 and 10, conclusions are an important feature of an essay, and a good conclusion will bring your ideas together in a way that demonstrates clearly your main points and (hopefully) leaves the reader convinced of your argument. It bears repeating that this is the last thing your instructor will read before assigning a grade, so make it a strong ending.

The steps given for writing essay drafts in Chapter 5 are relevant for book reviews as well. You will want to give yourself enough time to produce and rework several drafts of your review, to ensure it is logical and well structured, with no mistakes in grammar or presentation. Further, before you submit your review, it is always a good idea to reread your essay in the light of any available grading rubric or guidelines your teacher will employ. A generic rubric for book reviews might look something like the following:

Book Review Rubric

Student Name: _____ Student ID: _____

Assessment Criteria:

Understanding and explanation of the book (10 marks possible)

10 _____ Excellent understanding and explanation

8–9 _____ Very good . . .

7 _____ Good . . .

6 _____ Satisfactory . . .

5 _____ Marginal . . .

3 _____ Inadequate . . .

Critical engagement with and evaluation of the book (7 marks possible)

7 _____ Excellent engagement and exceptionally perceptive evaluation

6 _____ Very good engagement and perceptive evaluation

5 _____ Good engagement and evaluation

3 _____ Little engagement or evaluation

1 _____ No engagement or evaluation

Organization and overall presentation (5 marks possible)

5 _____ Outstanding, creative, and original; very well-constructed argument

4 _____ Competent and effective; well-constructed argument

3 _____ Adequate, reasonably clear, and logical

1 _____ Unsatisfactory, lack of organization, unclear in various places

The mechanics of the review: grammar, punctuation, spelling, etc. (4 marks possible)

4 _____ Very clear and fluent; correct grammar, punctuation, and spelling; no, or almost no, errors

3 _____ Clear and fluent; few errors in grammar, punctuation, or spelling

2 _____ Relatively clear and fluent; some errors in grammar, punctuation, or spelling; areas too informal in tone

1 _____ Lack of clarity; poor grammar, punctuation, and spelling; too informal in tone

Referencing and formatting (4 marks possible)

4 _____ Excellent referencing, well-formatted review

3 _____ Very good referencing, well-formatted review

2 _____ Satisfactory referencing and formatting

1 _____ Adequate or poor referencing and formatting

Total _____/30

Grade Scale:
(A) 25.5–30; (B) 22.5–25; (C) 19.5–22; (D) 15–19; (F) below 15

Comments:

_____

_____

_____

_____

_____

_____

POST-WRITING CHECKLIST

Once again, you will find it helpful to work through a post-writing checklist to ensure that you have put together the best review possible. Be sure you can answer each of the following:

- [ ] Am I being asked to write a book report or a book review?
- [ ] In my reading, have I been able to isolate the main point or argument that was put forward in the book?
- [ ] Have I read the book with an eye to the different sets of questions I will need to answer, specifically those related to *explanation* and *evaluation*?
- [ ] Does my review adequately answer the *explanation* questions?
  - What does the title say about the book?
  - What is the author's viewpoint and main purpose?
  - Is there a main thesis the author is arguing for?
  - What kind of evidence is used to back up the author's argument?
  - How is the book structured?
  - Do the chapters and sections flow into one another?
- [ ] Have I fairly evaluated the book (if asked to do so)?
  - Does the book fulfill its stated purpose? Why and how?
  - Do the author's argument(s) and evidence hold up to scrutiny?
  - Does the structure of the book further its argument? Is it logical and easy to follow?
- [ ] If a personal expression and reaction to the book is asked for, have I tried to remain objective with my language?
- [ ] Have I introduced and concluded my review?
- [ ] Have I taken the time to check the review for stylistic, grammatical, and spelling errors?

CONCLUSION: BOOK REVIEWS AND YOUR EDUCATION

Because books are one of the primary ways in which scholars and teachers communicate their research, you will encounter books at every stage of your university education. In some ways, books are the very nourishment of the academic world, a fact clearly seen in a visit to any professor's office. Books line the walls, clutter desks, and are usually bookmarked or open and used each day. The importance of acquiring the skills necessary to interact with these sources cannot be overstated. Book reviews offer one such example of this interaction, and they give your instructors a chance to see you engaging in several important academic practices: closely reading an entire book, comprehending its content and arguments, and expressing that understanding back to a new audience. On top of this, book reviews gauge your ability to interact with new material and to analyze and evaluate an extensive argument, something your instructors want you to be able to do intelligently and with some degree of sophistication. These skills are invaluable in becoming a better student and scholar in your own right.

CHAPTER 7

Writing Short Assignments: Chapter Summaries and Article Reviews

Objectives

- Determining the nature of the assignment
- Using steps of writing to produce good short assignments

In most humanities courses, including courses in religious studies, you may be asked to complete a short assignment, perhaps a chapter or article summary. These assignments are often given in order to ensure you have completed—and understood—a particular assigned reading. Such assignments generally do not require extensive research, or even outside reading. Further, they are usually short, sometimes no more than one page or 250 words. Don't be fooled, though! A short, non-research-based assignment does not necessarily mean you've been given a task that will be easy or will take you no time to complete. Accuracy, conciseness, and critical thinking become especially important, and these skills only come through practice. Further, such an assignment is often the first work you will submit to your instructor, work that has the potential to make an important impression early in the semester. Although your overall grade for the course will often be determined by your longer research essays and your exams, a consistently good impression made on your instructor in short assignments throughout the term can be an important factor if your final mark is hanging somewhere between two letter grades. All of this is to say that such assignments can be of great importance, even if they do not appear to account for a large percentage of your final course grade. In this chapter, then, we provide some guidelines for writing short assignments, particularly chapter and article summaries. (A sample summary can be seen in Appendix 2.)

DETERMINING THE NATURE OF THE ASSIGNMENT

Much of what we covered in chapters 5 and 6 regarding essay writing and book reviews applies here too, and the first thing to do is determine the nature of the assignment. Are you being asked to describe, analyze, or compare? Does your assignment ask that you determine and evaluate the main point of the article? Are you being asked to engage with one particular aspect of the reading, or are you being asked to summarize the reading as a whole?

The answers to these questions will take you a long way in your assignment and you should fully understand your task before you do any of the assigned reading. This will enable you to read with the relevant questions in mind, and it will also let you flag important ideas as you read, allowing you to take efficient and productive notes. Remember that sometimes when you are asked for a "summary" you may in fact be expected to *engage* with the piece under examination in an *evaluative* way. If you are in doubt, check with your instructor.

EIGHT STEPS FOR WRITING SHORT ASSIGNMENTS

We suggest working through the following eight steps, which should help you in any short reading assignment.

1. **Determine the genre (or type) and purpose of the chapter or article.** Before you begin to read the chapter or article closely, it's always a good idea to determine what sort of literature you are dealing with. Is it an article from an academic journal, which argues something specific about a narrow topic? Is it a dictionary article, intended to summarize scholarship on a broader topic? Is what you are reading a chapter of a book, perhaps an important chapter that really makes best sense as part of that larger whole? Further, what might the author's intention be in writing the piece? Sometimes the best way to determine these things is to scan the book's table of contents, the preface, or the introduction, and then give the piece you've been asked to summarize a quick skim to ascertain its particular purpose. Establishing the type of literature and its purpose will allow you to read and evaluate the piece more effectively.

2. **Begin a close reading, taking point-form notes.** This first, main read through the piece will form the basis of your summary. You may need to read things again to be sure you haven't missed or misunderstood anything, or even been wrong about the purpose of the chapter or article. When you make such a mistake—and inevitably you will—it is important to reread the piece with your newfound knowledge as a guide. Also, although we all like to think that we will remember key points or ideas, it is important to keep track of these through careful note-taking. Although some students prefer simply to underline important sentences or flag passages with Post-it Notes, it's still a good idea to jot down key ideas as you read, and to take note of relevant page numbers for later reference.

3. **Determine the thesis and the main points of the chapter or article.** After reading and rereading the piece, it's always a good idea to summarize the article or chapter in one or two sentences. What is the main point of the article? What is its thesis? After determining this, recount the main steps (or points) the author used to build his or her case. An ability to recount these briefly and accurately will not only show that you have read the material, but will also demonstrate that you have understood the argument.

4. **Draft a summary paragraph of the chapter or article, based on your outline.** Depending on the nature of your assignment, you will usually need to summarize, in varying amounts of detail, the article or chapter as a whole. This should take no more than one paragraph and will often be the first main paragraph of your assignment. It should be primarily *descriptive* (as opposed to *evaluative*) in approach. Further, you should use quotations carefully and sparingly. Proper use of the occasional quotation can make your summary interesting and compelling. Improper or excessive use of quotations can give the impression that you cannot summarize things adequately. It can also make your work tedious and uninspiring.

5. **Develop your own argument, or controlling idea, to use in your assessment.** Unless you are clearly instructed not to evaluate or engage with the argument in a critical way, you are almost always expected to offer a careful, critical assessment. This doesn't necessarily have to be a full-scale critique or advanced argument, but it should show that you are able to examine the relative persuasiveness of the author's arguments and to point out potential flaws

in logic or a lack of sufficient evidence to back up main points. Or, you may wish to put forward your own argument regarding how and why the piece is compelling, important to the field, or well written. A few questions may help you in this task:

- Does the author achieve what she or he set out to do?
- Is the evidence presented in a logical and well-ordered fashion? Is it relevant?
- Does the author misuse sources, ignore important data, or skirt issues?
- Can you find contradictions or holes in the author's argument?
- Is the writing clear and compelling? Why or why not?

You may want to focus on one aspect of the argument. This is usually acceptable, provided you do not lose sight of the author's main point. But be wary of turning a sub-point (or offhanded comment!) into a major point of contention that you will not let go. Doing this can give the impression that you have misunderstood the author's main point. Also, be sure to engage with the content of the article or chapter itself, not what you think the author *should* have written about.

6. **Bring your work together, often in two or three paragraphs total, using an introduction and conclusion when necessary.** If your piece feels like it needs an introduction and a conclusion, write them. These paragraphs can usually be one to three sentences, depending on the assignment. A good conclusion, tying your points together, can be the difference between getting an A or a B. However, there may be times in a short assignment when valuable words should not be wasted on separate introductions and conclusions. In these cases, use the opening and final sentences of your submission to introduce and conclude things for you.

7. **Read and reread your draft, making adjustments to length, content, and flow.** Often you will need to work within a page or word limit, and it is imperative that you do not write too much. Every word counts, and if you have repeated ideas or used unnecessary words, now is the time to cut them. Sometimes, entire sentences are best removed. If things feel disconnected or uneven, you can rework and polish things in the next stage.

8. **Give your assignment one or two more final readings, checking for grammar, spelling, and formatting mistakes, as well as overall readability.** In these final stages you will want to ensure that you are submitting a finished, polished product. Nothing distracts a reader—especially the one grading your work!—like glaring spelling errors or grammatical mistakes. These easy-to-avoid issues can often make a big difference in how your piece is received. A well-produced and properly formatted assignment allows the reader to focus on your content rather than your presentation.

Once you have completed these steps, you are nearly ready to submit your assignment. But before you do, make sure you've also included relevant details such as your name, course number, course title, and so on; it is surprising how often students will omit simple things like their name. Use an appropriate font, number pages if there is more than one, and ensure that you submit things on time. All of this will contribute to making your *ideas*, rather than unnecessary *faults*, stand out.

WRITING CHECKLIST: SHORT ASSIGNMENTS

- ☐ Have I determined the nature of the assignment?
- ☐ Have I determined the genre and purpose of the chapter or article under scrutiny?
- ☐ Have I isolated the thesis or main point of the chapter or article?
- ☐ Based on my reading and notes, am I able to summarize the chapter or article in one paragraph?
- ☐ Is my evaluation and assessment of the piece fair? Have I answered the following questions:
  - Does the author achieve what she or he set out to do?
  - Is the evidence presented in a logical and well-ordered fashion? Is it relevant?
  - Does the author misuse sources, ignore important data, or skirt issues?
  - Can you find contradictions or holes in the author's argument?
  - Is the writing clear and compelling? Why or why not?
- ☐ Is my final summary and evaluation clear and concise?
- ☐ Have I taken the time to ensure that my short assignment is grammatically correct, error free, and well presented?

CHAPTER 8

Reading Religious Texts and Writing Interpretive Essays

Objectives

- Recognizing different approaches to reading religious texts
- Understanding the role of languages and translation
- Interpreting poetry and art
- Understanding historical and literary elements of religious texts
- Developing your research on a religious text into an essay

Every academic discipline has its own set of specialty tasks and assignments, be they constructing lab reports, writing up fieldwork, or compiling statistical information. In religious studies, one such task (among many) has to do with religious, or *sacred*, texts. When dealing with religions that have sacred texts or influential books—such as the Qur'an, the Bhagavad Gita, the Bible, or the Book of Mormon—scholars often engage these texts in a critical, scholarly fashion. As a student in religious studies, you may be asked to do the same. These academic approaches may be very different from the way many religious believers approach the same texts (i.e., with a reverent attitude, a reluctance to question the text's authorship, or the belief that the text has only one "right" meaning). This chapter will outline some of the ways you can make the most of your interaction with religious texts in an academic context.

APPROACHES TO READING AND INTERPRETING RELIGIOUS TEXTS

Texts stand at the centre of the beliefs and practices of many religions. It's not surprising, therefore, that a lot of energy has been spent trying to understand these religious documents. The process of reading and understanding religious texts can be referred to in different ways. For example, in scholarship some refer to this exercise as *exegesis* and in some courses you may be asked to produce what is called an *exegetical paper*. The word *exegesis* simply means "to draw out" and is based on a Greek word made up of two parts, meaning "out of" and "to lead." Traditionally, the term was used almost exclusively in biblical studies, though it has come to gain currency in other areas and can apply more broadly to the critical study of any text. For the purposes of this chapter we will simply refer to this process as *interpretation*.

Sacred texts are sometimes called *holy books* or *scripture*. These texts are usually considered to be authoritative for a particular religious community. We should make clear, however, that not all religious groups view their sacred literature in the same way or attach authority to their writings in the ways other groups do. For example, within branches of Protestant Christianity, followers might view their scripture, the Bible, as a non-negotiable final authority for all matters of faith and practice. Others, such as adherents of Buddhism, view their sacred texts (e.g., the Tripitaka) with more fluidity; they may see their texts as containing important teachings but not refer to the documents as "scripture." Both groups deeply value their sacred texts, but they do so in distinct ways. Even within branches of the same religion, sacred texts are read and used in differing, at times competing, ways. Because these texts are of such value to religious groups, it's not surprising that one approach to understanding religious texts is to inquire how these texts might be read and used within their religious settings, or how they might function as authoritative for a particular community.

Scholars of religious studies also read and interpret these sacred texts. In religious studies, however, scholars tend to ask different kinds of questions about these texts—critical questions reflecting the non-confessional, interdisciplinary nature of religious studies (as outlined in Chapter 1). For example, some take a literary approach, reading religious texts as literature and investigating them with questions about genre, plot, and characterization. Others attempt to ascertain how the historical context of an ancient text can offer insight. Another section of scholarship focuses on the ways these texts have been interpreted throughout history, or how they have affected religious communities (often called the "reception history" of a text). Still others question how contemporary issues such as feminism, post-colonialism, queer theory, or environmentalism affect our reading of these texts. These are all valid academic approaches to reading and interpreting religious texts, and different classes may require you to employ different approaches and methods.

Examples of Academic Approaches to Interpreting Religious Texts

Comparative approach: Compares two or more religious texts, which may be drawn from either the same collection or a different set of texts (for more on this, see Chapter 9).

Ideological approach: Seeks to uncover how and why dominant ideologies might be silencing other voices in a particular text. Examples include feminist, Marxist, or post-colonial readings.

Reader-response approach: Focuses on the experience that the reader has when reading a particular text, as opposed to concentrating on the history *behind* a text. Reader-response is a recognition that all readers bring aspects of themselves (such as gender, class, or ethnicity) to a text, and these aspects affects the way in which we respond to texts.

Reception history approach: Also known as "history of interpretation," this approach explores how particular texts or ideas have been interpreted throughout history.

Social-scientific approach: Uses sociological and anthropological insights to interpret a text.

Historical approach: An approach that can take many forms. Such an essay might explore how to understand the passage or text based on its historical setting or other historical issues. Alternatively, it could explore the authorship of a text, how it was edited and arranged, or what sources the text draws from. Historical essays may also include discussion on archaeological data or social customs related to the text.

Literary-critical approach: Focuses on the text as literature, as it currently stands, focusing on literary, grammatical, and narrative aspects. This approach may highlight genre, narrative characterization, and/or plot development.

You might wonder: If there are so many valid approaches to reading and interpreting religious texts, where do I begin? This is a good question, and there is not necessarily one right answer; much depends on what types of assignments are set for you, or the preferences of your instructors. In order to provide a concrete example for you, we will use literary and historical approaches to highlight what the academic study of religious texts might look like. (We use these particular approaches not to privilege them above others, but rather for purposes of illustration, to give an example of academic interpretation.) Your instructor may have a preference for your essay and it is essential that you determine what this is before you begin.

For some students, any academic approach may raise questions about the sacredness of the text under study, and this is an understandable concern. Our goal here is not to diminish religious approaches or to replace them. Rather, we wish to explain how religious texts can be read in an academic context, and thus how your instructors might expect you to engage with such texts in your course assignments. Critical, academic study of religious texts is fundamental for understanding religions more generally—whether this be as a religious adherent or not. We hope our discussion will help get you started in the reading of religious texts, whatever your larger interpretive goals.

Religious texts and foreign languages

Before we look at some of the practical aspects of reading and interpreting religious texts, we should talk about language and translation. Very few of the sacred texts in today's world religions were written in English. To add to the challenge, many of the sacred texts used by major religious groups were composed many centuries ago, at times millennia ago, and often in languages that have either fallen out of use or have changed considerably. Here one need only think of the older English of Shakespeare to recognize how much a language can change in a relatively short time. All of this means that students who want to understand even one sentence of an ancient scripture must either learn to read another—at times ancient, "dead"—language or make use of a translation. Although scholars most often read texts in their original languages, they also regularly make use of translations. Each of these practices has its own difficulties, however. At least initially, most readers of this handbook will make use of translations, so we will focus our discussion there. (For more on issues related to learning languages, consult Chapter 13.)

Many readers will be familiar with the saying that something was "lost in translation." This common phrase suggests that with any translation, something gets sacrificed—a nuance or idiom, for example—because it simply cannot be communicated in the new language in the same way. Think about certain English phrases, ones we innately understand if English is our first language. For example, you may be thinking to yourself right now, "Come on, cut to the chase!" Translated literally to another language, this statement makes little sense. However, it has common usage in the English language meaning "Get to the point," or "Get to the good stuff." Although it may be possible to translate such sentences to capture the idiomatic idea or all of the phrase's nuances in its original language, doing so usually results in long, convoluted translations that quickly become unwieldy. "Cut to the chase," for example, is thought to have roots in the early days of the movie business, where a film producer or director would, when editing, skip (or "cut") the boring sections of the film and move right to the exciting scenes, which often included a chase.

Reading translated texts means that one is always at least one step removed from the original (and even the "original" may have involved a translation, for example, from Aramaic to Greek). This does not mean that we cannot understand or make use of translated texts. We simply need to keep in mind that sacred texts, in the original or in translation, sometimes use highly stylized, poetic, or culturally specific language, so it can be difficult to appreciate the nuances of these texts fully. Some of these problems can be overcome by consulting different translations or by using language dictionaries (or lexicons) and scholarly commentaries that engage with the primary languages of the texts themselves. The further you go in your studies, the more you will realize that reading a text in the original language is best. Of course, we recognize that this is not always possible. For now, simply be aware that these issues exist.

Working with Poetry and Art

Religious and sacred texts are by no means the only objects you might examine in your studies. You may be asked to interact with and interpret a variety of subjects, from a poem to a piece of art. Here are some tips for working with these media (see also our comments on reviewing film and fiction on pages 69–70).

Poetry and art are both unique forms, and at times students can find them daunting. Each medium has its own set of rules and assumptions when studied academically. However, if you are asked to engage with these forms as part of your religious studies curriculum, it may be helpful to divide the task into four steps, which we have labelled as *familiarize, describe, reflect,* and *relate.*[1]

- *Familiarize*: Both poetry and art can be demanding because they require us to use different senses and modes of thinking than, say, a dictionary article would require. Our visual and aural skills need to be engaged, as well as our appreciation for subtlety, metaphor, and emotion. One way of overcoming the distance you might feel from poetry and art is to familiarize yourself with the subject. This may mean giving yourself ample time to simply sit and study a piece of art, perhaps examining it from different vantage points and angles. Or it may require reading a poem several times, perhaps aloud. The more familiar you are with the subject, the more comfortable you will be when the time comes to describe and reflect on it.
- *Describe*: Once you've familiarized yourself with your subject, you will need to describe the poem or artwork. Here you will want to ask questions specific to the medium:
  - Poem: What do you know about the author? What does the poem seem to be about (theme)? What kind of poem is it (genre: epic, limerick, sonnet)? What is the metre or rhythm, and how does this affect the poem? What literary devices are employed (for example, metaphor)? How is the poem structured, and how does this affect the reading of it? Are there characters, repetitions, or key words of which you need to be aware?
  - Art: What do you know about the artist, and how does this piece fit into their larger body of work? What kind of piece is it (abstract, landscape, still life, portrait, sculpture)? What techniques and materials (paper, canvas, types of paint, stone) were used, and how does this affect the finished product? How would you describe the tone and composition (colours, space, patterns, organization)?

- *Reflect*: Your description of the subject should help determine your reflections on it. Here you will want to offer some analysis and interpretation of the poem or piece of art. What do you think this particular poem or piece of art is about? Why do you think the author or artist has chosen to craft the piece in this way? How does the historical setting of the author or artist affect what the piece communicates? We label this step *reflection* because there is a certain amount of freedom in interpreting both poetry and artwork. The way the piece is received by the audience—in this case you—informs much of the piece's meaning. However, your reflections should not be arbitrary; rather, they should flow out of your familiarization and description of the object under inspection.
- *Relate*: It is vital that you relate your reflections to the broader area of study for which the assignment has been given. Your instructors will want to see how you bring this particular expression, be it a painting or a poem, together with the subject you are studying.

The rules for writing essays highlighted throughout this handbook apply equally when working with art and poetry. Unless directed otherwise, you will be expected to use credible sources and to cite your work appropriately. You will also want to develop an argument, crafting a thesis that incorporates how you describe, reflect on, and relate the subject to the area of study.

EIGHT STEPS TO FOLLOW WHEN INTERPRETING RELIGIOUS TEXTS

When you read and interpret religious texts, there are a number of basic steps involved. We'd like to walk you through an example, with eight steps, that draws from literary and historical approaches. It's important to note that this isn't a comprehensive checklist: not all of the steps we're showing you will apply to every interpretive paper. The steps you use will depend on the genre of your passage. Further, the steps we offer are by no means the *only* approach to interpretation. You may vary the order, exclude some steps, or include others that work for you and the paper you are writing. These steps are simply a starting point and can be adapted as you gain experience.[2]

As you work through the following steps, take organized notes for later reference. You will use these notes as you draft your essay. Also, remember that interpretation is an *iterative* (that is, cyclical and repeated) process that requires you to revisit your earlier ideas in the light of your new findings. You will see that we suggest you go back and revisit these steps throughout the process.

Step One: Find a text of suitable length.

In an assignment like this, you will either be assigned a specific passage to interpret, or you will be allowed to choose something on your own. Picking your own passage may sound great and it will give you significant freedom, but you must take care to ensure you choose a suitable passage of an appropriate length. Sometimes it's actually simpler to interpret a predetermined passage, since your instructor will have done the hard work for you by choosing an appropriate passage that relates to your assignment.

You might stumble into the common problem of wanting to interpret too much text. It's tempting to choose a long passage to interpret, perhaps an entire chapter or more, because you might think that it will provide you with more "meat" to work with. In fact, a short passage will allow you to examine the material in more detail and with more care. Depending on the type of literature (and length of verses, should there be a versification system), 7–10 verses, or about one paragraph, is usually plenty for a student to examine in a standard university- or college-level paper of 10–20 pages. Sometimes as few as 4–5 verses will be enough, depending on their content. Remember that you will also examine the surrounding verses as part of your investigation of the passage's context. If you are in doubt about how to choose a passage, check with your instructor.

Step Two: Translate the passage or read it through in multiple translations.

This early stage of the process is simply a way to familiarize yourself with the passage and to jot down any initial thoughts you have as they arise. These initial readings are vital, but you will probably also need to do some general background reading during this process. Perhaps you are unfamiliar with how a particular religious text communicates its message or how it employs metaphor, poetic imagery, or song. You also don't want to make obvious errors in determining what your text is about, and doing some background reading can help you. Ask yourself the following questions:

- What is the larger book, poem, or chapter in which my passage is situated about?
- What do I already know about it?

Dictionary articles or introductions to the book or text can be especially helpful here. This background reading doesn't mean looking at secondary sources related *specifically* to your passage (such as commentaries or articles), because these could prematurely lead your interpretation in one particular direction. Specific sources should only be consulted later in the process (see Step Seven below as well as Chapter 5).

Background reading will help you to understand your passage, but your own reading of the primary literature is the most important part of an assignment like this. You don't just want to regurgitate what other people have said about the passage. Try instead to think about the passage in original ways. This kind of thinking is not only rewarding in itself but can often help you achieve a higher grade. Secondary sources are no substitute for the hard work of reading texts closely, carefully, and many times through. Religious texts often have deep layers of meaning and nuance that can only be uncovered through multiple, careful, and persistent readings. To put it another way, the more you look, the more you see.

Step Three: Determine the genre.

At times this can be the most difficult—but important—step in the interpretive process. The word *genre* here means "type" or "category," and thus to determine the genre of literature is to make a statement about how a particular passage should be classified, whether as poetry, narrative, law, or song (to name but a few). When we read newspapers, we know how to distinguish an advertisement from a business report, or letters to the editor from the comics page. We often take these distinctions for granted. But consider how confused or skewed your reading would be if you didn't make the distinction between a stock listing and funeral announcement!

Distinctions in genre become especially important when reading ancient or foreign literature, which may utilize a genre that is unfamiliar to modern Western readers. If a passage is primarily poetic, it should not be read as if it were definitive law or a report of history. If the passage you are reading employs a myth motif or a metaphor common in the ancient world, it is important that you discover this and read the passage appropriately. Your ability to differentiate genres will come with experience, and nothing can substitute for the hard work of reading multiple, parallel texts to get a sense of how ancient writers composed their literary works.

The following list is not definitive, but it represents many of the genres you may encounter when studying religious texts:

- poetry
- prayer
- psalm or song
- proverb or wisdom saying
- narrative or story
- law or commandment
- genealogy
- historical record
- mantra
- written letter (or *epistle*) to a person or a group
- dream or vision
- parable (a short story that teaches a lesson)
- ethical teaching
- philosophical argument
- will or last testament
- blessing or curse pronouncement
- romantic or erotic literature, or love poem
- sermon or homily
- ritual chant, canticle, or hymn
- prophecy
- legal agreement
- metaphysical speculation

Determining the genre of the literature will involve careful readings of the larger passage and, when stuck, consulting secondary sources for help. To make matters more difficult, some texts will have elements from several different genres, which may require extra care in your interpretation. For example, a will or last testament may also include a blessing or curse pronouncement, and it may be conveyed as poetry. In this case, an understanding of these various genres will be needed. Taking the time to identify and understand the genre of the text you are examining is crucial. If after your research you are still in doubt, it is once again a good idea to ask your instructor for guidance.

Step Four: Conduct literary analysis.

Once you've established the genre of your passage, you are now ready to begin literary analysis. This involves examining a number of elements, including the passage's *broader literary context, theme, structure, point of view, mood,* and *style*.

Literary context. Try to determine how your passage functions within its surrounding literature. You may have touched on this aspect when you were doing your background reading. Is the point of your passage part of a larger point within a chapter, section, tractate, or even the entire book? Or is it a digression, a passage that can stand apart from what surrounds it? Why might the author have written or placed your specific passage in this particular spot?

If you are able, you may also want to determine how your passage, and the larger book or document in which it stands, contributes to or affects the collection of writings that its religious community considers sacred. Does your passage play into larger themes, or does it challenge them? Is it part of a central teaching, or does it seem somewhat dispensable? Is it perhaps a rare instance in which an author or the larger collection brings up a difficult, or obscure, topic?

Theme. Before becoming immersed in the details of your text, it is necessary to get a sense of the larger whole. By now you will have read the passage a number of times, and you will have also looked at its wider literary context. It's time to determine what the theme of the passage is. You don't need to be too concrete here. You will revisit this step later in the process; for now, concentrate on a few key questions. How might you summarize the passage? What primary idea controls the passage? For example, is it a story about a specific event, or with a particular moral? Is it a sermon or admonition to a particular group of people? Is it a group of laws or commands all pointing to a common idea?

Structure. Next you should try to draft an outline of the passage. Just as you should make an outline of your essay before you begin to write it, so too should you be able to "reverse engineer" your passage and determine what its outline is. In some ways, you are now the detective, seeking to make sense of *how* the theme of your passage is made clear. Try to determine what steps, arguments, or methods are being used to convey the main point. What transitions are used? How does each part of your passage contribute to others and to the main idea? Some students find it helpful to diagram the passage or create a chart to visualize the passage's structure.

Point of view, mood, and style. At this point you should make note of the point of view being used, what the mood of the passage is, and what style the author is using to convey meaning. Is there a particular rhetorical tool, such as hyperbole or analogy, being employed by the author? Is the passage in first or third person? Who is speaking to whom?

Here we usually need to distinguish between the *implied author* and the real author, and between the *implied audience* and any real one. Although the actual author of your passage may be a religious scribe from the second century BCE, he or she may be trying to write as if from the fifth century BCE—as another person, in another area. You will deal with questions of when and where the text was composed later, so at this point you should simply seek to determine what the text itself might convey about these things.

Mood and style can contribute immensely to a passage. Is the language being used in the passage primarily figurative? Does it have a musical quality or rhythm? (This is often difficult to detect in a translation, but not impossible.) What *diction*, or choice of words, is used and how do these contribute to the passage? Is there an emotional element to the passage? Does the passage have a "feel" or style that can be described?

Step Five: Examine the historical context.

You have now spent time examining your passage in some detail and have noted its genre, theme, structure, point of view, mood, and style, as well as how it fits into the broader literary context. Next, it's time to take a deeper look at the historical context of your passage.

As a beginning student, you may find this step to be one of the more difficult ones. Don't worry too much, though. It's likely that your passage will fit into the material you are learning about in class in some way, perhaps regarding a religious group you may have already studied. You may have picked up some cues in class about when the text was written, to which group it is addressed, or whom it primarily affects. How does this information affect your reading? You will want to ask both broad and specific questions at this stage. Are there larger historical issues that affect how your text is understood (geographic, social, economic, or political issues)? And more specific to your particular passage, are there elements within the text itself that you might clarify by examining their history, such as a place name, a historical figure, or a reference to a type of weight or measurement? These broad and specific historical issues may help shed considerable light on the text you are attempting to interpret. You will need to dig into other sources at this stage, at least as they relate to the historical context of the text at hand.

Step Six: Examine the compositional history (when possible).

Sometimes the history of how a religious or sacred text was written is, or seems to be, well known. Sometimes it's a mystery. For example, in biblical scholarship it is generally agreed that the Christian apostle Paul wrote the New Testament book of Romans in the first century CE. There is a lot of debate, however, regarding other letters that were attributed to him but were likely not written by him; not all scholars agree who actually wrote these letters. This is true in other religions as well, where debate exists regarding the authorship of other texts, such as the Buddhist Pāli Canon, the Sikh Dasam Granth, or the Jewish Torah.

Information regarding authorship can be an important factor in your understanding of a passage. It can help you in the previous step dealing with historical context (which you can now revisit). It can also help you understand why and to whom a passage was written. Look to see if there is an introduction to your specific religious text; also check for dictionary articles on your particular book or text, as they can afford you a lot of insight. Provided they are trusted scholarly works (see Chapter 4), these resources will indicate, when possible, the scholarly consensus on a book's authorship and will also explain the various positions held by scholars so that you can better understand where this consensus comes from. You can now read your passage again in light of this information.

Step Seven: Consult secondary literature.

This is virtually your last step, even though it's the most tempting to do first. You might feel the urge to jump into a commentary or specific study to see what scholars or religious authorities have said about your passage before you start to work on it. As we mentioned earlier in the chapter, however, consulting secondary sources too early can skew your research or influence your thinking prematurely. It is important to come to an understanding of what a passage is about for yourself, what its key words are, how the argument is made, and so on *before* you read secondary sources.

To be clear, we are not suggesting that you stay away from secondary sources entirely; rather, you should do your own thinking first and then go to the experts. It is by standing on the shoulders of others that we are often able to see farther than before, so reading secondary sources will help you to clarify your thoughts on the passage. It will also guard against reading your passage idiosyncratically (or uniquely, that is, with peculiarities particular to you). You don't necessarily have to agree with all the secondary sources you consult, but you may find elements in these works that bolster your own ideas, that help give you further insight into an issue you have overlooked, or that persuade you to look at things in a different way. As with other essays, using and integrating secondary sources with your own ideas in interpretive work is a process that will take some time to learn.

In Chapter 4 we discussed how to go about selecting sources, which you can now use in this step. Remember, you must keep track of the names and page numbers of authors and their ideas so you can reference them properly in your paper. Teachers are more inclined to award a student a good mark for ideas that have been taken from other sources in a clear and well-documented fashion than for seemingly "original" ideas that are in fact not original and have been plagiarized (for more on plagiarism, see pages 37–39).

Step Eight: Revisit the above steps.

This is probably the last thing you feel like doing when you're pressed for time and you haven't even started writing your paper! But interpretation does not take place in a linear fashion. Rather, as we mentioned earlier, interpretation is an *iterative* process. If you revisit each step when interpreting texts, you will be able to refine your results and make necessary adjustments that would not have been possible without your subsequent research. Something that may have seemed clear when you started your research may now seem less defensible. Or, you may decide that you have fundamentally misunderstood the theme of the passage—for instance, if you have a better understanding of the text's historical context, you may see its meaning or mood in a new light. This is true for all stages of interpretation. You should continue this process for as long as is necessary, until you come to a sound conclusion regarding the passage's overall meaning.

A Word of Warning about Originality and "Meaning"

The reflections on interpretation offered above are meant to help you understand the historical and literary dimensions of sacred texts. However, there are two issues that warrant a word of warning as we conclude this section.

First, in arguing your case about a particular text, you may come to think that you understand something about your passage in a way that no one else before you has. As tempting as this position might be— especially after all the hard work of interpretation and all of the original thought you've put in!—it is always wise to err on the side of caution. Although it is possible that you have stumbled upon something brand new or unique, it is also possible that you have missed something or that you've inadvertently been influenced by something you have read or heard from another source. Especially when interpreting sacred texts that have been read carefully by countless people for many centuries, you need to respect that others may have observed what you do as well.

Second, and perhaps more common, it's easy to think that you have "mastered" a text and exhausted its meaning; that is, you have understood its meaning in the only way it can be understood. It is important to keep in mind, however, that any certitude about "meaning" is fraught with difficulties. Many books have been written about the problems of interpretation and meaning, and a good deal of postmodern scholarship would argue that no one can be absolutely certain about meaning, what an author of a passage "really meant," what a passage meant to the ancient audience, and so on. You will undoubtedly encounter more on these theoretical matters as you continue your undergraduate education. If you are interested in these issues, you can take classes on literary theory, hermeneutics (interpretational theory), and philosophy of language, among others. What you need to remember here is our earlier discussion regarding a balanced research mindset (see chapters 1 and 2); while you should confidently submit the findings of your research, it is also necessary to retain a level of academic and interpretive humility.

One way to think about these issues is to see yourself entering into an ongoing conversation that started long ago. You will (hopefully!) have something to contribute to the discussion concerning these texts, but the conversation is a complex one that has been going on for some time, with many voices, and will continue long after you. As such, build on the work that has been done before you, contribute what you can, and recognize that your contributions can never be seen as the final word.

DEVELOPING YOUR RESEARCH INTO AN ESSAY

You've done all of the hard work of interpretation. Now it's time to turn it into an essay. Writing an interpretative essay is similar to other types of essays you will encounter. You should go back to the steps in Chapter 5, paying particular attention to developing a thesis statement, an outline, and finally a finished, polished essay. You will want to use the information you have gathered in your research and turn it into a specific argument or thesis about the passage. As we discussed in the textbox above, your conclusions need not be entirely original or earth-shattering, especially at the undergraduate level. A modest thesis that is well argued and sound, with properly referenced sources for all of your ideas, will make for a much better essay than one that is based on leaps of conjecture or convoluted and undocumented argumentation.

Remember, while your essay may have implications for faith or for religious practice, your goal is not to create a sermon or a religious message. Rather, your essay is a chance to engage with and learn about a religious or sacred text on its own terms. While in some institutional contexts you may indeed be asked to reflect upon the spiritual nature or value of the text for a contemporary faith community, or to offer a critique of the text based on contemporary issues, be sure that this is indeed part of the assignment. Even here, you must take care in how this is done, and you should actively pursue the principles of objective and bias-free language (as discussed in Chapter 1).

Format and structure of an interpretive essay

Your interpretive essay will follow an overall structure similar to any other essay you will write (see Chapter 5). That means you need to ensure that you have a controlling theme or argument around which you organize your paper. However, there are a number of ways that you might structure an interpretive essay that will differ from standard approaches. For our purposes we will discuss two common types of interpretive essays: theme-oriented essays and essays that follow the natural progression of the text itself.

A theme-oriented interpretive essay is similar to a regular essay. You structure your essay around a theme, perhaps one that is assigned or one that you derive yourself from the passage you're studying. You might also be asked to trace a theme through a few passages or a particular writing within a sacred text. Generally, a theme-oriented paper is less detailed in its description of the text itself, but it should still engage with it in a serious way. An example of a theme-oriented essay topic could be "Discuss the use of the term *nomos* (law) in the New Testament writings of Paul."

An interpretive essay that is not theme-based usually follows the natural progression of the text instead, presenting a detailed, verse-by-verse (or section-by-section) explanation of the passage. With this approach, you will usually make an argument about a particular theme or topic in the end portion of your essay rather than explicitly from the start. This doesn't mean that you will ignore the steps we covered above or that you cannot make a nuanced argument in the body of your essay as you progress. It simply means that you will engage the text in a progressive step-by-step fashion and will then use this material to construct an argument in a section at the end of your essay. In this concluding section you will also draw from the research you did in the steps of interpretation.

As with all essays, your interpretive essay must have a strong introduction and conclusion. Keep in mind what we noted in Chapter 5: your introduction should clearly set out what the problem or issue is, why it is worth investigating, and how you will go about addressing it. The conclusion, meanwhile, should reiterate the question being addressed, how you approached it, and what conclusions can be drawn. As with other forms of essay writing, it is wise to leave the introduction and conclusion until you have completed the main body, so that you can be clear in these sections about the direction of your work.

CONCLUSION

Critical interaction with religious texts can be challenging, rewarding, even thrilling or scary—sometimes all at once. The task can seem all the more daunting because these texts are considered by many to be divine or at least authoritative, because they were penned in ancient languages, and because many were produced centuries ago. However, engaged interpretation need not be insurmountable. The steps outlined in this chapter will help you engage with particular dimensions of these texts, primarily historical and literary. As we highlighted throughout this discussion, there are various other aspects of religious texts that you can explore, and you may be asked to do so in your studies. As such, our guidelines are only that: guidelines. However, with experience and care, you should be able to adapt these for your specific needs as you explore the texts that stand at the heart of many of our world's religions.

ENDNOTES

1. There are many useful guides to writing about poetry and art available online. We draw here more generally from http://rwc.hunter.cuny.edu/reading-writing/on-line/writing-about-art. pdf; www.dartmouth.edu/~writing/materials/student/humanities/arthistory.shtml; http://owl. english.purdue.edu/owl/resource/615/01/; and www.hamilton.edu/writing/writing-resources/ poetry. For further help on these issues, see Sylvan Barnet, *A Short Guide to Writing about Art*, 10th ed. (Upper Saddle River, NJ: Prentice Hall, 2010), and Frank Madden, *Exploring Literature: Writing and Arguing about Fiction, Poetry, Drama, and the Essay*, 4th ed. (New York: Longman, 2008).

2. For further help in this area, consult Scott G. Brown's section on "Approaching Ancient Texts" (pp. 54–62) in *A Guide to Writing Academic Essays in Religious Studies* (London/New York: Continuum, 2008). The basic structure of what follows has been adapted from Craig C. Broyles (ed.), *Interpreting the Old Testament: A Guide for Exegesis* (Grand Rapids, MI: Baker Academic, 2001), 21–23.

CHAPTER 9

Writing Comparative Essays

INTRODUCTION

As noted in the previous chapter, a distinctive element of religious studies is the analysis of religious texts. In the study of religion, scholars also regularly engage in *comparative analysis*—a subset within "comparative religion"—meaning they analyze the similarities and differences of religious groups, concepts, themes, rituals, or myths, all with a view toward a deeper understanding of one religion or several. In this chapter, we look specifically at comparative essays (for more on general essay-writing guidelines, see Chapter 5).

A comparative essay is, quite simply, an essay that compares things. Sometimes you will be assigned subjects to compare, while in other instances you might be given the freedom to choose topics. As we discussed in Chapter 8, care must be taken to ensure that your selection is appropriate to the assigned length of your paper, to ensure that you have enough space to examine your topic in detail. Examples of things you might compare and contrast can include:

- **Texts**: perhaps a comparison of texts in one collection, such as teachings on the soul in the Upanishads; or a comparison of different texts, such as the Babylonian creation epic Enuma Elish and the biblical creation stories in Genesis;

- **Individuals or groups**: Sikh communities in Yuba City, CA, and Richmond Hill, NY;
- **Historical events**: The events surrounding the assassinations of Mohandas Karamchand Gandhi and Martin Luther King Jr.;
- **Issues or theories**: religious pluralism in Canada and in India; or the sociology of religion as seen in the works of Emile Durkheim and Max Weber; or
- **Religious practices or beliefs**: Hinduism and Islam in India.

As your studies progress, the subjects you will be asked to compare may become more intricate and involved. For the purposes of introducing you to comparative essays, this chapter will provide broad-based examples.

FINDING COMPONENTS FOR YOUR COMPARATIVE ESSAY

Approaching comparative essays might initially feel overwhelming. You might be tempted to come up with a long list of similarities and differences, and simply put these down on paper. But this isn't comparing, it is cataloguing. Comparison involves looking at the two (or more) topics together. Much of what we discussed in Chapter 5 regarding general essay writing applies here as well; for example, the general principle of limiting your research to retain a narrow focus is still paramount. Therefore, in order to compare and contrast your subjects you will need to isolate specific components or issues on which to base your research. Some instructors will isolate these components for you through an essay title or question; others will expect you to do this on your own. Whatever your situation, the components you choose will provide a framework around which to structure your essay, and they will help you develop your thesis. Within the limited space of an essay, choosing fewer components gives you room for a richer comparison.

To take one of the examples from above, you may be asked to write a comparative essay on religion in India by comparing two of its major religions, Hinduism and Islam. As you begin your research you will discover that trying to say everything about these religions is impossible; these are vast topics, much too broad to cover comprehensively in a short undergraduate essay. As such, you will need to focus your essay on particular components of these religions. For example, you may decide to investigate 1) the historical development of these religions in India, 2) their core beliefs or a particular belief, and 3) their respective practices and rituals. Alternatively, you may opt to look at how these religious systems are practised in India today, focusing on 1) typical places and forms of worship, 2) syncretism (the intricate fusion of beliefs or practices) between the two religions, and 3) the role of religion in contemporary Indian life. But as you look at these topics, you may decide that they are still too broad, and you may choose to focus solely on places of worship, comparing elements of Hindu and Muslim sacred sites.

As you research, you may find similarities and differences in the depictions of the components you have chosen to focus on; or you may realize that you need to break the components down into further categories, or simply focus on one. Regardless, finding components (such as places of worship, texts, holy persons, or the ritual year) on which to base your essay will give you a framework that will make the comparison much more manageable. If you aren't sure whether your framework is narrow enough, ask your instructor for advice before you make too much progress, to ensure you are on the right track.

To take another example, you may be required to compare the sociological approaches to religion in the works of Emile Durkheim and Max Weber. Once again, it would be a lifetime's work to cover every aspect of this comparison in depth, so if your instructor does not ask you to concentrate on particular aspects or teachings of these theorists, you will need to identify specific issues or components to examine yourself. One approach would be to 1) place each of these thinkers in their historical context, 2) explain their respective approaches to how religion affects social life, and 3) outline their main contributions to the broader study of religion. Another approach would be to focus on particular methodological issues in relation to each theorist, such as 1) views concerning scientific knowledge in sociological research, 2) approaches to collecting and using data, and 3) how these matters affect these thinkers' conclusions regarding religion.

Finally, let's say you are asked to compare certain aspects of two ancient texts, for example the biblical accounts of creation in Genesis 1–2 and the Babylonian account of creation in the Enuma Elish. Into what components might you be able to break down your comparison? After carefully reading the texts themselves, you might decide that it would be helpful to compare how the two texts depict 1) the deities, 2) humanity, and 3) the cosmos. Alternatively, you might explore how these texts depict 1) the human–divine relationship, and 2) the relationship between humanity and the created world. Again, you may feel the need to break these down into further categories, or you may choose to focus on only one for the sake of space or clarity. The key is to find components around which you can frame your comparison, and to do so in a way that allows you to discuss them intelligently and efficiently. Hopefully you will find a topic that interests you as a student, too!

STRUCTURING A COMPARATIVE ESSAY

Having identified the components you will use in your comparative essay, you need to consider how you will organize your research. There are three main ways that you can structure a comparative essay. The first is a *subject-based* approach, where you deal with each of the subjects in their entirety on their own (all of A then all of B), followed by a comparison of these elements. The second approach is *component-based* (or theme-based), meaning that you structure your essay around your components or individual points, alternating between the subjects (the aspects of both A and B for component one, then A and B for component two, and so on). The third option is the *lens* approach, where you investigate one subject in light of, or through the "lens" of, the other. This latter approach is particularly useful if you want to explore one subject in more detail than the other, or if one subject is illuminated by another.

Here are some ways you could structure comparative essays, using examples from above:

FOCUS: Sacred sites of Hinduism and Islam in India

Subject-based approach:

    I. Hinduism
        A. Historical development (brief survey)
        B. Core beliefs (brief survey)
        C. Description of key sacred sites and their use
    II. Islam
        A. Historical development (brief survey)
        B. Core beliefs (brief survey)
        C. Description of key sacred sites and their use
    III. Comparison of subjects

Component-based approach:

    I. Historical development
        A. Hinduism
        B. Islam
    II. Core beliefs
        A. Hinduism
        B. Islam

   III. Description of key sacred sites
      A. Hinduism
      B. Islam

Lens approach:
    I. Brief introduction to Hinduism and Islam in India
   II. A closer look at Islam in India
      A. Historical development, in light of Hinduism
      B. Core beliefs, in light of Hinduism
      C. Discussion of sacred sites, in light of Hinduism
  III. Conclusion: how Islam's sacred sites have developed in India, in relation to Hinduism

FOCUS: Sociological approaches to religion as seen in the work of Emile Durkheim and Max Weber:

Subject-based approach:
    I. Durkheim
      A. Historical context
      B. Approach to how religion affects social life
      C. Main contributions to the sociological study of religion
   II. Weber
      A. Historical context
      B. Approach to how religion affects social life
      C. Main contributions to the sociological study of religion
  III. Comparison of subjects

Component-based approach:
    I. Views concerning scientific knowledge in sociological research
      A. Durkheim
      B. Weber
   II. Approaches to collecting and using data
      A. Durkheim
      B. Weber
  III. Ramifications for the study of religion
      A. Durkheim
      B. Weber

Lens approach:
    I. A brief introduction to the sociological approaches of Durkheim and Weber

II. A closer look at Durkheim's methodology, in light of Weber
  A. Views concerning scientific knowledge, in light of Weber
  B. Approaches to collecting data, in light of Weber
III. Ramifications of Durkheim's understanding of religion, in light of Weber

FOCUS: Creation accounts in Genesis and the Enuma Elish

Subject-based approach:
  I. Genesis creation accounts
    A. Deities
    B. Humanity
    C. Cosmos
  II. Enuma Elish creation account
    A. Deities
    B. Humanity
    C. Cosmos
  III. Comparison of subjects

Components-based approach:
  I. Deities
    A. Enuma Elish
    B. Genesis
  II. Humanity
    A. Enuma Elish
    B. Genesis
  III. Cosmos
    A. Enuma Elish
    B. Genesis

Lens approach:
  I. Summary of Enuma Elish creation account
  II. Genesis creation accounts, with reference to Enuma Elish
    A. Deities in Genesis, with reference to Enuma Elish
    B. Humanity in Genesis, with reference to Enuma Elish
    C. Cosmos in Genesis, with reference to Enuma Elish
  III. Conclusions on Genesis, in light of Enuma Elish

All of these approaches are acceptable, though be aware that your instructors may have a preference for one or feel that your specific essay would be best handled in a particular way.

CONTROLLING IDEA OR THESIS

As is true of general essay writing, when writing a comparative essay it is not enough simply to identify components and choose the way you would like to structure your essay. An essay is above all an argument: you are trying to convince your reader of something. It is fundamental that you develop a thesis or controlling idea for your essay, so that it is not simply a collection of data showing similarities and differences. Your essay needs to argue something specific. This might seem difficult at first, but a thesis or argument is vital for a strong comparative essay.

For comparative essays based on texts, many of the guidelines discussed in the previous chapter regarding interpreting religious texts will assist you in reading and comparing your texts. When comparing groups, events, theories, or issues, you will need to exercise the same critical judgment that we discussed in Chapter 5, as your paper will involve research similar to that engaged in a general essay. The difference will rest primarily in the fact that your thesis or controlling theme will now be dependent upon a difference or similarity in the things you are comparing, rather than a particular, stand-alone idea.

Let's return to the example of Hinduism and Islam in India. In your essay comparing these religions you might come up with a thesis statement like this: "India's two largest religions are helpfully understood in light of syncretism, which highlights the flexibility of, but also the tension between, Hinduism and Islam as religions." In this case, the controlling idea for your paper is that the syncretism of the two religions is a useful way of exploring these subjects with relation to India; this might work best in an essay whose structure is component-based. Another thesis might read: "While Islam is usually considered as a Middle Eastern religion, its development and current form in India can only be understood if the prior existence of Hinduism in the country is taken into account." This thesis may need some further tightening or narrowing, but it provides a preliminary framework from which to approach your essay. Given its content, this thesis would probably be best suited for an essay with a lens structure because you are proposing to understand one of India's religions (Islam) in light of another (Hinduism).

To take the example of the sociology of religion in the works of Durkheim and Weber, a thesis statement might be shaped like this: "Despite their differences, Durkheim and Weber both reflect the historical era they shared in that they both attempted to make sense of religion in an increasingly rationalistic, scientific, and secular age." Having determined this thesis you are now able to structure your essay in a variety of ways, depending on your preference and what you think will allow you to make the most convincing case. Again, your thesis may be refined or made more specific as you continue, and this is perfectly acceptable.

In relation to the comparison of the Genesis and Enuma Elish creation accounts, you might come up with the following thesis: "Although both the Genesis and Enuma Elish creation accounts make reference to deities, humanity, and the cosmos, the differences in how these elements are portrayed point toward the ideological and political interests of the communities that produced these texts." For the lens approach, you might focus on how reading Genesis alongside Enuma Elish brings to light factors that might otherwise be missed: "When read in light of Enuma Elish, it becomes evident that the Genesis creation account employs themes common to a mythological worldview found throughout the ancient Near Eastern world."

Once you have developed a thesis or controlling idea, you must ensure that it serves as the overarching focus of your comparative essay, as in general essay writing. Take special care to ensure that your components and structure enhance, not detract from, your thesis.

BALANCE AND CLARITY

As we note throughout this handbook, balance and clarity are of utmost importance for all of your work. However, these two principles are particularly important in writing comparative essays. First, strive for *balance*, both in content and in tone. As instructors, one of the most frequent problems we encounter in comparative essays is the lack of balance on the subjects being compared and contrasted. If your essay leans more heavily on one subject than the other (for instance, if you have employed the "lens" approach), or if you are more generous with one subject and more critical of the other, you will need to state why this is the case, and have good reasons for doing so. Do not assume that your reader will necessarily agree with your decision to give preference to any one group, event, text, or idea. You need to *demonstrate* (as part of your argument) why you have approached the essay in this manner.

Second, in your essay overall, and especially in your thesis statement and conclusion, aim for *clarity* and *precision*. That is, try and offer substantial information; to say that two subjects have both similarities and differences is neither a thesis nor a conclusion; the reader is left none the wiser. It is important to make a larger point in your conclusion, but remember, this is not necessarily something exceptional or groundbreaking. What you want to do is summarize how you have demonstrated your point or points by way of careful research and a well-documented argument.

To help you in the task of making your thesis clear and precise, you should learn how to make use of transition markers. Terms and phrases you may find helpful in comparative essays include:

- On the one hand/on the other hand
- Like, just as, similar to
- Whereas, alternatively, conversely

These and other transitions will make clear to your reader when you are comparing and when you are contrasting your subjects. Anything you can do to make your writing as clear and precise as possible will contribute to a more readable and convincing essay.

WRITING CHECKLIST: COMPARATIVE ESSAYS

Once again we present a list of things to check as you write your essay, in this case a comparative essay:

- ☐ What am I being asked to compare (texts, theories, beliefs, people, groups)?
- ☐ Have I isolated components or issues that can be used as the basis for my comparison? Are these appropriate for the length and nature of the essay assigned?
- ☐ What approach will I take in this essay (subject-based, component-based, lens approach)? Am I clear and consistent with this approach?
- ☐ Do I have a controlling idea or thesis that can serve as a framework for the essay?
- ☐ Have I offered a balanced comparison of my topics?
- ☐ Is my focus clear?

CONCLUSION

As with interpretive essays, well-written and convincing comparative essays come only with time and practice. Pay attention to the components, structure, and thesis of your comparison, because these key elements will give your essay focus and clarity. Learning to compare matters efficiently, accurately, and fairly will prove to be invaluable as you continue in your studies.

CHAPTER 10

Writing with Style

Objectives

- Being clear in your writing
- Being concise in your writing
- Being forceful in your writing
- Making the most of introductions and conclusions

In the previous chapters we have explored how to go about planning and crafting your essays and other writing assignments. We will now look at several ways you can improve the quality of your writing.

Writing with style does not mean inflating your prose with fancy words and extravagant images. Any style, from the simplest to the most elaborate, can be effective depending on the occasion and intent. Writers known for their style are those who have projected their own personality into their writing; we can hear a distinctive voice in what they say. Obviously it takes time to develop a unique style. To begin with, you have to decide what general effect you want to create.

Taste in style reflects the times. In earlier centuries, many respected writers wrote in an elaborate style that we would consider much too wordy. Today, journalists have led the trend toward short, easy-to-grasp sentences and paragraphs. Writing in an academic context, you may expect your audience to be more reflective than the average newspaper reader, but the most effective style is still one that is clear, concise, and forceful.

BE CLEAR

Use clear diction

A dictionary is a wise investment. A good dictionary will help you understand unfamiliar words or archaic and technical senses of common words. Some dictionaries help you use words properly by offering example sentences that show how certain words are typically used. A dictionary will also help you with questions of spelling and usage. If you aren't sure whether a particular word is too informal for your writing or if you have concerns that a certain word might be offensive, a good dictionary will give you this information.

If you are at a Canadian institution, usage and spelling may follow either Canadian (similar to British) or American convention, or you may be asked to use a combination of both. There are a number of Canadian dictionaries available today that will help you to be consistent in your approach. It's also a good idea to make sure that the Language feature of your word-processing program is set to the appropriate setting, *English (Canada, United Kingdom,* or *United States),* depending on your context.

A thesaurus lists words that are closely related in meaning. It can help when you want to avoid repeating yourself or when you are fumbling for a word that's on the tip of your tongue. Your word-processing program may also have a thesaurus feature, which allows you to look up synonyms and antonyms easily. But be careful: make sure you distinguish between *denotative* and *connotative* meanings. A word's denotation is its primary or "dictionary" meaning. Its connotations are any associations that it may suggest; they may not be as exact as the denotations, but they are part of the impression the word conveys. If you examine a list of synonyms in a thesaurus, you will see that even words with similar meanings can have dramatically different connotations. For example, alongside the word *indifferent* your thesaurus may give the following: *neutral, aloof, callous, moderate, unenthusiastic, apathetic, unprejudiced,* and *fair.* Imagine the different impressions you would create if you chose one or the other of those words to complete this sentence: "Questioned about his interpretation of this text, he was _____ in his response." In order to write clearly, you must remember that a reader may react to the suggestive meaning of a word as much as to its "dictionary" meaning. As a rule of thumb, use a thesaurus to jog your memory for a familiar term rather than to come up with a new and unfamiliar term, one you will potentially misuse.

USE PLAIN ENGLISH

Plain words are almost always more forceful than fancy ones. If you are not sure what plain English is, think of the way you talk to your friends (apart from swearing, slang, and abbreviations or acronyms that come from texting and messaging!). Many of our most common words—the ones that sound most natural and direct—are short. A good number of them are also among the oldest words in the English language. By contrast, most of the words that

English has derived from other languages are longer and more complicated; even those that have been used for centuries can sound artificial. For this reason you should beware of words loaded with prefixes (*pre-*, *post-*, *anti-*, *pro-*, *sub-*, *maxi-*, etc.) and suffixes (*-ate*, *-ize*, *-tion*, etc.). These Latinate attachments can make individual words more precise and efficient, but putting a lot of them together will make your writing seem dense and hard to understand. There may be times when the use of these words is necessary for your field of study; however, in many cases you can substitute a plain word for a fancy one:

Fancy	*Plain*
accomplish	do
cognizant	aware
commence	begin, start
conclusion	end
determinant	cause
fabricate	build
finalize	finish, complete
firstly	first
infuriate	anger
maximization	increase
modification	change
numerous	many
obviate	prevent
oration	speech
prioritize	rank
remuneration	pay
requisite	needed
sanitize	clean
subsequently	later
systematize	order
terminate	end
transpire	happen
utilize	use

Suggesting that you write in plain English does not mean that you should never pick an unfamiliar word, a "fancy" term, or a foreign derivative; sometimes these words are the only ones that will convey precisely what you mean. Inserting an unusual expression into a passage of plain writing can also be an effective means of catching the reader's attention—as long as you don't do it too often.

USE JARGON CAREFULLY

All academic subjects have their own terminology; it may be unfamiliar to outsiders, but it helps specialists explain things to each other. The trouble is that people sometimes use jargon—special, technical language—unnecessarily, thinking it will make them seem more knowledgeable. Too often the result is not clarity but complication. The principle is easy: use specialized terminology only when it's a kind of shorthand that will help you explain something more precisely and efficiently. If plain prose will do just as well, stick to it.

BE PRECISE

Always be as specific as you can. Avoid all-purpose adjectives like *major*, *significant*, and *important* and vague verbs such as *involve*, *entail*, and *exist* when you can be more specific:

> **orig.**   Mahatma Gandhi was involved in the civil rights movement in South Africa in the early twentieth century.

> **rev.**   Mahatma Gandhi was a key figure in organizing and leading the civil rights movement in South Africa in the early twentieth century.

Another example:

> **orig.**   Martin Luther's views on Judaism have had a significant influence on his legacy.

> **rev.**   Martin Luther's views on Judaism have had a costly influence on his legacy.

AVOID UNNECESSARY QUALIFIERS

Qualifiers such as *very*, *rather*, and *extremely* are overused. Saying that something is *extremely profound* may have less impact than saying simply that it is *profound*. For example, compare these sentences:

> This is a profound statement.

> This is an extremely profound statement.

Which has more impact? When you think that an adjective needs qualifying—and sometimes it will—first see if it's possible to change either the adjective or the phrasing. Instead of writing

> The Muslim population of Europe has experienced very large growth in the past decade,

write a precise statement:

> The Muslim population of Europe has seen unprecedented growth in the past
> decade.

In some cases, qualifiers not only weaken your writing but are redundant because the adjectives themselves are absolutes. To say that something is *very unique* makes as little sense as saying that someone is *slightly pregnant* or *extremely dead.*

Create clear paragraphs

Paragraphs come in so many sizes and patterns that no single formula could possibly cover them all. The two basic principles to remember are these:

1. a paragraph is a means of developing and framing an idea or impression;
2. the divisions between paragraphs are not random but indicate a shift in focus.

DEVELOP YOUR IDEAS

You are not likely to sit down and consciously ask yourself, "What pattern shall I use to develop this paragraph?" What comes first is the idea you intend to develop; the structure of the paragraph should flow from the idea itself and the way you want to discuss or expand it.

You may take one or several paragraphs to develop an idea fully. For a definition alone you could write one paragraph or ten, depending on the complexity of the subject and the nature of the assignment. Just remember that ideas need development, and that each new paragraph signals a change in idea.

CONSIDER THE TOPIC SENTENCE

Skilled skim readers know that they can get the general drift of a book simply by reading the first sentence of each paragraph. The reason is that most paragraphs begin by stating the central idea to be developed. If you are writing your essay from a formal plan, you will probably find that each section and subsection will generate the topic sentence for a new paragraph.

Like a thesis statement for an essay as a whole, a topic sentence is not obligatory; in some paragraphs the controlling idea is not stated until the middle or even the end, and in others it is not stated at all but merely implied. Nevertheless, it's a good idea to think out a topic sentence for every paragraph. That way you'll be sure that each one has a readily graspable point and is clearly connected to what comes before and after. When revising your initial draft, check to see that each paragraph is held together by a topic sentence, either stated or implied. If you find that you can't formulate one, you should probably rework the whole paragraph.

MAINTAIN FOCUS

A clear paragraph should contain only those details that are in some way related to the central idea. It should also be structured so that the connection between these details and the main idea can be readily seen. One way of showing these relationships is to keep the same grammatical subject in most of the sentences that make up the paragraph (for example, if you are referring to Ananda in biographies of the Buddha, make sure that each sentence revolves around Ananda in some way). When the grammatical subject keeps shifting, a paragraph loses focus. However, when you focus on and use one grammatical subject, you will assist your readers to keep things clear in their minds and follow the logic behind your ideas.

Naturally it's not always possible to retain the same grammatical subject throughout a paragraph. If you were comparing the religious affiliation of college-aged males and females, for example, you would have to switch back and forth between males and females as your grammatical subject. In the same way, you have to shift when you are discussing examples of an idea or exceptions to it.

AVOID MONOTONY

If most or all of the sentences in your paragraph have the same grammatical subject, how do you avoid boring your reader? There are two easy ways:

1. **Use substitute words**. Pronouns, either personal (*I*, *we*, *you*, *he*, *she*, *it*, *they*) or demonstrative (*this*, *that*, *those*), can replace the subject, as can synonyms (words or phrases that mean the same thing). Most well-written paragraphs have a liberal sprinkling of these substitute words.
2. **"Bury" the subject by putting something in front of it**. When the subject is placed in the middle of the sentence rather than at the beginning, it's less obvious to the reader. You might make use of phrases or introductions for this, though at times even a single word, such as *first*, *then*, *lately*, or *moreover*, will do the trick. Ensuring that you balance, and thus do not overuse, these phrases or words is key to effective writing.

LINK YOUR IDEAS

To create coherent paragraphs, you need to link your ideas clearly. Linking words are those connectors—conjunctions and conjunctive adverbs—that show the relationship between one sentence, or part of a sentence, and another. They are also known as transition words, because they form a bridge from one thought to another. Make a habit of using linking words when you shift from one grammatical subject or idea to the next, whether the shift occurs within a single paragraph or as you move from one paragraph to another. The following are some of the most common connectors and the logical relations they indicate:

Linking word	Logical relation
and also again furthermore in addition likewise moreover similarly	addition to previous idea
alternatively although but by contrast despite, in spite of even so however nevertheless on the other hand rather yet	change from previous idea
accordingly as a result consequently hence for this reason so therefore thus	summary or conclusion

Numerical terms such as *first*, *second*, and *third* also work well as links.

VARY PARAGRAPH LENGTH, BUT AVOID EXTREMES

Ideally, academic writing will have a balance of long and short paragraphs. However, it's best to avoid the extremes—especially the one-sentence paragraph, which can only state an idea without explaining or developing it. A series of very short paragraphs is usually a sign that you have not developed your ideas in enough detail or that you have started new paragraphs unnecessarily. On the other hand, a succession of long paragraphs can be difficult to read. In deciding when to start a new paragraph, consider what is clearest and most helpful for the reader.

Use headings

One way to be clear in your writing is to use headings. Like paragraphs, section headings are signposts for the reader, offering direction as to where the essay is going. Headings are especially helpful in longer pieces of work. While care should be taken not to go overboard with the number of headings used, it is reasonable to place headings over the introduction and conclusion of your essay, as well as the main points or components of the body of the essay. As with other stylistic issues, the use of headings depends on the formatting requirements in your department or institution. Not all instructors like or allow the use of headings in essays, particularly in shorter undergraduate essays, so be sure to follow the required conventions for your particular context.

BE CONCISE

At one time or another, you will probably be tempted to pad your writing. Whatever the reason—because you need to write two or three thousand words and have only enough to say for one thousand, or because you think length is strength and hope to get a better mark for the extra words—padding is a mistake.

Strong writing is always concise. It leaves out anything that does not serve some communicative or stylistic purpose, and it says as much as possible in as few words as possible. Concise writing will help you do better on both your essays and your exams.

Use adverbs and adjectives sparingly

Don't sprinkle adverbs and adjectives everywhere and don't use combinations of modifiers unless you are sure they clarify your meaning. One well-chosen word is always better than a series of synonyms:

orig.   As well as being <u>costly</u> and <u>financially extravagant</u>, the venture was <u>reckless</u> and <u>risky</u>.

rev.   The venture was <u>risky</u> as well as <u>costly</u>.

Avoid noun clusters

A recent trend in some writing is to use nouns as adjectives (as in the phrase *noun cluster*). This device can be effective occasionally, but frequent use can produce a monstrous pile of nouns. Breaking up noun clusters may not always result in fewer words, but it will make your writing easier to read:

orig.   doctrinal position revision summary

rev.   summary of the revised doctrinal position

Avoid chains of relative clauses

Sentences full of clauses beginning with *which*, *that*, or *who* are usually wordier than necessary. Try reducing some of those clauses to phrases or single words:

orig.   The Rastafarian movement <u>that</u> developed in the 1930s is considered an Abrahamic religious movement, <u>which</u> means there are elements of continuity with Judaism and Christianity.

rev.   The Rastafarian movement developed in the 1930s and is considered an Abrahamic religious movement, exhibiting elements of continuity with Judaism and Christianity.

Try reducing clauses to phrases or words

Independent clauses can often be reduced by subordination. Here are a few examples:

orig.   The creed was formulated in a clear and concise manner, and it was widely used.

rev.   Formulated in a clear and concise manner, the creed was widely used.

rev.   Clear and concise, the creed was widely used.

orig.   His plan was of a radical nature and was a source of embarrassment to his followers.

rev.   His radical plan embarrassed his followers.

Eliminate clichés and circumlocutions

Trite or roundabout phrases may flow from your pen automatically, but they make for stale prose. Unnecessary words are deadwood; be prepared to slash ruthlessly to keep your writing vital:

Wordy	Revised
due to the fact that	because
at this point in time	now
consensus of opinion	consensus
in the near future	soon
when all is said and done	[omit]
in the eventuality that	if
in all likelihood	likely
it could be said that	possibly, maybe
in all probability	probably

Avoid "it is" and "there is" beginnings

Although it may not always be possible, try to avoid beginning sentences with *It is . . .* or *There is (are) . . .* Your sentences will be crisper and more concise:

orig. There is little time remaining for the preservation of these archaeological artifacts.

rev. Little time remains for the preservation of these archaeological artifacts.

BE FORCEFUL

Developing a forceful, vigorous style simply means learning some common tricks of the trade and practising them until they become habit.

Choose active over passive verbs

An active verb creates more energy than a passive one does:

passive: The ritual <u>was investigated</u> by her.

active: She <u>investigated</u> the ritual.

Moreover, passive constructions tend to produce awkward, convoluted phrasing. However, passive verbs are appropriate in four cases:

1. When the subject is the passive recipient of some action:

   The rabbi <u>was heckled</u> by the angry crowd.

2. When you want to emphasize the object rather than the person acting:

   The process of reconciliation <u>will be discussed</u>.

3. When you want to avoid an awkward shift from one subject to another in a sentence or paragraph:

   The Jesuits began to convert the Hurons but <u>were attacked by</u> the Iroquois band before they had completed the mission.

4. When you want to avoid placing responsibility or blame:

   Several errors <u>were made</u> in the calculations.

When these exceptions do not apply, make an effort to use active verbs for a livelier style.

Use personal subjects

Most of us find it more interesting to learn about people than about things. Wherever possible, therefore, make the subjects of your sentences personal. This trick goes hand in hand with the use of active verbs. Almost any sentence becomes livelier with active verbs and a personal subject:

orig.   The <u>outcome</u> of the panel <u>was</u> the <u>decision</u> to continue the study.

rev.   The <u>panel decided</u> to continue the study.

Use concrete details

Concrete details are easier to understand—and to remember—than abstract theories. Whenever you are discussing abstract concepts, therefore, always provide specific examples and illustrations; if you have a choice between a concrete word and an abstract one, choose the concrete. Consider this sentence:

The Irish monastic communities helped preserve ancient documents.

Now see how a few specific details can bring the facts to life:

> With their careful copying methods and vigilant storage techniques, the Irish monastic communities helped preserve ancient Christian documents.

Adding concrete details doesn't mean getting rid of all abstractions. Just try to find the proper balance. The above example is one instance where adding words, if they are concrete and correct, can improve your writing.

Make important ideas stand out

Experienced writers know how to manipulate sentences in order to emphasize certain points. The following are some of their techniques.

PLACE KEY WORDS IN STRATEGIC POSITIONS

The positions of emphasis in a sentence are the beginning and, above all, the end. If you want to bring your point home with force, don't put the key words in the middle of the sentence. Save them for the end:

> **orig**.   People are more likely to consider themselves "spiritual" than "religious" in Western society today.

> **rev**.   In today's Western society, people are more likely to consider themselves "spiritual" than "religious."

SUBORDINATE MINOR IDEAS

Small children connect incidents with a string of *and*s, as if everything were of equal importance:

> Our bus was delayed, and we were late for school, and we missed the test.

As they grow up, however, they learn to *subordinate*—that is, to make one part of a sentence less important in order to emphasize another point:

> Because the bus was delayed, we were late and missed the test.

Major ideas stand out more and connections become clearer when minor ideas are subordinated:

> **orig**.   The first generation passed away and the movement developed more structure.

rev. As the first generation passed away, the movement developed more structure.

Make your most important idea the subject of the main clause, and try to put it at the end, where it will be most emphatic:

orig. I was relieved when I saw my marks.

rev. When I saw my marks, I was relieved.

VARY SENTENCE STRUCTURE

As with anything else, variety adds spice to writing. One way of adding variety, which will also make an important idea stand out, is to use a periodic rather than a simple sentence structure.

Most sentences follow the simple pattern of subject–verb–object (plus modifiers):

The church lost some members.
    S   V   O

A *simple sentence* such as this gives the main idea at the beginning and therefore creates little tension. A *periodic sentence*, on the other hand, does not give the main clause until the end, after one or more subordinate clauses:

Because of personal conflicts and doctrinal issues, membership at the
                                                    S
church declined.
      V

The longer the periodic sentence is, the greater the suspense and the more emphatic the final part. Since this high-tension structure is more difficult to read than the simple sentence, your reader would be exhausted if you used it too often. Save it for those times when you want to make a compelling point.

VARY SENTENCE LENGTH

A short sentence can add impact to an important point, especially when it comes after a series of longer sentences. This technique can be particularly useful for conclusions. Don't overdo it, though—a string of long sentences may be monotonous, but a string of short ones can make your writing sound like a children's book.

Still, academic papers usually have too many long sentences rather than too many short ones. Since short sentences are easier to read, try breaking up clusters of long ones. Check any sentence over 20 words or so to see if it will benefit from being split.

USE CONTRAST

Just as a jeweller highlights a diamond by displaying it against dark velvet, so you can highlight an idea by placing it against a contrasting background:

orig. Sikhism discourages its followers from using translations of sacred texts.

rev. Unlike Christianity, Sikhism discourages its followers from using translations of sacred texts.

Using parallel phrasing will increase the effect of the contrast:

Although the chaplain often spoke in prisons, she seldom spoke in schools.

USE A WELL-PLACED ADVERB OR CORRELATIVE CONSTRUCTION

Adding an adverb or two can sometimes help you dramatize a concept:

orig. Although I dislike the proposal, I must accept it as the practical answer.

rev. Although <u>emotionally</u> I dislike the concept, <u>intellectually</u> I must accept it as the practical answer.

Correlatives such as *both . . . and* or *not only . . . but also* can be used to emphasize combinations as well:

orig. The professor was a good instructor and a good friend.

rev. The professor was <u>both</u> a good instructor <u>and</u> a good friend.

(or)

rev. The professor was <u>not only</u> a good instructor <u>but also</u> a good friend.

USE REPETITION

Repetition is a highly effective device for adding emphasis:

He fought injustice and corruption. He fought complacent bishops and religious abuses. He fought hard, but he always fought fairly.

Of course, you would only use such a dramatic technique on rare occasions. Used infrequently, repetition adds great emphasis. But used too often, it becomes tiresome and contrived.

INTRODUCTIONS AND CONCLUSIONS

One final way to add force to your essay is by carefully choosing what you include in your introduction and conclusion. As we noted in Chapter 5, your introduction should present your reader with the question or problem you are addressing and how you will go about answering that question. However, if space permits, the introduction can also be a good time to grab the reader's attention and whet their appetite for the rest of your essay. This can be done in several ways. First, consider ways to elaborate on the question or problem you are addressing, highlighting why it is an important issue. For instance, if writing about the history and significance of the Hajj, Islam's annual pilgrimage to Mecca, you might note in your introduction that roughly two million people take part in this pilgrimage every year and that all Muslims are expected to make it at least once in their lifetime. Alternatively, you might find a quotation that helpfully summarizes the significance of your topic and why it needs to be addressed. However, when using quotations, make sure that you understand what the statement says, and that it actually helps bolster your case.

The same principles apply to your conclusion. We noted in Chapter 5 that your conclusion should summarize your findings and draw conclusions; no new information should be brought into the essay at this stage. Yet, a well-placed anecdote or quotation in your conclusion can be rhetorically effective. Moreover, these can often serve as your *clincher*, a statement that sums up your argument in a pithy or forceful way.

SOME FINAL ADVICE

Write before you revise

No one expects you to sit down and put all this advice into practice as soon as you start to write. You would feel so constrained that it would be hard to get anything down on paper at all. You will be better off if you begin concentrating on these guidelines during the final stages of the writing process when you are looking critically at what you have already written. Some experienced writers can combine the creative and critical functions, but most of us find it easier to write a rough draft first before starting the detailed task of revising and editing. (See our comments on writing drafts in Chapter 5.)

Use your ears

Your ears are probably your best critics; make good use of them. Before producing a final copy of any piece of writing, read it out loud in a clear voice. The difference between cumbersome and fluent passages will be unmistakable. If you are simply too tired to do this in the final stages of your essay composition, use the software built into your word processor (or computer's operating system) to read the text back to you.

CONCLUSION

Following the suggestions offered above is just one way to improve your style. Another way is by reading a variety of different writers to pick up on their distinctive ways of writing. Remember, however, that any style you develop should be your own and should reflect who you are. Indeed, some of the most forced writing we encounter as teachers is from students who are attempting to adopt what they assume is a more academic tone, resulting in stiff and stilted writing. As with many other areas we have explored in this book, writing with style is a skill that you will develop over time, so allow for the fact that you will need time to let your unique voice develop.

CHAPTER 11

Tests and Examinations

Objectives

- Preparing for exams
- Writing an essay exam
- Writing an open-book exam
- Writing a take-home exam
- Taking an objective test

The mere thought of an exam makes many people nervous and it can send some into a state of panic. It's not surprising. After all, the words "test" and "examination" conjure up uncomfortable images of inspection and scrutiny, and few of us enjoy the pressure of being examined. On top of this, writing an essay exam imposes special pressures. You can't write and rewrite the way you can in a regular essay, you must often write on topics you would otherwise choose to avoid, and you must observe strict time limits. On the surface, objective tests—involving multiple-choice or true–false questions—may look easier because you don't have to compose the answers, but they force you to be more decisive about your answers than essay exams do and they require very detailed and precise knowledge of the subject. But there are some upsides to taking exams. You cannot be expected to give very long or detailed answers, especially in comparison to your research essays, and you are not expected to write out references or bibliographies. Further, examiners tend to be more generous on exams when it comes to minor grammatical errors, spelling, and structure than they are with research essays. As with so many other areas of your education, perspective is key to understanding and excelling in exams.

Why do we have tests and exams? This is a valid question, and there has been much debate on the purpose and usefulness of exams in recent years. However, the main purpose of tests and exams is for your instructor to verify that you have understood the course material and that the work you've done that demonstrates this is entirely your own. To do your best, you need to be prepared and feel calm—but how? These general guidelines will help you approach any test or exam with confidence.

PREPARING FOR THE EXAM

Review regularly

Exam preparation has to begin long before the exam period itself. A weekly review of lecture notes and texts will help you remember important material and relate new information to old. If you don't review regularly, at the end of the year you'll be faced with relearning rather than remembering.

Retain perspective

Studying can be hard work. At times you may find the pressure so overwhelming, or you may be too mentally drained, to focus on the material. Keep this in mind, and aim to work in short spells of time with small, attainable goals. In other words, don't attempt to study an entire course's material in one sitting! There is little chance that you'll be able to digest it all properly.

Ask for help

If you are given class time for an exam review, ask your instructor what she or he is looking for in your exam answers. Also, it doesn't hurt to attempt to squeeze your instructor for all the information you can about which topics or themes are especially important or might feature in the exam. If possible, study with other students and ask them for their ideas on what might be key areas of emphasis in the course. Be able to explain material to one another in an understandable manner, test one another on *memory triggers* (see below), and compare notes you have taken. Engaging in course-specific discussions with your classmates is always a helpful tool in exam preparation.

Set memory triggers

As you review, condense and focus the material by writing in the margin key words or phrases that will trigger whole sets of details in your mind. The trigger might be a concept word that names or points to an important theory or definition, or it might be a quantitative phrase such as "three holy sites in Islam" or "four reasons for the Protestant Reformation."

Sometimes you can create an acronym or a nonsense sentence that will trigger an otherwise hard-to-remember set of facts—something like the acronym HOMES

(*Huron, Ontario, Michigan, Erie, Superior*) for the Great Lakes. Since the difficulty of memorizing increases with the number of individual items you are trying to remember, any method to reduce that number will increase your effectiveness.

Ask questions

Think of questions that will get to the heart of the course material and force you to examine the relations between various subjects or issues; then think about how you would answer them. For example, reviewing the components of a subject could mean focusing on the main parts of an issue or on the definitions of major terms or theories. Alternatively, you might explore change in a subject, asking yourself what the causes or results of those changes are. Often the most useful review questions are not the ones that require you to recall facts but the ones that force you to analyze, integrate, or evaluate information.

Identify any special needs you may have

Educational institutions are now making a concerted effort to recognize and accommodate the special needs of students who have learning disabilities such as dyslexia or other perceptual problems or physical disabilities. If you think you fall into this category, be sure to make your instructor and the appropriate school officials aware of your situation. You may be able to complete a test in a computer lab or under special conditions that will give you the best chance to demonstrate your knowledge.

Stay healthy

Though it may sound trite, it is vitally important that you eat and sleep well in the weeks coming up to your exams. Make sure you relax and take plenty of breaks—overdoing it in long sessions will not help you in the long run. On the day before an exam, don't pull an all-nighter! There are numerous horror stories of students who have tried this; in the end, it just isn't worth it. Your mind and body need rest in order to think clearly.

Avoid last-minute cramming

If you have given yourself enough time to review and study the material leading up to the exam, then last-minute cramming should not be necessary. In point of fact, cramming can have adverse effects on your exam performance. To begin with, spending too much energy on last-minute study may drain your energy for the exam itself, especially if you get little (or no) sleep. On top of this, waiting until the last minute to study for your exam can be distressing, as you may realize how much you do not yet know about the subject. Instead, you will be better off getting a good night's sleep and using the time directly before the exam as a chance to refresh yourself on key memory triggers, questions, and issues you have already studied.

Allow extra time

Give yourself lots of time to get to the exam. Nothing is more nerve-wracking than thinking you're going to be late because your alarm didn't go off or you got caught in traffic. Remember Murphy's Law: "Whatever can go wrong will." Anticipate any potential difficulties and allow yourself a good margin of time.

WRITING AN ESSAY EXAM

Many exams in post-secondary education are essay-based, that is, they ask you to answer questions by writing what are in essence short essays. On an essay exam, you may be given several questions and be expected to answer a percentage of them (for instance, you may be given five questions and be instructed to answer three of them). Often, you will write your answers in a separate booklet or notebook provided for you. Essay exams require careful planning and preparation, even once you are in the exam itself. Here are a few ways to make the most of these exams.

Read the exam and apportion your time

Remember that an essay exam is not a hundred-metre dash. Instead of starting to write immediately, take time at the beginning to read through each question and create a plan. A few minutes spent thinking and organizing will bring better results than the same time spent writing a few more lines. Read the instructions carefully to find out how many questions you must answer and to see if you have any choice. Believe it or not, many students answer more questions than required because they fail to read things carefully. Determine the amount of time you will need for each question; subtract five minutes or so for the initial planning, and then divide the time you have left by the number of questions you have to answer. If possible, allow for a little extra time at the end to reread and edit your work. If the instructions on the exam indicate that not all questions are of equal value, be sure to apportion your time accordingly.

Choose your questions

Decide which questions you want to answer and the order in which you will tackle them. You don't have to answer the questions in the order they appear on the paper. If you think you have lots of time, it's a good idea to place your best essay answer first, your worst answer in the middle, and your second-best answer at the end, in order to leave the reader on a high note. If you think you will be rushed, though, it's wiser to work from best to worst; that way you will be sure to get all the marks you can on your good answers, and you won't have to cut a good answer short at the end.

Stay calm

If your first reaction on reading the exam is "I can't do any of this!" force yourself to be calm; take several slow, deep breaths to relax; then decide which question you can answer best. Even if the exam seems impossible at first, you can probably find one question that looks manageable; that's the one to begin with. It will get you rolling and increase your confidence. By the time you have finished your first answer, you will probably find that your mind has worked through the answer for another question.

Read each question carefully

As you turn to each question, read it again carefully and underline all the key words. The wording will probably suggest the number of parts your answer should have. For example, a question that says "Compare and contrast the rise of Lutheranism to the rise of Anabaptism in Germany in the sixteenth century" is asking you to examine at least two things. Be sure you don't over-look anything—this is a common mistake when people are nervous. Since the verb used in the question is usually a guide for the approach to take in your answer, it's especially important that you interpret the key words in the question correctly. In Chapter 5 we summarized what you should do when you are faced with instructions like *explain*, *compare*, *discuss*, and so on; it's a good idea to review this list before you go to the exam (see page 45).

Make notes

Before you even begin to organize your answer, jot down key ideas and information related to the topic on rough paper or the unlined pages of your answer book. These notes will save you the worry of forgetting something while you are writing. Next, arrange those parts you want to use into a brief plan or outline.

Be direct

Get to your points quickly and use examples to illustrate them. In an exam, as opposed to an essay, it's best to use a direct approach. Don't worry about composing a graceful introduction, though a brief introduction is certainly appropriate; simply state the main points that you are going to discuss and then get on with developing them. Remember that your exam will likely be one of many read and marked by someone who has to work quickly; the clearer your answers are, the better they will be received. For each main point give the kind of specific details that will prove you really know the material. General statements will show you are able to assimilate information, but they need examples to back them up.

Write legibly

Poor handwriting makes readers cranky. When the person marking your paper has to struggle to decipher your ideas, you may get poorer marks than you deserve. If for some special reason (such as a physical disability) your writing is hard to read, you should be able to make special arrangements to use a computer. If your writing is not very legible, consider printing. Also, write on every second or third line of the booklet; this will not only make your writing easier to read but also leave you space to make changes and additions if you have time later on. For those with very small writing, you may want to consider writing your answers in bigger lettering than would normally be the case, as miniscule letters are often difficult for graders to decipher.

Stick to your time plan

Stay on your drafted schedule, and try to write something in response to each question you need to answer. Remember that it's easier to score half marks for a question you don't know much about than it is to score full marks for one you could write pages on. If you find yourself running out of time on an answer and still haven't finished, summarize the remaining points and go on to the next question. Leave a large space between questions so that you can go back and add more if you have time.

Reread your answers

No matter how tired or fed up you are, reread your answers at the end if there's time. Check especially for clarity of expression; try to get rid of confusing sentences and improve your transitions so that the logical connections between your ideas are as clear as possible. Don't be afraid to rewrite or clarify an illegibly written word. Revisions that make answers easier to read are always worth the effort.

WRITING AN OPEN-BOOK EXAM

If you think that permission to take your books into the exam room is an "Open Sesame" to success, be forewarned: do not fall into the trap of relying too heavily on your reference materials. You may spend so much time riffling through pages and looking things up that you won't have time to write good answers. The result may be worse than if you hadn't been allowed books at all.

If you want to do well, use your books only to check information and look up specific, hard-to-remember details for a topic you already know a good deal about. For instance, you might look up exact dates, or quotations, or an author's exact definition of a key concept—if you know where to find these details quickly. In other words, use the books to make sure your answers are precise and well illustrated, but never use them to replace study and careful exam preparation.

WRITING A TAKE-HOME EXAM

The benefit of a take-home exam is that you have time to plan your answers and consult your texts and other sources. The catch is that the amount of time you have to do this is usually less than you would have for a research essay. Don't work yourself into a frenzy trying to respond with a polished research essay for each question; instead, aim for well-written exam answers. Keep in mind that you were given this assignment to test your overall command of the course material; your reader is likely to be less concerned with your specialized research than with evidence that you have understood and assimilated the material.

The guidelines for a take-home exam are similar to those for a regular exam; the only difference is that you don't need to keep such a close eye on the clock:

- Keep your introductions short and get to the point quickly.
- Organize your answers so they are straightforward and clear, and the reader can easily see your main ideas.
- Use concrete examples to back up your points.
- Where possible, show the range of your knowledge of course material by referring to a variety of sources rather than constantly using the same ones.
- Try to show that you can analyze and evaluate material—that you can do more than simply repeat information.
- If you are asked to acknowledge the sources of any quotations you use, be sure to jot them down as you go rather than trying to track down sources at the end.
- Ask your instructor if the exam is to be typed or handwritten and if there are any other formatting guidelines that you should follow.

WRITING AN OBJECTIVE TEST

Objective tests are particularly common in entry-level courses, though they can surface in almost any religious studies course. You are likely quite familiar with this kind of test from high school. Objective tests usually feature multiple-choice questions, and they sometimes contain true–false or fill-in-the-blank questions as well. The main difficulty with these tests is that the questions are designed to confuse the student who is not certain of the correct answers. If you tend to second-guess yourself or if you are the sort of person who readily sees two sides to every question, you may find objective tests particularly hard at first. Fortunately, practice almost always improves performance.

Preparation for objective tests is the same as for other exams. Here, though, it is especially important to pay attention to definitions and unexpected or confusing pieces of information, because these are the kinds of details that are often used in questions for objective tests. Although there is no sure recipe for doing well on an objective test—other than a thorough knowledge of the course material—the following suggestions may help you do better.

Determine the marking system

If marks are based solely on the number of right answers, you should pick an answer for every question, even if you aren't sure it's the right one. For a true–false question, you have a 50 per cent chance of being right. Even for a multiple-choice question with four possible answers, you have a 25 per cent chance of getting it right, more if you can eliminate one or more answers that you know are wrong.

On the other hand, if there is a penalty for wrong answers—if marks are deducted for errors—you should guess only when you are fairly sure you are right, or when you are able to rule out most of the possibilities. In this case, don't make wild guesses.

Do the easy questions first

Go through the test at least twice. On the first round, don't waste time on troublesome questions. Since the questions are usually of equal value, it's best to get all the marks you can on the ones you find easy. You can tackle the more difficult questions on the next round. This approach has two advantages: first, you won't be forced, because you have run out of time, to leave out any questions that you could easily have answered correctly; second, when you come back to a difficult question on the second round, you may find that in the meantime you have figured out the answer.

Make your guesses educated ones

If you have to guess, at least increase your chances of getting the answer right. Forget about intuition, hunches, and lucky numbers (and forget that old chestnut that if you have to guess, you should always answer "C"). More importantly, forget about so-called patterns of correct answers—the idea that if there have been two "A" answers in a row, the next one can't possibly be "A" as well, or that if there hasn't been a "true" for a while, "true" must be a good guess. Many test-setters either don't worry about patterns at all or else deliberately elude pattern-hunters by giving the right answer the same letter or number several times in a row.

Remember that constructing good objective tests is a special skill that not all instructors have mastered. In many cases the questions they pose, though sound enough as questions, do not produce enough realistic alternatives for answers. In such cases the test-setter may resort to some less realistic options, and if you keep your eyes open you can spot them. James F. Shepherd[1] has suggested a number of tips that will increase your chances of making the right guess:

- Start by weeding out all the answers you know are wrong rather than looking for the right one.
- Avoid any terms you don't recognize. Some students are taken in by anything that looks like sophisticated terminology and may assume that such answers must be correct. In fact, these answers are usually wrong; the unfamiliar term may well be a red herring, especially if it sounds close to the correct one.
- Avoid absolutes, especially on questions dealing with people. Few aspects of human life are as certain as is implied by such words as *everyone*, *all*, *no one*, *always*, *invariably*, or *never*. Statements containing these words are usually false.
- Avoid jokes or humorous statements.
- Avoid demeaning or insulting statements. Like jokes, these are usually inserted simply to provide a full complement of options.
- Consider choosing options that make a specific statement, as opposed to those that are very general in nature. Generalizations are often too sweeping to be true.
- Don't overlook the "all of the above" option. Test-setters know that students with a patchy knowledge of the course material will often fasten on the one fact they know. Only those with a thorough knowledge will recognize that all the answers listed are correct. If

you see two options that you *know* are correct, and you think the third might be as well, it is probably safe to go with the "all of the above" answer.

Two final tips

If you have time at the end of the exam, go back and reread the questions. One or two wrong answers caused by misreading can make a significant difference to your score. That said, don't start second-guessing yourself either, changing a lot of answers at the last minute. Studies have shown that when students make changes they are often wrong. Stick with your original decisions unless you know for certain that you've made a mistake.

CONCLUSION

There is no denying that exams are intimidating. Preparation is key, but little things such as reading questions carefully to ensure you answer what is asked will also take you a long way on the road to success. The art of writing exams comes with practice, but hopefully the tips outlined above will help you approach even your first exams with confidence.

ENDNOTE

1.   James F. Shepherd, *College Study Skills*, 6th ed. (Boston: Houghton Mifflin, 2002) and *RSVP: The College Reading, Study, and Vocabulary Program*, 5th ed. (Boston: Houghton Mifflin, 1996).

CHAPTER 12

Giving an
Oral Presentation

Objectives

- Preparing presentations
- Giving your talk
- Taking questions on your presentation
- Making the most of visual aids

Jerry Seinfeld once remarked: "According to most studies, people's number one fear is public speaking. Number two is death. Death is number two? Does that seem right? To the average person that means that if they have to go to a funeral, they'd be better off in the casket than giving the eulogy."[1]

For some students the prospect of standing in front of a class to give a presentation can be terrifying. The reason is almost always that they are afraid of appearing foolish by not knowing what to say or how to answer questions. But you *can* give a good presentation, even if you're nervous when you begin—you just have to be prepared.

If you think about all the bad presentations you've heard in class, you'll probably find that you couldn't follow what was going on because the speaker jumped from topic to topic, or omitted crucial segments of an argument, or took for granted things that you didn't know about. The good presentations you have heard were more likely well organized and systematic, leading you through the material being discussed in a logical manner. Some people are naturally more comfortable in front of an audience than others, and these students do have a slight advantage. Even if public speaking is not one of your natural talents, however, you can still achieve good grades by following a few simple rules. Above all, remember: *be prepared and be organized.*

MAKING PREPARATIONS

Know your topic

For the purposes of an in-class presentation or seminar, you are the expert and will probably know more about your topic than any of the other students. You need to show your audience that your grasp of the subject matter goes beyond what you include in your talk. If you don't know any more than what you present, you won't be able to answer questions. The more background reading you do, the more information you will have to fall back on when someone asks you a question. This can be a serious confidence booster.

Consider your audience

It is a mistake to prepare your presentation based only on what you know about your topic. In fact, you should approach the talk from precisely the opposite direction: put yourself in the position of your audience. Imagine you are sitting in class instead of standing up at the front. What do you expect of the speaker? How much will the typical audience member know about this topic? What will the typical audience member find most interesting? Most relevant? What can be taken for granted as common knowledge in the context of the course? Are there terms in the presentation, religious or otherwise, with which your fellow students will be unfamiliar? If you combine these with your own question—*What do I want my audience to know?*—then you have the basis for setting up your talk.

Plan your presentation

Giving a presentation involves much more than writing an essay and then reading it out to the class. In fact, doing that is a terrible idea. Remember that talking to people requires a very different style of presentation than simply reading aloud. By the time you are asked to give an in-class presentation, it is likely that you will have sat through hundreds of lectures. Think about the ones you enjoyed most: What was it about them that made them interesting? If you do that, you will realize that your best lecturers were the ones who seemed the most prepared, who spoke without reading directly from their notes, who used a range of visual aids, and who seemed animated and genuinely interested in what they were talking about. You can be just as interesting by following some of these suggestions:

- **Don't write out everything you plan to say.** You should not write out your whole talk. Unless you are a skilled reader, the presentation will sound laboured and monotonous. Instead, draw up an outline that will serve as a guide as you move through your talk. This will help keep you on track. You can also prepare notes—perhaps on index cards—for each of the points that you are planning to discuss. These will allow you to use your own words and, likely, a more natural speaking style. If this sounds just too intimidating or you are worried that you may freeze when you first begin, write out the first few sentences you want to say, just to get you started. If you feel that you *must* write out a portion of your presentation, practice reading it so often that it is virtually memorized and does not feel like it is being read.

- **Consider preparing an outline for your audience.** Having a copy of your outline will give your audience something to follow along with as you talk. Typically, you should base this outline on the one you use to organize your talk, but you may want to include additional detail and a bibliography for your audience.

- **Use visual aids.** Having visual aids serves several purposes. First, whether an overhead, a PowerPoint slide, or an actual object, visual aids can attract and focus the audience's attention. If you are likely to become self-conscious when standing in front of a group, you will be more at ease when all eyes are on your visual aids and not on you. Second, visual aids provide another form of notes to remind you of what you need to say. However, as we discuss below, you need to make sure that these aids are in fact *aids*, not hindrances in your presentation.

- **Rehearse your talk**. The more you rehearse your talk, the smoother your presentation will be when you deliver it to your audience. A couple of practice runs will show you where the weak points in your presentation are and will also let you know if you are running over or under time. Knowing exactly how long your presentation will take can give you much-needed confidence. As teachers, we find that time management is often the most difficult obstacle students face in their presentations, so it's important that you have rehearsed it a few times in advance.

GIVING YOUR TALK

Dress comfortably

Dressing comfortably means not overdressing—but don't take that to mean dressing down for the occasion either. A suit may suggest the importance of your talk, but it may look odd to give your presentation in a suit if you ordinarily wear jeans and a short-sleeved shirt to class. The key is to wear something that will not distract your listeners, whether too formal or too casual. When in doubt, find out what is expected. Just don't go too far with informal dress: ripped jeans and an old T-shirt can seem disrespectful to the audience. Something that's casual but clean and neat will set a better tone.

Give yourself time at the beginning

If you have equipment to set up or other preparations to make, try to do this before the class begins. If everything is ready, you won't get flustered trying to resolve technical problems with your classmates looking on. Also, it's important to check with your instructor well in advance (not 10 minutes before the class begins!) what equipment is available or how you should access your PowerPoint presentation.

Try to relax

Take a deep breath before you begin and remind yourself that almost everyone gets nervous when speaking in front of an audience. Letting yourself become too nervous will be counterproductive, so relax! Consider injecting some humour into your presentation, possibly by way of an introductory quotation or short joke that is appropriate and connected to your topic. Not only have studies shown that humour is a useful tool to foster participation and retain your audience's attention, but a little laughter will put you at ease as well.

Begin with an overview

If the audience knows how the talk is structured, they will be able to understand what you are doing as you move from one point to the next. Introduce your topic and then give a brief statement of the main areas you will discuss. Again, an overhead, PowerPoint slide, or handout with the topic outline is useful because the audience can refer to it as your talk progresses.

Project your voice

When you speak, be sure you are loud enough so that everyone in the classroom can hear you. This is especially important to remember because, since you will likely be nervous, you will also likely be quieter or more hesitant in tone than usual. Also, try to put some feeling into what you say. It is difficult to remain attentive to even the most interesting presentation delivered in a monotone. Vary your speed and use emphasis to your advantage.

Don't be apologetic

The *worst* way to start a talk is by saying: "You'll have to forgive me, I'm really nervous about this," or "I hope this projector is going to work properly." Even if you are nervous, try to create an air of confidence.

Maintain eye contact with your audience

Look around the room as you speak. When you look at individuals, you involve them in what you are saying. Looking up, away from your notes, will let the audience know that you are well prepared and familiar with your material. Also, as you scan the faces in front of you, you can monitor for signs of boredom or incomprehension and can adjust your talk accordingly.

Work with your visual aids

If you have visual aids, take advantage of them; just remember that the visual material should enhance your talk, not distract the listener or deliver your presentation for you. At times, visual "aids" can actually become barriers when they are not seamlessly integrated with what you are saying or if you fumble to find your place in your notes after referencing them. Here are some guidelines that may help you to use visual aids:

- When you are making a point from your overhead or slide, try to use different words and expand on what is there.
- Give your audience enough time to read through and absorb each visual. They will find it frustrating to see images, text, or figures flash by before they've had a chance to take them in.
- Explain any figures you use. If it's a graph, describe what the x- and y-axes represent, and then explain what the graph shows. If it's a diagram, take the audience through it step by step; while you may be familiar with the material, your audience might not be.
- Don't forget to speak to your audience. At the beginning of your presentation, try to establish a rapport with the audience by talking briefly without a slide. Then, after you finish your last slide, try to put the focus back on you by summarizing your conclusion without the use of a slide.

Later in this chapter you will find some tips on how to prepare visual materials to make the strongest impression and to ensure that these are properly integrated with what you are saying.

Don't go too fast

A good talk is one that is well paced. However, keep in mind that nervousness causes some people to speak faster than they realize. If you think this might be something you do, make a conscious effort to speak slowly and clearly, perhaps even remind yourself in your cue cards or notes to maintain a steady pace throughout the presentation. If you're discussing background information that everyone is familiar with, you can go over it a little faster; if you're describing something complex or less familiar, go slowly. It often helps to explain a complicated point a couple of times in slightly different ways. Also, don't be afraid to ask your audience if they understand. Almost certainly, someone will speak up if there is a problem.

Monitor your time allotment

As well as pacing your delivery, you should try to ensure that you aren't going to finish too quickly or, worse (and more common), go over your allotted time. Once you have rehearsed your talk, you should know roughly how long it will take. You may want to bring a watch to place on the table beside you. You should also consider putting time reminders in the margins of your outline to help you stay on track. Remember to allow extra time for questions that people might ask during or after your talk. Ideally, you should plan to make your talk a little shorter than the amount of time you have available so that you have some leeway to answer questions.

Make your ending strong

Don't let your talk fade away at the end. Use your tone and emphasis to give people the cue that you have finished. You should finish by summarizing the main points you have made and by drawing some conclusions. These conclusions should be available on your visual material so that they can be left there for the discussion. Similar to the idea of the "clincher" in your essays, make this conclusion strong in content, as these are the last words of your presentation. Certainly don't end by saying, "Well, that's it." If you can find a way to raise some questions in your conclusions, this will set you up for the question period to follow.

Be prepared for questions

The question period is a time when you can really make a good impression. This is an opportunity for you to demonstrate your thorough understanding of the topic and even to reinforce one or two points that you think you may have missed. If you know your material well, you should have no problem dealing with the content of the questions, but the manner in which you answer these questions is important, too:

- It's a good idea to repeat a question if you are in a large room where everyone may not have heard it. This should also solidify the question in your mind and give you a few extra moments to consider it before answering.
- If you didn't hear or didn't understand a question, don't be afraid to ask the person who asked it to repeat or clarify it.
- Keep your answers short and to the point. Rambling answers are not helpful to anyone.
- If you don't know an answer, say so. It's okay to admit that you don't know everything—as long as you don't do this for every question. And, certainly, it's better to admit that you don't know an answer than to guess or to make up a response that everyone will know is not correct.

PREPARING VISUAL AIDS

With the availability of graphic presentation software such as Microsoft Power-Point, Adobe Photoshop, and others, as well as laptop computers and video projectors, your ability to use visual aids in a presentation is limited only by your own ingenuity and your instructor's willingness to let you use the technology in class.

For instance, you could develop a PowerPoint presentation that includes video clips and sound as well as animated diagrams. Even if you do not have access to PowerPoint or similar software, you can type up the main points of your talk and print them on transparencies along with any pictures and diagrams you have.

The suggestions that follow apply to any visuals that you might want to display during your talk.

Keep it simple

This is the cardinal rule and applies to every aspect of your visual aids. It is much better to put too little material on a slide than too much. Here are some specific ways to keep it simple:

- **Use plain fonts**. Unless you need a fancy one for a specific reason, stick with fonts that are easy to read, such as Arial, Verdana, Helvetica, or Times New Roman. Avoid fonts that are too elaborate, since they have reduced readability and can become irritating after a few slides.

- **Choose an appropriate font size**. The last thing you want on your slides or overheads is text that is too small to decipher. The regular 12-point font you use for your papers will almost certainly be too small when it is projected on a screen. The minimum size you can use will depend to some extent on how far the projector is from the screen, but one rule of thumb suggests 36 points for titles and 24 for body text. It's always a good idea to test-drive your presentation in the room where you'll be presenting your talk so that you can make adjustments if necessary.
- **Use a simple background**. If you're using PowerPoint to make your slides, choose a plain background and use the same one on every slide.
- **Don't overuse colour or animation**. Unless you have a good reason for doing so, avoid multicoloured slides or animation effects that are too busy or distracting.
- **Don't put too much information on one slide**. If you treat your slides as a script, then you'll be tempted to read directly from them. Instead, make your point briefly on the slide and then expand on the material as you talk. This will make your presentation sound much more natural and professional. If you have a diagram or graph, use the simplest version that you can.
- **Don't use too many slides**. A common weakness in presentations is overuse of slides, suggesting that the speaker cannot manage to talk without a prop. In many cases, three or four slides will be plenty for a short presentation (no more than one slide per minute of speech is a good rule of thumb).

Keep it organized

The second fundamental rule of using visual aids is to make sure your material is well organized. If you use a consistent organizational scheme, the audience will become used to it and will be able to follow along more easily.

- **Begin with a title slide**. A title slide sets the tone and orients the audience to your topic. It should contain the title, your name, and the name of the course.

- **Create a summary slide**. This will give an outline of your talk so that your audience knows what to expect. Remember to give your audience enough time to read through this slide before moving on.
- **Use headings**. Most of your slides should be in point form, using numbers or bullets, with headings and subheadings. If you do this, the audience will be able to tell which are your main points and which are elaborations.
- **Consider section breaks**. If your talk falls naturally into several sections, you could start each one with a new title slide. Anything that allows the audience to see the structure of your talk is worth doing.
- **Keep your overheads in order**. If you are using overhead transparencies, make sure that they are in the correct order—and in the correct orientation—when you start, and be sure to place your transparencies in an ordered pile as you use them. You may have to refer to one later, and you don't want to be shuffling through a disorganized pile in order to find the one you want.

CONCLUSION

Although it may be hard to remember while giving your presentation, try to relax and enjoy yourself. A presentation is a unique opportunity to present what you are learning while also developing speaking skills that are important for so many occupations and other aspects of life. The skills you learn will stay with you. Using the guidelines outlined in this chapter will enable you to be prepared and organized, present confidently, and thus achieve the highest grade possible, even if you are the most timid of students.

ENDNOTE

1.   Jerry Seinfeld, *SeinLanguage* (New York: Bantam, 1993), p. 120.

CHAPTER 13

Learning Languages

Objectives

- Recognizing the importance of languages
- Understanding ways to succeed in language learning

By now it should be clear that religious studies is concerned with, among many other things, both history and texts. Any study of history and textual traditions quickly comes to an issue that we mentioned in Chapter 8: much of the historical and textual material relating to various religions (and religious studies) originated in languages other than English. As such, scholars of religion find themselves dealing with languages ranging from Akkadian, to Japanese, to Syriac, to Old Norse. While you probably won't have to become proficient in Old Norse in your undergraduate studies, you may well have the chance (or be required) to learn an ancient language such as Latin, Greek, Sanskrit, or Hebrew, not to mention contemporary languages such as Spanish, German, or French, in the course of your studies. Although each language is different, there are a few underlying principles that apply to all language acquisition, particularly reading skills. With this in mind, in this chapter we offer a few suggestions for how you can excel in this rewarding, but sometimes difficult, task.

THE IMPORTANCE OF LANGUAGES

First, a brief word on why you should take languages seriously. Over the years friends and acquaintances have often asked us why we bother with learning languages—particularly ancient or "dead" languages—when so much material is available in English translation. This issue has become even more pressing in recent years with the development of translation tools and technologies, including web-based resources. Why bother with learning the original when so much is available in English?

There are several reasons why one might learn another language. There's no denying that learning a language can be hard work. However, the corollary of this is that being able to use an ancient or foreign language is fulfilling and can bring great personal satisfaction. To know that you have put in the time learning parts of speech and vocabulary and can now read the Qur'an in Arabic or St. Patrick's *Confession* in Latin is rewarding indeed.

Second, anyone who has worked with texts in another language knows that every *translation* is in fact an *interpretation*. That is to say, there are no perfect translations that directly transmit meaning from one language to another. We touched on this briefly in Chapter 8. Languages are full of nuance, whether in the range of meanings a word might have or the various ways the tense of a verb can be understood. A translator has to make certain choices about how to present these words and phrases in the translated language, choices that another translator might have made differently. Thus, to work with a text in its original language is to push past the interpretive choices made by translators to see for yourself how that text functions.

Finally, as you progress in your studies, you will find that more obscure resources are not always available in your language. A lot of vital secondary sources and commentaries will only be accessible in German or French. This will become especially apparent if you continue into graduate studies, where acquiring several ancient and modern languages is the norm. Demonstrating that you can interact with a broad spectrum of scholarship—a key aspect of graduate research—will often entail engaging with sources that are not in your native tongue.

To be sure, there are many reasons one might come up with for *not* learning a language in today's world. However, being able to interact with primary materials in languages other than your own remains a vital aspect of religious studies. With this in mind, here are some things to consider as you embark on this journey.

TIPS FOR SUCCEEDING IN LANGUAGE LEARNING

Like many people, you may find the idea of learning a new language to be quite frightening. This can be true for a number of reasons. Perhaps you have never attempted to learn another language, so the whole concept seems scary—especially when you have to learn an entirely new alphabet before you can even start to learn vocabulary. Or you may have had a less-than-successful experience with learning a language in the past, so it's not a pleasant prospect to try it out again. While these concerns are understandable, our experience is that people who want to do well and succeed in learning a language can indeed thrive, given the right circumstances, tools, and choice. In what follows we offer some basic concepts to help you start off on the right foot in learning a new language.

Brush up on grammar

In the initial stages of learning a language, you may feel lost in the grammatical jargon as much as in the language itself. Although you might recall what a noun, verb, or adjective is from your high school days, you may be a little fuzzier when it comes to a predicate or an indefinite article, not to mention a demonstrative pronoun, an intransitive verb, or a passive participle. These issues are compounded by the fact that the English language does not employ all the grammatical aspects you may encounter in the languages you are learning. For example, English does not differentiate second-person singular from second-person plural, while many other languages do. In French, you can use the word "tu" to mean a singular you, or "vous" to address a group of people, whereas in English you would use "you" in both instances. As another example, the form and function of words in relation to other words in a sentence, called their *case*, does not often change in English. However, many languages make use of a number of cases, meaning that words can change in form, sometimes dramatically, depending on their relation to other words.

Our point is not to scare you off from other languages because of their grammatical differences, nor to claim that everyone needs to be an expert in grammar. Rather, we simply wish to note that the more you understand grammar, the basic building blocks and tools of language, the easier it will be for you to focus on the new language itself. Accordingly, we suggest that before you begin learning a language, you brush up on your English grammar. Take some time to refresh your memory on the parts of speech and how language functions. There are many helpful resources that can assist you with this (including the glossary at the back of this book).

Put in the necessary time

You may find that learning a language requires a different set of habits and a different kind of self-control than other subjects. For instance, it is difficult, if not impossible, to "cram" when learning a language, both for class and for exams. Languages are learned best over time, as new aspects are incorporated into what has previously been learned. Consequently, you must put in the necessary time when learning a language. This requires diligence on your part, and may demand more of a routine from you than other subjects you are studying. Put aside time on a daily basis for studying the language in question. You don't have to devote hours every single day, seven days a week; perhaps 45 minutes to an hour, four to five days a week, will be sufficient. However, it is vital that you continually review what you have learned previously, while staying on top of new information you need to assimilate.

Find your own system

A lot has changed in the teaching and learning of languages over the past few decades. Instructors are more aware than ever that students need to engage with a language in a variety of ways if they are truly to learn the subject. As such, your language instruction may now include a wide variety of learning experiences, incorporating multimedia and emerging technologies. That said, languages still have large vocabularies, many rules, and often many exceptions to these rules, all of which simply need to be learned and memorized. And while your instructors will do their best to help you with these aspects of the language, the responsibility still lies with you to master all of them.

As with many other tasks that we have covered in this book—such as taking notes or writing essays—it is likely that over time you will develop your own unique system for how you study and learn languages. We suggest that you find a method that works for you and remain consistent. You may engage with a variety of learning methods:

- **Vocabulary flash cards** have been a staple of language learning for a long time and continue to be useful today.
- **Computer programs** have become useful tools for language learning, offering a helpful combination of grammar and vocabulary tools. They often include flash card programs and quizzes.
- **Studying with others** can be a helpful exercise, as it forces you to verbalize your learning to others while getting feedback on areas in which you might need help. Studying with others can also help you to practise pronunciation, which can be particularly important if speaking is part of your learning program.

Whatever shape your personal study and learning takes, do it often, and do it consistently.

Stay up to speed

This leads to our final suggestion: do all you can to keep up with the tempo of your course. Falling behind in language classes can be devastating, as it is difficult to catch up on a language if you have missed a step, even if that step seems inconsequential. Make sure that you do all the required assignments, and don't be afraid to ask for help from your instructor if you feel like you're falling behind. If you do happen to miss a session or an assignment, do not skip over what you missed and assume you can pick up with everyone else at the next topic. Do your best to catch up on the missed material so that you are ready for the next stage of your learning. Failure to keep up to speed with a class is often the main reason students drop out of language courses. Committing ahead of time to stay on task may be the single best thing you can do to ensure success in learning a language.

CONCLUSION

Learning a language can be exhilarating and exasperating, often in close succession. Although this task will without doubt be demanding and at times frustrating, we believe that the payoff is well worth the work. The first time you open a foreign or ancient text and are able to read even a few sentences for yourself, you will understand why you have invested the time and energy you have. A whole world can open up to you. No longer will you be one of the many who are forced to read something in which the meaning is "lost in translation."

CHAPTER 14

Receiving Feedback and Reflecting on Your Studies

Objectives

- Maximizing feedback for personal improvement
- Approaching instructors and professors
- Understanding the process of personal reflection

Whether we're awkwardly accepting a compliment or feeling devastated after critical assessment, many of us find the process of receiving feedback to be an uncomfortable one. And yet, receiving feedback and using it constructively is an integral part of how we develop in all aspects of life, our studies included. Indeed, throughout this book we have encouraged you to become an engaged learner, making the most of your learning opportunities and taking an active role in your education. This engaged approach has obvious implications for receiving criticism, as engaged learners will want to receive and absorb feedback in order to help them continue to grow and learn. This chapter will explore some of the issues involved in responding to feedback, as well as the importance of self-reflection in higher education.

USING FEEDBACK FOR IMPROVEMENT AND INTELLECTUAL DEVELOPMENT

Without a doubt, you will receive a lot of feedback throughout your post-secondary education. The most common form is in written notes from your instructor or grader, whether in your essay and assignment margins or on your exams. Here are some issues to keep in mind when you receive this type of feedback.

Because you are now studying at the university level, your instructors may feel it is appropriate to give you more *critical* feedback than you have received in the past. To be frank, the response you are given may seem quite harsh at times. While this type of feedback may initially be distressing, you should strive to keep some perspective. To begin with, while your high school teachers saw you as, well, a high school student, your post-secondary instructors may assume that as an adult you are able to deal appropriately with critical appraisal. Furthermore, your instructors want you to engage with, enjoy, and learn the subjects they are teaching. The feedback they give is not criticism of you as a person, nor is it a personal attack. Rather, it is *constructive criticism*, aimed at helping you develop so that you don't keep repeating shortcomings in your work. With this in mind, you need to ask yourself how you can best take in the response you have been given and use it as a chance to grow and learn. Resist the urge to take it personally and instead focus on how you can improve.

Next, you need to realize that different instructors give different kinds and amounts of feedback. Some instructors will comment on both your strengths and weaknesses, while others will assume your strengths do not need to be pointed out and will only highlight the areas in which you need to improve. In addition, some instructors will give extensive feedback, while others will offer little interaction with your work. To put it plainly, you may end up with a better understanding in some subjects than in others about the grades that you receive and how you can improve on them.

If you are unsure about the reasoning for your grades, check your professor's grading rubric or the list of criteria for your essay, assignment, or exam; you could also consult your university's standard grading scale, which might explain your letter grade (see the sample grading guide on the facing page). But if these tools are not available and you are still unsure why you received the grade you did, or if some of the feedback you have received is unclear, you can seek further explanation from your instructor. That leads us to our next issue: approaching your instructors.

APPROACHING INSTRUCTORS

Approaching your instructors can be a daunting experience, particularly as you begin your college or university education. There are a few issues that, if kept in mind, will make these encounters less intimidating and more useful.

As we've noted earlier in this book, your instructors are an amazing resource that you can learn from, and one of their primary functions is to guide you in your education. What you may not realize is that your instructors have many

Grade	Grade Interpretation Guidelines
A+	**Outstanding, excellent work.** Exceptional performance with strong evidence of original thinking; clear capacity to analyze, synthesize, evaluate, and elaborate; eloquence and insight in written expression; a masterful grasp of the subject matter and its implications; evidence of an extensive and detailed knowledge base. (A+ is reserved for truly exceptional, outstanding accomplishment.)
A	
A-	
B+	**Good, competent work.** Laudable performance with evidence of some original thinking; careful organization; satisfactory critical and analytical capacity; reasonably error-free written expression, supported with arguments and well documented; a good grasp of the subject matter, both concepts and key issues; overall, shows a serious, responsible engagement with the course content.
B	
B-	
C+	**Reasonably satisfactory work.** Fair performance but limited evidence of original thinking; limited capacity to analyze, synthesize, or evaluate course material; undue reliance on rote memory; fairly clear but uninspiring written expression, with problems in mechanics or syntax; weak in documented support; satisfactory grasp of basics, but lacks detailed understanding of the course content.
C	
C-	
D+	**Minimally acceptable work.** Relatively weak performance with little evidence of original thinking or ability to analyze and synthesize course material; written expression frequently lacks a coherent argument; ideas are undeveloped; an inadequate grasp of (or confusion in) basic elements of the course.
D	
D-	
F	**Inadequate work.** Poor performance indicating a lack of understanding of essential subject matter; written expression is poorly organized, often incoherent, with mechanical and diction errors; shows little evidence of even basic competency in the course content.

Figure 14.1   Sample grading scale

Source: Adapted, with permission, from "What Does My Letter Grade Mean?" *Trinity Western University Academic Pages,* available online at http://twu.ca/academics/resources/faq/lettergrade.html. Note that these criteria are given for illustrative purposes only, as different institutions will have different grading guidelines.

other responsibilities, both inside and outside the institution. For instance, most of your instructors are expected to carry out their own research and to publish articles or books as part of their academic obligations. Moreover, instructors often have various administrative responsibilities for their department or institution, or for larger professional bodies such as the Canadian

Society for the Study of Religion or the American Academy of Religion. Instructors must carry out their research and administrative duties alongside their teaching—and instructors will often teach as many as eight separate courses per year. This is to say nothing about their personal lives outside of the academy, which may involve family, community, and civic duties. Why do we bring all of this up? It's simply to make you aware that your instructors may have a lot on their plates. You are encouraged to approach your instructors when you need help, but bear in mind that *appropriate expectations* are an important part of student–teacher interaction. In light of this, here are a few things to keep in mind when approaching your instructors.

- *Make an appointment or use office hours.* You may not always be well received if you show up unannounced or detain your instructor in the hallway. This is not to say that you cannot interact with your teachers outside the classroom. Just be aware that most instructors are not prepared to discuss the intricacies of one of your essays directly before or after a lecture, let alone in the cafeteria lunch line. If you're approaching your instructor without an appointment, it's always a good rule of thumb to ask if it is a good time to discuss your question or concern, rather than just launching into it. Also, if an instructor has particular office hours (usually a specific time slot each week, indicated on your syllabus, when the instructor will always be in his or her office) dedicated to meeting with students, you may drop in to discuss your concerns at those times. That's what they're there for. If you schedule an appointment, make sure you arrive on time.
- *Don't be offended if your instructor does not remember your name.* This is particularly the case at the beginning of the year, and in larger institutions, where your instructors may be dealing with hundreds of students, many of whom are new to them. One way to approach this issue is to politely offer your name as you greet your instructor, and perhaps mention the course name or number to which your question pertains. (If you want your professor to remember your name, show that you are critically and carefully engaged with the course material, either by asking insightful questions in class or by turning in exemplary work. Instructors are more likely to remember students who demonstrate effort or acquired understanding in their subjects.)
- *Be prepared.* Your instructors will appreciate it if you are prepared for meetings you have with them. You may want to have a list of

questions or topics ready for discussion, in case you go blank in the moment. Show your instructor that you have given some thought to the meeting and that you have a clear purpose for being there.

None of this should be seen as an excuse for an instructor treating a student poorly, and we would never want to justify such action. However, the main point we want to convey is that your instructors are human. There are times when they will be busy and frazzled, and they are allowed to have good and bad days like everyone else. If you are respectful, engaged, and prepared, your instructors should respond in kind.

THE PROCESS OF PERSONAL REFLECTION

While your instructors may give you individualized feedback on particular subjects and assignments, you are less likely to receive specific input on your overall personal development and progress. Even when instructors do give you feedback, they are not in a position to tell you why, for instance, you did not do adequate research for your essay. In many cases, this type of reflection rests on you and you alone.

Set aside time for this kind of personal reflection on your work; even half an hour may be sufficient depending on the subject or length of assignment. When to do this depends on you: ideal times may be after you have received feedback on individual assignments or at the end of a semester or year when you can reflect on your body of work as a whole. Here are some issues you may wish to consider:

- Are you happy with the grades you have received? Why or why not?
- Based on your grades and the feedback you have received, what are some of your strengths? How can you continue to develop, and build upon, these strengths?
- What might be some weaknesses that you need to improve on? How might you go about improving these areas?
- What factors contributed to your success or lack of success in particular areas? Are these factors that you can do something about?

Let's say, for example, that you just got back an essay for which you were awarded an average grade ("C"). Your instructor notes that your writing is clear and your essay is structurally sound. However, your essay suffered from insufficient research and a lack of quality sources, as well as poor footnoting and formatting. These issues resulted in a "C" rather than a "B" or even an "A". How might you personally reflect on this result?

First, even though you may be disappointed with the grade, you should still recognize the positives that were highlighted. Your instructor has pointed out that your writing is good, as is your essay structure. These are important elements of essay writing, and it is good to know that you can build on this foundation in later assignments.

What about the issues of research and formatting? It may be that you had various assignments all due around the same time, and you simply didn't allow yourself enough time to collect and read quality sources or to properly footnote and format your essay. In hindsight, these are fixable issues. Upon reflection, you may decide to allocate yourself an extra week for collecting and reading sources and an additional day for properly checking your notations and style for all future essays.

CONCLUSION

Setting up appropriate meeting times with your professors and working to better understand and learn from the grades you receive are important parts of the post-secondary learning process. Self-reflection, too, is a necessary—though not necessarily difficult—task. Spending a short amount of time reflecting on your strengths and weaknesses can help you address issues which need attention. Remember: no one is going to do this type of reflection for you—the responsibility lies with you and you alone. Engaged learning entails taking the time to reflect on your learning experiences so you can continue to build on your strengths.

CHAPTER 15

Documenting Your Sources

Objectives

- Being aware of different documentation styles and manuals
- Understanding Chicago style notes and bibliography
- Understanding MLA style citations and works cited
- Understanding APA style citations and bibliography

Documenting your sources is one of the most vital aspects of academic research and writing. The intricacies of citing your sources in notations and bibliographies may seem complex and strange as you begin writing essays. Academics take these things very seriously, however, and you should do your best to learn these conventions early in your degree.

STYLESHEETS AND MANUALS

Documentation styles can differ from institution to institution, department to department, and even instructor to instructor. Before you start your research, find out whether your university or department follows a particular style. If there is no required style, you may choose to follow one of the options set out below.

Academics in religious studies tend to use one of three systems to document their sources. The first, known as the Chicago style, makes use of footnotes or endnotes, usually in addition to a complete bibliography. The other two most common approaches are the MLA (Modern Language Association) style and the APA (American Psychological Association) style. These styles use author–date citations, which occur inside parentheses within the text of your essay, along with a full list of references at the end. Don't worry if this sounds confusing: in this chapter we will look at some of the more practical issues involved with documenting your sources in these styles. We will also offer examples from the Chicago, MLA, and APA styles so that you may learn how to document different types of sources.

A word of caution before we go on, however: most documentation styles are continually changing and adapting, particularly with the growth of electronic and online literature. This means you will need to keep up to date with all of the latest changes. For more on this see Janice Walker and Todd Taylor's *The Columbia Guide to Online Style* (2nd ed., New York: Columbia University Press, 2006). You may also want to investigate bibliographic software, such as EndNote, that helps you organize your sources and can aid you in the formatting of styles as well.

CHICAGO STYLE

For humanities disciplines, including religious studies, the Chicago style recommends the use of footnote and endnote notations, as well as bibliographies, for documenting sources. This style is outlined in *The Chicago Manual of Style* (16th ed., Chicago: University of Chicago Press, 2010), and more specifically for post-secondary students in Kate Turabian's *A Manual for Writers of Research Papers, Theses, and Dissertations* (6th ed., Chicago: University of Chicago Press, 1996). Be aware that various disciplines within religious studies may have their own particular styles. For instance, students in biblical studies may wish to consult *The SBL Handbook of Style; For Ancient Near Eastern, Biblical, and Early Christian Studies* (ed. Patrick H. Alexander, et al., Peabody: Hendrickson, 1999), which is built upon *The Chicago Manual of Style*.

You can also go online to the "Chicago-Style Citation Quick Guide" (www.chicagomanualofstyle.org/tools_citationguide.html), which gives examples of different Chicago style references. The Chicago style does also allow for in-text citations, and these are similar to the APA style, which is outlined below. Hence, if you do consult the online "Chicago-Style Citation Quick Guide", you will note that it gives information on both systems, under separate tabs:

Notes and Bibliography

Author Date

As a Humanities student, you will use the first of these two styles, and that is what we will discuss in this chapter.

Chicago style notations: footnotes and endnotes

In the Chicago style, sources cited within the essay are documented in either footnotes or endnotes. These notations provide a record of where you have gleaned your information. You may notice that some writers add extra content to footnotes or endnotes, usually to clarify something that might be too tangential to or not appropriate in the text itself. However, most instructors will tell you that if something is worth saying, it should be said in the text itself. This is particularly the case in undergraduate essays. Though it can be tempting to use footnotes as a place to expand or qualify your research, remember that their primary purpose is the acknowledgment of sources. Therefore, the majority of your notations should be for citations, not extra content.

Footnotes and endnotes are indicated by a small, superscripted number at the end of a sentence, as you will have seen throughout this book. Footnotes occur at the bottom of the page where the superscripted note appears, while endnotes occur all together at the end of the essay, prior to the bibliography. Word-processing programs have made working with footnotes quite easy, allowing you to insert and format notes with ease. Indeed, most word processors can easily convert between footnotes and endnotes if need be, and some newer versions can even format sources for you based on various styles.

In your footnotes and endnotes, you should provide enough information to identify the work being cited, including author, title, publishing details, date of publication, and the specific page numbers to which you are referring. Unlike bibliographic entries, footnotes and endnotes should read like sentences. As such, commas are usually used instead of periods, the author's names are given in their natural order, and the publishing details are placed in parentheses before the page numbers. Your instructors may allow you to use abbreviations in your notes (such as standardized acronyms for periodicals or book series) if you include a list of abbreviations at the beginning of your essay, or include the full details in the bibliography. In the Chicago style, the first line of a footnote is usually indented (though some writers choose to keep their notes aligned to the left margin). Unless instructed otherwise, footnotes should remain single-spaced, and the font size is typically 10 point.

Let's look at some specific examples of how to cite sources in Chicago style footnotes.

BOOK WITH ONE AUTHOR

1. Jonathan Z. Smith, *Relating Religion: Essays in the Study of Religion* (Chicago: University of Chicago Press, 2004), 1–5.

Avoid unnecessary repetition in second and subsequent citations for a source, but remember to be clear and accurate. The traditional Latin abbreviations—*ibid.*, *op. cit.*—are still used in some institutions. However, many feel that these tend to create more confusion than clarity in the reading process. You may or may not be familiar with them at all. In the Chicago style, second and subsequent citations include only the author's last name, a shortened version of the book's title, and the relevant page numbers. Hence a subsequent citation to the above book would be abbreviated to look like this:

2. Smith, *Relating Religion*, 6–10.

A book with one author is the simplest type of source to footnote. When the resources you are working with contain more documentable elements, the notations become more complex. For example, notations for books with more than one author, books in a series, edited books, journal articles, and chapters within a book will all vary from the example above. Below are a few such examples, though be aware that this list is not exhaustive. Consult the *Chicago Manual* or Turabian's manual for further guidance, and make sure you are aware of any specifications your own institution or department might require.

BOOK WITH TWO AUTHORS, IN A SUBSEQUENT EDITION

3. Lawrence S. Cunningham and John Kelsay, *The Sacred Quest: An Invitation to the Study of Religion*, 5th ed. (Upper Saddle River, NJ: Prentice Hall, 2010), 121–23.

Subsequent citations

4. Cunningham and Kelsay, *Sacred Quest*, 124–27.

BOOK IN TRANSLATION

5. Maria Rosa Antognazza, *Leibniz on the Trinity and the Incarnation: Reason and Revelation in the Seventeenth Century*, trans. Gerald Parks (New Haven, CT: Yale University Press, 2007), 32–35.

Subsequent citations

6. Antognazza, *Leibniz on the Trinity*, 36–40.

BOOK IN SERIES
The series is placed after the title, but is not italicized.

7. Serif Mardin, *Religion, Society, and Modernity in Turkey*, Modern Intellectual and Political History of the Middle East (Syracuse: Syracuse University Press, 2006), 1–12.

Subsequent citations

8. Mardin, *Religion, Society, and Modernity*, 13–15.

BOOK WITH AN EDITOR

9. Steven M. Cahn, ed., *The Essential Texts in the Philosophy of Religion: Classics and Contemporary Issues* (Oxford: Oxford University Press, 2005), 12.

Subsequent citations

10. Cahn, *Essential Texts*, 13.

ARTICLE IN BOOK

11. Courtney S. Campbell, "Boundary Crossings: The Ethical Terrain of Professional Life in Hospice Care," in *Caring Well: Religion, Narrative, and Care Ethics*, ed. David H. Smith (Louisville, KY: Westminster John Knox Press, 2000), 201–20.

Subsequent citations

12. Campbell, "Boundary Crossings," 201–203.

JOURNAL ARTICLE

While Chicago recommends giving a journal's title in full, some institutions may recommend that you abbreviate such titles. Thus, in the following instance, you would use the abbreviation *JAAR* in place of the journal's title:

13. Mark C. Taylor, "Refiguring Religion," *Journal of the American Academy of Religion* 77, no. 1 (2009): 105–19.

Subsequent citations

14. Taylor, "Refiguring Religion," 105–106.

DICTIONARY OR ENCYCLOPEDIA ENTRY

It is generally acknowledged that well-known reference works, such as the *Encyclopaedia Britannica*, do not need to be listed in the bibliography of your paper; the footnote citations need only to give the work's full title, set in italics; the edition number, if not the first; and the article's title, set in quotation marks. However, if you are dealing with a specialized reference work, as often happens in religious studies, you should give the full details.

15. G.J. Riley, "Demon," in *Dictionary of Deities and Demons in the Bible*, ed. Karel van der Toorn, Bob Becking, and Pieter W. van der Horst, 2nd ed. (Leiden: Brill, 1999), 235–40.

Subsequent citations

16. Riley, "Demon," 235.

ELECTRONIC SOURCES
Article in an online journal or database

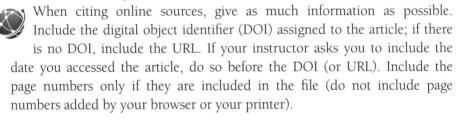

When citing online sources, give as much information as possible. Include the digital object identifier (DOI) assigned to the article; if there is no DOI, include the URL. If your instructor asks you to include the date you accessed the article, do so before the DOI (or URL). Include the page numbers only if they are included in the file (do not include page numbers added by your browser or your printer).

17. Robert A. Segal, "Mysticism and Psychoanalysis," *Religious Studies Review* 37, no. 1 (2011): 1-18, doi: 10.1111/j.1748-0922.2011.01477.x.
18. Rebecca Margolis, "Culture in Motion: Yiddish in Canadian Jewish Life," *Journal of Religion and Popular Culture* 21 (2009), accessed March 1, 2011, http://www.usask.ca/relst/jrpc/art(se)-Yiddish.html.

Subsequent citations

19. Margolis, "Culture in Motion."

Website

20. "Internet Guide to Religion," Wabash Center for Teaching and Learning in Theology and Religion, accessed March 1, 2011, http://www.wabashcenter .wabash.edu/resources/guide_headings.aspx.

Subsequent citations

21. "Internet Guide to Religion."

Chicago style bibliographies

Bibliographies should provide information similar to that found in the notations. However, while footnotes and endnotes provide a quick reference for the reader, including specific page numbers, a bibliography is an alphabetized list of all the sources you have cited in your research. Thus, bibliographies are formatted differently to reflect this specific purpose.

To begin with, bibliographies are alphabetized according to the authors' last names. Second, the various sections of a bibliographic entry tend to be separated by periods, not commas. Finally, specific page numbers are not required in a bibliography; the exception to this rule is when referencing chapters in books, journal articles, and reference-work articles. In these cases, all of the page numbers of the referenced work are needed in the bibliography.

Bibliographies are usually typed in a 12-point font, are single spaced, and have an extra line space between entries. They also employ a unique formatting structure called a *hanging indent,* where the first line of each entry is at the left margin, but the second and subsequent lines are all indented by five spaces.

Here are some examples, using the same sources as above.

BOOK WITH ONE AUTHOR

Smith, Jonathan Z. *Relating Religion: Essays in the Study of Religion*. Chicago: University of Chicago Press, 2004.

AUTHOR WITH MORE THAN ONE WORK IN LIST

If an author occurs more than once in your bibliography, Chicago style recommends that you list the author's full name the first time and replace the name with three full dashes in the second and subsequent entries. (Note that some instructors recommend an alternative option in which you list the author's full name in each entry.)

Smith, Jonathan Z. *Imagining Religion: From Babylon to Jonestown*. Chicago Studies in the History of Judaism. Chicago: University of Chicago Press, 1982.
———. *Relating Religion: Essays in the Study of Religion*. Chicago: University of Chicago Press, 2004.

BOOK WITH TWO AUTHORS, IN A SUBSEQUENT EDITION

In this case only the first author's names are inverted. Second and subsequent authors are presented in their natural order.

Cunningham, Lawrence S., and John Kelsay. *The Sacred Quest: An Invitation to the Study of Religion*. 5th ed. Upper Saddle River, NJ: Prentice Hall, 2010.

In the above example, note than the city "Upper Saddle River" is lesser known and so the state name (abbreviated) is also included. If in doubt, include the state or province (or country).

BOOK IN TRANSLATION

Antognazza, Maria Rosa. *Leibniz on the Trinity and the Incarnation: Reason and Revelation in the Seventeenth Century*. Translated by Gerald Parks. New Haven, CT: Yale University Press, 2007.

BOOK IN SERIES

Mardin, Serif. *Religion, Society, and Modernity in Turkey*. Modern Intellectual and Political History of the Middle East. Syracuse, NY: Syracuse University Press, 2006.

BOOK WITH AN EDITOR

Cahn, Steven M., ed. *The Essential Texts in the Philosophy of Religion: Classics and Contemporary Issues*. Oxford: Oxford University Press, 2005.

ARTICLE IN BOOK

Campbell, Courtney S. "Boundary Crossings: The Ethical Terrain of Professional Life in Hospice Care." In *Caring Well: Religion, Narrative, and Care Ethics*, edited by David H. Smith, 201–20. Louisville, KY: Westminster John Knox Press, 2000.

JOURNAL ARTICLE

Keep in mind that even if you have used abbreviations for periodicals in your notations you need to supply the full name in the bibliographic entry.

Taylor, Mark C. "Refiguring Religion." *Journal of the American Academy of Religion* 77, no. 1 (2009): 105–19.

DICTIONARY OR ENCYCLOPEDIA ENTRY

Riley, G.J. "Demon." In *Dictionary of Deities and Demons in the Bible*, 2nd ed., edited by Karel van der Toorn, Bob Becking, and Pieter W. van der Horst, 235–40. Leiden: Brill, 1999.

ELECTRONIC SOURCES
Article in an online journal or database

> Margolis, Rebecca. "Culture in Motion: Yiddish in Canadian Jewish Life."
> *Journal of Religion and Popular Culture* 21 (2009). Accessed March 1,
> 2011. http://www.usask.ca/relst/jrpc/art(se)-Yiddish.html.
> Segal, Robert A. "Mysticism and Psychoanalysis." Religious Studies Review 37,
> no. 1 (2011): 1–18. doi: 10.1111/j.1748-0922.2011.01477.x.

Website

> "Internet Guide to Religion." Wabash Center for Teaching and Learning in
> Theology and Religion. Accessed March 1, 2011. http://www
> .wabashcenter.wabash.edu/resources/guide_headings.aspx.

MLA STYLE

The MLA style uses in-text citations, which give the author's last name and
the page number in parentheses after the information cited. Complete bibliographical information is then given in an alphabetical list, titled "Works Cited,"
on a separate page at the end of the essay or report. Further information on this
style can be found in the *MLA Handbook for Writers of Research Papers* (7th ed.,
New York: Modern Language Association, 2009). Some guidelines, including
tips for documenting electronic sources, are also available on the FAQ page of
the MLA website: www.mla.org/handbook_faq.

MLA in-text citations

The following examples illustrate some of the most common types of references
as they would appear in citations, using the same sources shown above in the
Chicago style.

BOOK OR ARTICLE WITH ONE AUTHOR

Put in parentheses (round brackets) only the information needed to identify a
source clearly—usually the author's (or editor's) last name and the page number
of the text referred to:

> His early interest in these issues "led directly to a concern with comparison"
> (Smith 19).

Place the parenthetical reference where a pause would naturally occur,
preferably at the end of the sentence or clause it documents. Note that there is

no punctuation between the author's name and the page number, and that the citation falls before the final period.

If the author's name is already given in the text, put in parentheses only the place of the reference:

> In his work, Smith has refused to separate comparison and classification (20).

If you are citing an entire work, try to include the author's (or editor's) name in the text rather than in parentheses:

> In *Relating Religion*, Jonathan Z. Smith begins with an account of his own journey into religious studies, followed by various essays that show the development of his thought.

BOOK OR ARTICLE WITH MORE THAN ONE AUTHOR

If the work has two or three authors, include all of the names in the citation:

> As already noted, several definitions of religion have been laid out (Cunningham and Kelsay 12–13).

If the work has four or more authors, either use only the first author's last name and "et al." or give all the last names.

TWO OR MORE WORKS BY THE SAME AUTHOR

If you need to refer to more than one work written by the same author, use a shortened version of the appropriate title with each citation:

> The "manipulation of difference" is a recurring theme in his discussion of taxonomy and comparison (Smith, *Relating* 25).

If the author's name appears in the text, include only the title and page number(s) in parentheses. If the author's name and the title appear in the text, indicate only the page number(s) in parentheses:

> In *Relating Religion*, Smith discusses his early years in teaching religious studies (9–12).

ELECTRONIC SOURCES

In-text citations for electronic sources use the same formatting principles outlined above for print sources. However, since many electronic sources do not have page numbers, you may have to cite a paragraph or section number instead. If the citation begins with the author's name, insert a comma after the name:

("Internet Guide," sec. 2)

(Margolis, pars. 12–15)

If your source has no page, section, or paragraph numbers, include only the name of the author or a shortened version of the work's title (if there is no listed author) in your parenthetical references. Do not use page numbers of a printout of the source, as the pagination may vary in different printouts.

MLA Works Cited list

Your list of works cited should contain only those works you have actually referred to in the text; do not include works that you consulted but did not cite directly in your essay. The following are some formatting guidelines, followed by examples of common entries in a Works Cited list. If the kind of source you are using is not shown in any of the examples here, consult the *MLA Handbook* or the MLA website.

- Begin your Works Cited section on a separate page but continue the page numbering from the last page of your essay.
- Double-space the entire list, both between and within entries and between the title and the first entry.
- Do not number entries, but list them alphabetically by the author's or editor's surname. If no author is given, begin with the first significant word in the title.
- Format with hanging indents: begin each bibliographic entry at the margin and indent any subsequent line five spaces.
- Separate the main divisions with periods.
- Note the medium of the publication you consulted (generally "Print" or "Web").

BOOK WITH ONE AUTHOR

Smith, Jonathan Z. *Relating Religion: Essays in the Study of Religion*. Chicago: University of Chicago Press, 2004. Print.

BOOK WITH MORE THAN ONE AUTHOR

If a book you have cited was written by two or three authors, list all of the authors in the order in which they appear on the title page, separated with commas, with only the first author's name inverted:

Cunningham, Lawrence S., and John Kelsay. *The Sacred Quest: An Invitation to the Study of Religion.* 5th ed. Upper Saddle River, NJ: Prentice Hall, 2010. Print.

If the book has four or more authors, you may either list all the names in full in the order in which they appear on the title page or give only the first author's name, inverted, followed by a comma and "et al."

Alexander, Patrick H., et al. *The SBL Handbook of Style: For Ancient Near Eastern, Biblical, and Early Christian Studies.* Peabody: Hendrickson, 1999. Print.

TWO OR MORE BOOKS BY THE SAME AUTHOR

Entries for two or more books by the same author are arranged alphabetically by the first significant word in the title. List the author's name in the first entry only; in subsequent entries, use three hyphens followed by a period:

Smith, Jonathan Z. *Imagining Religion: From Babylon to Jonestown.* Chicago: University of Chicago Press, 1982. Print. Chicago Studies in the History of Judaism.

- - -. *Relating Religion: Essays in the Study of Religion.* Chicago: University of Chicago Press, 2004. Print.

BOOK WITH AN EDITOR

Cahn, Steven M., ed. *The Essential Texts in the Philosophy of Religion: Classics and Contemporary Issues.* Oxford: Oxford University Press, 2005. Print.

If the book has more than one editor, follow the guidelines given above for a book with more than one author, listing the editors' names followed by "eds."

BOOK WITH A TRANSLATOR

Antognazza, Maria Rosa. *Leibniz on the Trinity and the Incarnation: Reason and Revelation in the Seventeenth Century.* Trans. Gerald Parks. New Haven, CT: Yale University Press, 2007. Print.

CHAPTER IN AN EDITED BOOK

Campbell, Courtney S. "Boundary Crossings: The Ethical Terrain of Professional Life in Hospice Care." *Caring Well: Religion, Narrative, and Care Ethics.* Ed. David H. Smith. Louisville, KY: Westminster John Knox Press, 2000. 201–20. Print.

Note that you are required to give inclusive page numbers for the entire piece, not just for the material you have used.

ARTICLE IN A JOURNAL

When listing a journal article, give the author, the title of the article, the journal title, the volume number, the issue number, the year of publication, and the inclusive page numbers. Omit introductory articles in the journal title:

> Taylor, Mark C. "Refiguring Religion." *Journal of the American Academy of Religion* 77.1 (2009): 105–19. Print.

ELECTRONIC SOURCES

Article in an online journal or database

When referencing an article retrieved from an online journal, list the author's name, the title of the article, the name of the journal, the volume number, and the issue number, as you would for a print journal. If the article does not have page numbers, insert "n. pag." in place of the inclusive page range. Give the medium and the date you retrieved the article; you may also include the URL in angle brackets. If you have to break the URL at the end of a line, do so after a slash. If you access the article through an online database, use a similar format, but include the relevant page numbers and the name of the database.

> Margolis, Rebecca. "Culture in Motion: Yiddish in Canadian Jewish Life." *Journal of Religion and Popular Culture* 21 (2009): n. pag. Web. 1 Mar. 2011. <http://www.usask.ca/relst/jrpc/art(se)-Yiddish.html>.
> Segal, Robert A. "Mysticism and Psychoanalysis." *Religious Studies Review* 37.1 (2011): 1–18. Project *MUSE*. Web. 1 May 2011.

Website

References to original content from online sources should contain as much of the following information as possible: the name of the author, editor, or compiler; the title of the article or web page; the publisher of the site; the date the material was posted (or "n.d.", if the date is unavailable); the medium; and the date you accessed the site. You can also include the URL at the end of the entry.

> "Internet Guide to Religion." Wabash Center for Teaching and Learning in Theology and Religion, n.d. Web. 1 Mar. 2011. <http://www.wabashcenter.wabash.edu/resources/guide_headings.aspx>.

APA STYLE

The American Psychological Association system of documentation is the one most commonly used in the social sciences. Like the MLA style, the APA style uses parenthetical citations within the text that refer to a more complete list of references at the end. One key difference is that the APA system includes the publication date in the in-text citations, and this date is placed more prominently in the bibliographic entries. For more detailed information, consult the *Publication Manual of the American Psychological Association* (6th ed., 2010) or visit the APA website (http://apastyle.apa.org/).

APA in-text citations

BOOK OR ARTICLE WITH ONE AUTHOR

If the author's name is given in the text, cite only the year of publication in parentheses. Otherwise, give both the name and the year:

> In this volume, Smith (2004) outlines his own journey into religious studies as well as the development of his thought. This volume also picks up on themes common in his earlier work (1982).

BOOK OR ARTICLE WITH MORE THAN ONE AUTHOR

If the work you are citing has two authors, include both names every time you cite the reference in the text. The APA uses an ampersand (&) when the names are in parentheses but the word *and* in the text:

> The complexity of coming up with a definition of "religion" has been dealt with extensively (Cunningham & Kelsay, 2010).

If there are three, four, or five authors, cite all the names when the reference first occurs, and afterwards cite only the first author, followed by "et al." If the work you are citing has six or more authors, cite only the surname of the first author followed by "et al."

SPECIFIC PARTS OF A SOURCE

If you are referring to a particular part of a source, you must indicate the page, chapter, figure, table, or equation. Always give page numbers for quotations:

> (Smith, 2004, p. 23)

> (Cunningham & Kelsay, 2010, pp. 12–13)

> (Antognazza, 2007, Chapter 2)

Note that the APA prefaces page numbers with "p." for a single page and "pp." for several pages; it does not abbreviate "Chapter.".

ELECTRONIC SOURCES

In-text citations for electronic sources use the same formatting principles outlined above for print sources, with the following exceptions. If your source has no page numbers, use the paragraph number preceded by the abbreviation "para." When citing an entire website, give the URL in the text:

(Margolis, 2009, para. 10)

According to the Wabash Center (http://www.wabashcenter.wabash.edu) . . .

APA References list

Entries in an APA References section are similar to those in an MLA Works Cited list with the following exceptions:

- Entries begin with the author's surname, followed by his or her initials; full given names are not used.
- For works with multiple authors, all names are reversed; the name of the last author is preceded by an ampersand (&) rather than *and*.
- The date of publication appears immediately after the authors' names.
- Entries for different works by the same author are listed chronologically. Two or more works by the same author with the same publication date are arranged alphabetically by title.
- For titles of books and articles, capitalize only proper nouns and the first word of the title and of the subtitle if there is one.
- Titles of articles or selections in books are not enclosed in quotation marks.
- For works published in Canada or the US, always include the city as well as the province, territory, or state in which the book was published. For works published outside of Canada or the US, include the city followed by the name of the country.

BOOK WITH ONE AUTHOR

Smith, J.Z. (2004). *Relating religion: Essays in the study of religion.* Chicago, IL: University of Chicago Press.

BOOK WITH MORE THAN ONE AUTHOR

Cunningham, L.S., & Kelsay, J. (2010). *The sacred quest: An invitation to the study of religion* (5th ed.). Upper Saddle River, NJ: Prentice Hall.

BOOK WITH AN EDITOR

Cahn, S.M. (Ed.). (2005). *The essential texts in the philosophy of religion: Classics and contemporary issues*. Oxford, UK: Oxford University Press.

CHAPTER OR SELECTION IN AN EDITED BOOK

Campbell, C.S. (2000). Boundary crossings: The ethical terrain of professional life in hospice care. In D.H. Smith (Ed.), *Caring well: Religion, narrative, and care ethics* (pp. 201–220). Louisville, KY: Westminster John Knox Press.

Note that the page numbers of the selection are given, preceded by "pp."

ARTICLE IN A JOURNAL

Taylor, M.C. (2009). Refiguring religion. *Journal of the American Academy of Religion, 77*, 105–119.

Note that the page numbers are given but are not preceded by "pp." When a journal has continuous pagination, the issue number should not be included. If each issue begins on page 1, give the volume number, followed immediately (with no space) by the issue number in parentheses, then a comma, then the page numbers. The volume number is italicized; the issue number and its brackets are not:

Margolis, R. (2009). Jewish immigrant encounters with Canada's Native peoples: Yiddish writings on Tekahionwake. *Journal of Canadian Studies/Revue d'études canadiennes 43*(3), 169–193.

ELECTRONIC SOURCES

Article in an online journal or database

 Include the same elements as you would for a printed journal article. In addition, include a DOI whenever one has been assigned to the article; if no DOI is available, include the URL. Do not include a retrieval date or the name of the database:

> Margolis, R. (2009). Culture in motion: Yiddish in Canadian Jewish life. Journal of Religion and Popular Culture 21. Retrieved from http://www.usask.ca /relst/jrpc/art(se)-Yiddish.html
> Segal, R.A. (2011). Mysticism and psychoanalysis. Religious Studies Review 37(1): 1–18. doi 10.1111/j.1748-0922.2011.01477.x

If you need to break the URL or DOI at the end of a line, do so before an existing punctuation mark. Do not insert a hyphen at the end of a line, and do not add a period at the end of the entry.

CONCLUSION

Appropriately documenting sources can take time. It can also seem tedious. However, if you learn from the start how to reference your sources correctly, the task will become second nature and soon you will be doing it with little time or effort. Furthermore, your instructors are aware of the difficulties here (they were once students too, and they continue to use these conventions in their research) and they know that proper documentation is a necessary part of scholarship. Your thoroughness and precision in this area will signal to your teacher that you are committed to academic excellence, and your careful practice will most assuredly contribute to a higher mark in your assignments.

CHAPTER 16

Common Errors in Grammar and Usage

Objectives

- Understanding sentence unity
- Recognizing subject–verb agreement
- Being aware of verb tenses
- Employing pronouns correctly
- Using modifiers
- Using pairs and parallels

This chapter is not a comprehensive grammar lesson; it's simply a survey of those areas where students most often make mistakes. It will help you pinpoint weaknesses as you edit your work. Once you get into the habit of checking your work, it won't be long before you are correcting potential problems as you write.

The grammatical terms used here are the most basic and familiar ones; if you need to review some of them, see the Glossary. If you're interested in a more exhaustive treatment, consult one of the many books that deal exclusively with grammar and usage.

SENTENCE UNITY

Sentence fragments

To be complete, a sentence must have both a subject and a verb in an independent clause; if it doesn't, it's a fragment. There are times in informal writing when it is acceptable to use a sentence fragment in order to give emphasis to a point:

✓ Will the government reinstate the death penalty to appease religious fundamentalists? <u>Not likely</u>.

Here the sentence fragment *Not likely* is clearly intended to be understood as a short form of *It is not likely that it will do so*. Unintentional sentence fragments, on the other hand, usually seem incomplete rather than shortened:

✗ I enjoy studying religious pluralism. <u>Being a student who is interested in diversity</u>.

The last "sentence" is incomplete because it lacks an independent clause with a subject and a verb. (Remember that a participle such as *being* is a verbal, or "part-verb," not a verb.) The fragment can be made into a complete sentence by adding a subject and a verb:

✓ <u>I am</u> a student who is interested in diversity.

Alternatively, you could join the fragment to the preceding sentence:

✓ Being a student who is interested in diversity, I enjoy studying religious pluralism.

✓ I enjoy studying religious pluralism, since I am a student who is interested in diversity.

Run-on sentences

A run-on sentence is one that continues beyond the point where it should have stopped:

✗ Some religious groups practice polygamy, but it is not legal in most countries, and in Canada some groups are testing polygamy laws, but they face an uphill battle.

This run-on sentence could be fixed by removing the word *and* and adding a period or semicolon after *countries*.

Another kind of run-on sentence is one in which two independent clauses are wrongly joined by a comma. An independent clause is a phrase that can stand by itself as a complete sentence. Two independent clauses should not be joined by a comma without a coordinating conjunction:

✗ Siddhartha Gautama is considered to be the Supreme Buddha, he was the spiritual teacher from India who founded Buddhism.

This error is known as a *comma splice*. There are three ways of correcting it:

1. by putting a period after *Buddha* and starting a new sentence:

   ✓   . . . the Supreme Buddha. He . . .

2. by replacing the comma with a semicolon:

   ✓   . . . the Supreme Buddha; he . . .

3. by making one of the independent clauses subordinate to the other, so that it doesn't stand by itself:

   ✓   Siddhartha Gautama, who is considered to be the Supreme Buddha, was the spiritual teacher from India who founded Buddhism.

The one exception to the rule that independent clauses cannot be joined by a comma arises when the clauses are very short and arranged in a tight sequence:

✓   I opened the document, I saw the error, and I changed it immediately.

You should not use this kind of sentence very often.

Contrary to what many people think, words such as *however, therefore*, and *thus* cannot be used to join independent clauses:

✗   Two of my friends started out in philosophy, however they quickly realized they didn't like learning symbolic logic.

This mistake can be corrected by beginning a new sentence after *Philosophy* or (preferably) by replacing the comma with a semicolon:

✓   Two of my friends started out in philosophy; however, they quickly realized they didn't like learning symbolic logic.

Another option is to join the two independent clauses with a coordinating conjunction—*and, or, nor, but, for, yet, so*, or *whereas*:

✓   Two of my friends started out in philosophy, but they quickly realized they didn't like learning symbolic logic.

Faulty predication
When the subject of a sentence is not grammatically connected to what follows (the predicate), the result is *faulty predication*:

✗   The <u>reason</u> he failed <u>was because</u> he couldn't handle multiple-choice exams.

The problem with this sentence is that *the reason* and *was because* mean essentially the same thing. The subject is a noun and the verb *was* needs a noun clause to complete it:

✓   The <u>reason</u> he failed <u>was that</u> he couldn't handle multiple-choice exams.

Another solution is to rephrase the sentence:

✓   He failed because he couldn't handle multiple-choice exams.

Faulty predication also occurs with *is when* and *is where* constructions:

✗   The climax of the documentary <u>is when</u> the researcher finally deciphers the hieroglyphs.

Again, you can correct this error in one of two ways:

1. Follow the *is* with a noun phrase to complete the sentence:

    ✓   The climax of the documentary <u>is the decipherment</u> of the hieroglyphs by the researcher.

2. Change the verb:

    ✓   The climax of the documentary <u>occurs</u> when the researcher finally deciphers the hieroglyphs.

SUBJECT–VERB AGREEMENT

Identifying the subject

A verb should always agree in number with its subject. Sometimes, however, when the subject does not come at the beginning of the sentence or when it is separated from the verb by other information, you may be tempted to use a verb form that does not agree:

✗   The <u>interpretation</u> of the church fathers <u>were flawed</u> from the beginning.

The subject here is *interpretation*, not *church fathers*; therefore, the verb should be singular:

✓   The <u>interpretation</u> of the church fathers <u>was flawed</u> from the beginning.

Either, neither, each

The indefinite pronouns *either*, *neither*, and *each* always take singular verbs:

✓   Neither of the movements <u>has</u> a singular leader.

✓   Each of them <u>has</u> a council.

Compound subjects

When *or*, *either . . . or*, or *neither . . . nor* is used to create a compound subject, the verb should usually agree with the last item in the subject:

✓   Neither the professor nor <u>her students were</u> able to make sense of the inscription.

✓   Either the students or <u>the TA was</u> misinformed.

You may find, however, that it sounds awkward in some cases to use a singular verb when a singular item follows a plural item:

orig.   Either my history books or my Eastern religions <u>text is</u> going to gather dust this weekend.

In such instances, it's better to rephrase the sentence:

rev.   This weekend, I'm going to ignore either my history books or my Eastern religions text.

Unlike the word *and*, which creates a compound subject and therefore takes a plural verb, the phrases *as well as* and *in addition to* do not create compound subjects; therefore the verb remains singular:

✓   Judaism <u>and</u> Islam <u>are</u> technically Western religions.

✓   Judaism, <u>as well as</u> Islam, <u>is</u> technically a Western religion.

Collective nouns

A collective noun is a singular noun that comprises a number of members, such as *family*, *army*, *team*, or sometimes *people*. If the noun refers to the members as one unit, it takes a singular verb:

✓   The first <u>class is</u> preparing for its religion and ethics debate.

If, in the context of the sentence, the noun refers to the members as individuals, the verb becomes plural:

✓   The <u>class are</u> receiving their scorecards after the debate.

✓   The <u>majority</u> of immigrants to Canada <u>are</u> religious.

Titles

The title of a book or a movie or the name of a business or organization is always treated as a singular noun, even if it contains plural words; therefore, it takes a singular verb:

✓   *The Ways of Religion* <u>was</u> in the university bookstore.

✓   Smyth & Helwys <u>is</u> publishing the commentary series.

VERB TENSES

Native speakers of English usually know without thinking which verb tense to use in a given context. However, a few tenses can still be confusing.

The past perfect

If the main verb is in the past tense and you want to refer to something that happened before that time, use the *past perfect* (*had* followed by the past participle). The time sequence will not be clear if you use the simple past in both clauses:

✗   He <u>hoped</u> that she <u>read</u> the article.

✓   He <u>hoped</u> that she <u>had read</u> the article.

Similarly, when you are reporting what someone said in the past—that is, when you are using *past indirect discourse*—you should use the past perfect tense in the clause describing what was said:

✗   He <u>told</u> the TA that he <u>wrote</u> the essay that week.

✓   He <u>told</u> the TA that he <u>had written</u> the essay that week.

Using "if"

When you are describing a possibility in the future, use the present tense in the condition (*if*) clause and the future tense in the consequence clause:

✓   If he <u>tests</u> us on Sikh religious festivals, I <u>will fail</u>.

When the possibility is unlikely, it is conventional—especially in formal writing—to use the *subjunctive* in the *if* clause, and *would* followed by the base verb in the consequence clause:

✓   If he <u>were</u> to cancel the test, I <u>would cheer</u>.

When you are describing a hypothetical instance in the past, use the *past subjunctive* (it has the same form as the past perfect) in the *if* clause and *would have* followed by the past participle for the consequence. A common error is to use *would have* in both clauses:

✗   If he would have been clearer, I would have mastered the material much sooner.

✓   If he had been clearer, I would have mastered the material much sooner.

Writing about literature

When you are describing a literary work in its historical context, use the past tense:

✓   Sarvepalli Radhakrishnan wrote *The Reign of Religion in Contemporary Philosophy* at a time when Max Müller's *Introduction to the Science of Religion* was persuading scholars to adopt a comparative approach.

To discuss what goes on within a work of literature, however, you should use the present tense:

✓   The author retells the story and tries to emphasize the wisdom of the guru.

PRONOUNS

Pronoun reference

The link between a pronoun and the noun it refers to must be clear. If the noun doesn't appear in the same sentence as the pronoun, it should appear in the preceding sentence:

✗   The textbook supply in the bookstore had run out, so we borrowed them from the library.

Since *textbook* is used as an adjective rather than a noun, it cannot serve as referent or antecedent for the pronoun *them*. You must either replace *them* or change the phrase *textbook supply*:

✓   The textbook supply in the bookstore had run out, so we borrowed the texts from the library.

✓   The bookstore had run out of textbooks, so we borrowed them from the library.

When a sentence contains more than one noun, make sure there is no ambiguity about which noun the pronoun refers to:

✗   The clergy members want more <u>programs</u> and larger <u>buildings</u>, but the congregants do not favour <u>them</u>.

What does the pronoun *them* refer to: the programs, the buildings, or both?

✓   The clergy members want more <u>programs</u> along with larger <u>buildings</u>, but the congregants will not support any further <u>building projects</u>.

Using "it" or "this"
Using *it* or *this* without a clear referent can lead to confusion:

✗   Although the leaders wanted to meet in January, <u>it</u> didn't take place until May.

✓   Although the leaders wanted to meet in January, <u>the council</u> didn't take place until May.

Make sure that *it* or *this* clearly refers to a specific noun or pronoun.

Using "one"
People often use the word *one* to avoid overusing *I* in their writing. Although in Britain this is common, in Canada and the United States frequent use of *one* may seem too formal:

orig.   If <u>one</u> were to apply for the grant, <u>one</u> would find <u>oneself</u> engulfed in so many bureaucratic forms that <u>one's</u> patience would be stretched thin.

While there is nothing grammatically incorrect in this example, it may strike the North American reader as stiff. The best thing to do is to recast the sentence with a plural subject:

rev.   If <u>researchers</u> were to apply for grants, <u>they</u> would find <u>themselves</u> engulfed in so many bureaucratic forms that <u>their</u> patience would be stretched thin.

Use *one* sparingly, and don't be afraid of the occasional *I*. Just remember to avoid the pitfall of mixing the third person *one* with the second person *you*:

✗   When <u>one</u> visits the Dome of the Rock, <u>you</u> are impressed by the magnificence of the architecture.

Using "me" and other objective pronouns

Remembering that it is wrong to say "Nikhil and me were invited to present our findings to the delegates" rather than "Nikhil and I were invited . . .", many people use the subjective form of the pronoun even when it should be objective:

✗   The delegates invited Nikhil and I to present our findings.

✓   The delegates invited Nikhil and me to present our findings.

The verb *invited* requires an object; *me* is the objective case. A good way to tell which form is correct is to ask yourself how the sentence would sound with only the pronoun. You will know by ear that the subjective form—"The delegates invited I"—is not appropriate.

The same problem often arises with prepositions, which should also be followed by a noun or pronoun in the objective case:

✗   Between you and I, this result doesn't make sense.

✓   Between you and me, this result doesn't make sense.

✗   Eating well is a problem for we students.

✓   Eating well is a problem for us students.

There are times, however, when the correct case can sound stiff or awkward:

orig.   To whom was the award given?

Rather than using a correct but awkward form, try to reword the sentence:

rev.   Who received the award?

EXCEPTIONS FOR PRONOUNS FOLLOWING PREPOSITIONS

The rule that a pronoun following a preposition takes the objective case has exceptions. When the preposition is followed by a clause, the pronoun should take the case required by its position in the clause:

✗   The students showed some concern over whom would be selected as Dean.

Although the pronoun follows the preposition *over*, it is also the subject of the verb *would be selected* and therefore requires the subjective case:

✓   The students showed some concern over who would be selected as Dean.

Similarly, when a gerund (a word that acts partly as a noun and partly as a verb) is the subject of a clause, the pronoun that modifies it takes the possessive case:

✗   We were surprised <u>by him dropping</u> out of school.

✓   We were surprised <u>by his dropping</u> out of school.

✗   He was tired <u>of me reminding</u> him.

✓   He was tired <u>of my reminding</u> him.

MODIFIERS

Adjectives modify nouns; adverbs modify verbs, adjectives, and other adverbs. Do not use an adjective to modify a verb:

✗   He played <u>good</u>. (adjective with verb)

✓   He played <u>well</u>. (adverb modifying verb)

✓   He played <u>really well</u>. (adverb modifying adverb)

✓   He had a <u>good</u> style. (adjective modifying noun)

✓   He had a <u>really good</u> style. (adverb modifying adjective)

Squinting modifiers

Remember that clarity depends largely on word order: to avoid confusion, the connections between the different parts of a sentence must be clear. Modifiers should therefore be as close as possible to the words they modify. A *squinting modifier* is one that, because of its position, seems to look in two directions at once:

✗   She expected <u>after the announcement</u> a protest from the pacifists.

Was *after the announcement* the time of expectation or the time of the protest? Changing the order of the sentence or rephrasing it will make the meaning clearer:

✓   <u>After the announcement</u>, she expected a protest from the pacifists.

✓   She expected a protest from the pacifists <u>after the announcement</u>.

Other squinting modifiers can be corrected in the same way:

✗ Our Japanese religions professor gave a lecture on the Ise Grand Shrine, which was elaborate.

✓ Our Japanese religions professor gave an elaborate lecture on the Ise Grand Shrine.

Often the modifier works best when placed immediately in front of the phrase it modifies. Notice the difference that this placement can make:

Only she guessed the motive for the request.

She only guessed the motive for the request.

She guessed only the motive for the request.

She guessed the motive for the request only.

Dangling modifiers

Modifiers that have no grammatical connection with anything else in the sentence are said to be *dangling*:

✗ Walking around the campus in June, the river and trees made a picturesque scene.

Who is doing the walking? Here's another example:

✗ Reflecting on the results of the poll, it was decided not to announce the new marriage legislation right away.

Who is doing the reflecting? Clarify the meaning by connecting the dangling modifier to a new subject:

✓ Walking around the campus in June, Nina thought the river and trees made a picturesque scene.

✓ Reflecting on the results of the poll, the clergy decided not to announce the new marriage legislation right away.

PAIRS AND PARALLELS

Comparisons

Make sure that your comparisons are complete. The second element in a comparison should be equivalent to the first, whether the equivalence is stated or merely implied:

✗ That new text is a boring book and so are the lectures.

The lectures may be boring, but they are not a boring book; to make sense, the two parts of the comparison must be parallel:

✓ The new text is <u>boring</u> and so are the lectures.

Correlatives
Constructions such as *both . . . and, not only . . . but also,* and *neither . . . nor* are especially tricky. For the implied comparison to work, the two parts that come after the coordinating term must be grammatically equivalent:

✗ He <u>not only drinks lager but also ale</u>.

✓ He drinks <u>not only lager but also ale</u>.

Parallel phrasing
A series of items in a sentence should be phrased in parallel wording. Make sure that all the parts of a parallel construction are in fact equal:

✗ We had to turn in <u>our rough notes</u>, <u>our essay outlines</u>, and <u>finished assignments</u>.

✓ We had to turn in <u>our rough notes</u>, <u>our essay outlines</u>, and <u>our finished assignments</u>.

Once you have decided to include the pronoun *our* in the first two elements, the third must have it too.

For clarity as well as stylistic grace, keep similar ideas in similar form:

✗ He <u>failed</u> philosophy and <u>barely passed</u> religious studies, but history <u>was</u> a subject he did well in.

✓ He <u>failed</u> philosophy and barely <u>passed</u> religious studies but <u>did well</u> in history.

Faulty parallelism is a common problem in bulleted or numbered lists:

✗ There are several reasons for joining the university's debating club:

- low <u>membership cost</u>
- <u>there is</u> a member's lounge
- <u>offered</u> public speaking opportunities
- <u>getting</u> unlimited access to university-sponsored debates

✓   There are several reasons for joining the university's debating club:

- low cost
- member's lounge
- public speaking opportunities
- unlimited access to university-sponsored debates

CHAPTER 17

Punctuation

Objectives

- Understanding and correctly employing punctuation

Punctuation causes students so many problems that it deserves a chapter of its own. If your punctuation is faulty, your readers will be confused and may have to backtrack; worse still, they may be tempted to skip over the rough spots. Punctuation marks are the traffic signals of writing; use them with precision to keep readers moving smoothly through your work.

(Items in this chapter are arranged alphabetically: *apostrophe, brackets, colon, comma, dash, ellipsis, exclamation mark, hyphen, italics, parentheses, period, quotation marks,* and *semicolon.*)

APOSTROPHE [']

1. **Use an apostrophe to indicate possession.** The following rules are the easiest to remember:

    a. To illustrate the possessive, create an "of" phrase:

the Jesuits monastery	→	the monastery of the Jesuits
the girls fathers	→	the fathers of the girls
the childrens parents	→	the parents of the children
Augustines writings	→	the writings of Augustine

b. If the noun in the "of" phrase ends in "s" add an apostrophe:

the Jesuits' monastery

the girls' fathers

c. If the noun in the "of" phrase does not end in "s", add an apostrophe plus "s":

the children's parents

Augustine's writings

2. **Use an apostrophe to show contractions of words, but try to limit the use of contractions in formal essays or assignments**:

isn't   we'll   he's   shouldn't   I'm

Caution: don't confuse *it's* (the contraction of *it is*) with *its* (the possessive of *it*), which has no apostrophe. Again, because you should avoid contractions in your essays and assignments, as a rule of thumb "it's" should rarely appear in your submitted work. Also, remember that possessive pronouns never take an apostrophe: yours, hers, its, ours, yours, theirs.

BRACKETS [ ]

Brackets are square enclosures, not to be confused with parentheses (which are round). **Use brackets to set off a remark of your own within a quotation**. The brackets indicate that the words enclosed are not those of the person quoted:

Žižek maintains, "This extraction [of religion from the social order] enables religion to globalize itself."

Brackets are sometimes used to enclose *sic*, which is used after an error such as a misspelling to show that the mistake was in the original. *Sic* may be italicized:

The leader, in a letter to his followers, wrote about "these dagnerous [*sic*] times of instability."

COLON [:]

A colon indicates that something is to follow.

1. **Use a colon before a formal statement or series**:

   ✓   The religions in question are the following: Sikhism, Buddhism, Hinduism, and Jainism.

   Do not use a colon if the words preceding it do not form a complete sentence:

   ✗   The religions in question are: Sikhism, Buddhism, Hinduism, and Jainism.

   ✓   The religions in question are Sikhism, Buddhism, Hinduism, and Jainism.

   On the other hand, a colon often precedes a vertical list, even when the introductory part is not a complete sentence:

   ✓   The religions in question are: Sikhism
                                         Buddhism
                                         Hinduism
                                         Jainism

2. **Use a colon for formality before a direct quotation or when a complete sentence precedes the quotation**:

   The leaders of the anti-nuclear group repeated their message: "The world needs bread before bombs."

3. **Use a colon between numbers expressing time and ratios**:

   4:30 p.m.

   The local ratio of Shi'a to Sunni is 8:1.

   In North America, colons are also used when referencing particular ancient texts. For instance, most biblical texts use a colon to separate chapter and verse:

   Genesis 1:1

   Matthew 2:2

COMMA [,]

Commas are the trickiest of all punctuation marks; even the experts differ on when to use them. Most agree, however, that too many commas are as bad as too few since they make writing choppy and awkward to read. Certainly recent writers use fewer commas than earlier stylists did. Whenever you are in doubt, let clarity be your guide. The most widely accepted conventions are these:

1. **Use a comma to separate two independent clauses joined by a co-ordinating conjunction (*and, but, for, or, nor, yet, so, whereas*).** By signalling that there are two clauses, the comma will prevent the reader from thinking that the beginning of the second clause is the end of the first:

   ✗   The study explores sexual ethics and family patterns are also investigated.

   ✓   The study explores sexual ethics, and family patterns are also investigated.

   When the second clause has the same subject as the first, you have the option of omitting both the second subject and the comma:

   ✓   The argument is rhetorically persuasive, but it contains fallacies.

   ✓   The argument is rhetorically persuasive but contains fallacies.

   If you mistakenly punctuate two sentences as if they were one, the result will be a *run-on sentence*; if you use a comma but forget the co-ordinating conjunction, the result will be a *comma splice*:

   ✗   The works of Descartes are often cited, they are rarely read carefully.

   ✓   The works of Descartes are often cited, but they are rarely read carefully.

   Remember that words such as *however, therefore*, and *thus* are conjunctive adverbs, not conjunctions; if you use one of them to join two independent clauses, the result will again be a comma splice:

   ✗   She was accepted into graduate school, however, she took a year off to earn her tuition.

   ✓   She was accepted into graduate school; however, she took a year off to earn her tuition.

   Conjunctive adverbs are often confused with conjunctions. You can distinguish between the two if you remember that a conjunctive adverb's position in a sentence can be changed:

✓   She was accepted into graduate school; she took a year off, however, to earn her tuition.

The position of a conjunction, on the other hand, is invariable; it must be placed between the two clauses:

✓   She was accepted into graduate school, but she took a year off to earn her tuition.

A good rule of thumb, then, is to *use a comma when the linking word can't move*.

When, in rare cases, the independent clauses are short and closely related, they may be joined by a comma alone:

✓   I came, I saw, I conquered.

2. **Use a comma between items in a series**. Place a coordinating conjunction before the last item:

✓   She found the text to be clear, concise, and powerful.

✓   This is due to its vocabulary, grammar, and rhetorical force.

3. **Use a comma to separate adjectives preceding a noun when they modify the same element**:

✓   He was a passionate, eloquent communicator.

However, when the adjectives *do not* modify the same element, you should not use a comma:

✗   It was an enjoyable, evening lecture.

Here *evening* modifies *lecture*, but *enjoyable* modifies the whole phrase *evening lecture*. A good way of deciding whether you need a comma is to see if you can reverse the order of the adjectives. If you can reverse them (*passionate, eloquent communicator* or *eloquent, passionate communicator*), use a comma; if you can't (*evening enjoyable lecture*), omit the comma:

✓   It was an enjoyable evening lecture.

4. **Use commas to set off an interruption (or "parenthetical element")**:

✓   The study, I hear, isn't nearly as good as past publications.

✓   The cleric, however, couldn't answer the question.

Remember to put commas on both sides of the interruption:

✗   The cleric however, couldn't answer the question.

✗   The concept, they say was adapted from a poem by Rumi.

✓   The concept, they say, was adapted from a poem by Rumi.

5. **Use commas to set off words or phrases that provide additional but non-essential information**:

✓   Our president, Dr. Stephens, does her job well.

In this example, *Dr. Stephens* is an *appositive*: it gives additional information about the noun it refers to (*president*), but the sentence would make sense without it. Here's another example:

✓   His first book, which decisively shaped the study of religion, was published just before the Second World War.

The phrase *which decisively shaped the study of religion* is a *non-restrictive modifier* because it does not limit the meaning of the word it modifies (*book*). Without that modifying clause the sentence would still specify what was published. Since the information the clause provides is not necessary to the meaning of the sentence, you must use commas on both sides to set it off.

In contrast, a *restrictive modifier* is one that provides essential information; it must not be set apart from the element it modifies, and commas should not be used:

✓   The man who assisted us was the bishop.

Without the clause *who assisted us*, the reader would not know which man was the bishop.

To avoid confusion, be sure to distinguish carefully between essential and additional information. The difference can be important:

Faith organizations, which are unwilling to comply, should not receive charitable status. (All faith organizations are unwilling to comply and should not receive charitable status.)

Faith organizations which are unwilling to comply should not receive charitable status. (Only those which are unwilling to comply should be denied charitable status.)

6. **Use a comma after an introductory phrase when omitting it would cause confusion**:

   ✗   On the shelf above the rare books are stored.

   ✓   On the shelf above, the rare books are stored.

   ✗   As they concluded the study became clear.

   ✓   As they concluded, the study became clear.

7. **Use a comma to separate elements in dates and addresses**:

   ✓   February 2, 2011 (Commas are often omitted if the day comes first: 2 February 2011.)

   ✓   117 Hudson Drive, Edmonton, Alberta

   ✓   They lived in Dartmouth, Nova Scotia.

8. **Use a comma before a quotation in a sentence**:

   ✓   He said, "Life is too short to worry."

   ✓   "The children's safety," he warned, "is in your hands."

   For more formality, or if the quotation is preceded by a complete sentence, you may use a colon.

9. **Use a comma with a name followed by a title**:

   ✓   Phyllis Trible, President

   ✓   David Black, Ph.D.

10. **Do not use a comma between a subject and its verb**:

    ✗   Her most demanding subject, is philosophy of religion.

    ✓   Her most demanding subject is philosophy of religion.

11. **Do not use a comma between a verb and its object**:

    ✗   He immediately decided, what he must do.

    ✓   He immediately decided what he must do.

12. **Do not use a comma between a coordinating conjunction and the following clause**:

    ✗   Ellen got honours but, Daniel failed the course.

    ✓   Ellen got honours, but Daniel failed the course.

DASH [—]

A dash creates an abrupt pause, emphasizing the words that follow. Never use dashes as casual substitutes for other punctuation; overuse can detract from the calm, well-reasoned effect you want to create.

1. **Use a dash to stress a word or phrase**:

   The community—without prompting—decided to raise awareness of the issue.

   The authenticity of the artifact was unquestioned—at first.

2. **Use a dash in interrupted or unfinished dialogue**:

   "But I thought—" Donald tried to explain, but Mario cut him off: "You were wrong."

You can type two hyphens together, with no spaces on either side, to show a dash; your word processor may automatically convert this to a solid line as you continue typing. Alternatively, you can insert an *em dash* from the list of special characters in your word-processing program.

En Dash [–]

An en dash looks shorter than a full dash, and slightly longer than a hyphen (it is about the width of a letter "n").

Use an en dash rather than a hyphen to separate parts of inclusive number or date ranges:

   the years 1890–1914

   pages 3–10

ELLIPSIS [. . .]

1. **Use an ellipsis (three dots) to show an omission from a quotation**:

   For an ellipsis within a sentence, use three periods with a space before each and a space after the last:

   > "The committee reported that the position paper . . . would need to be adjusted."

   If the omission comes at the beginning of the quotation, an ellipsis is not necessarily used:

The position paper, it was reported, "would need to be adjusted."

To omit a full line of a poem, use a full line of periods:

Cedar and jagged fir

. . . .

against the gray

and cloud-piled sky

2. **Use an ellipsis to show that a series of numbers continues indefinitely**:

1, 3, 5, 7, 9 . . .

EXCLAMATION MARK [!]

An exclamation mark helps to show emotion or feeling. It is usually found in dialogue:

"Woe is me!" she cried.

In academic writing, exclamation marks should be used sparingly, if at all.

HYPHEN [-]

1. **Use a hyphen to separate the parts of certain compound words**:

- compound nouns:

  sister-in-law; vice-consul

- compound verbs:

  self-aggrandize; dive-bomb

- compound modifiers:

  a well-considered plan; forward-looking attitudes

Note that compound modifiers are hyphenated only when they precede the part modified; otherwise, omit the hyphen:

The plan was well considered.

His attitudes are forward looking.

Also, do not hyphenate a compound modifier that includes an adverb ending in *-ly*:

✓ a well-written essay

✗ a beautifully-written thesis

✓ a beautifully written thesis

Spell-checking features today will help you determine which compounds to hyphenate, but there is no clear consensus even from one dictionary to another. We recommend you choose one current dictionary and use it throughout your paper. As always, consistency in your writing style is most important.

2. **Use a hyphen with certain prefixes (*all-*, *self-*, *ex-*) and with prefixes preceding a proper name**. Again, practices vary, so when in doubt consult a dictionary:

    all-star; self-imposed; anti-American

3. **Use a hyphen to emphasize contrasting prefixes**:

    The guest speaker agreed to take both pre- and post-lecture questions.

4. **Use a hyphen to separate written-out compound numbers from one to ninety-nine, and compound fractions**:

    eighty-one years ago; seven-tenths full; two-thirds of a cup

ITALICS [*ITALICS*]

1. **Use italics for the titles of works published independently, such as books, long poems that are complete books, plays, films, albums, and long musical compositions**:

    East of Eden is one of my favourite novels.

    For articles, essays, short poems, or songs, use quotation marks. If the title itself contains the title of another work, be sure to set it off in the correct style:

    • When both titles are books (or book-length poems), use quotation marks for the internal one:

    Her latest book is *Western Philosophy since Derrida's "Of Grammatology."*

- When the internal title is a book but the main title is not, use italics:

    For more detail, see his recent article, "Comments on the *Encyclopedia of Religion and Nature.*"

2. **Use italics to emphasize an idea**:

    It is important that *all* viewpoints be taken into consideration.

    Be sparing with this use, interspersing it with other, less intrusive methods of creating emphasis.

3. **Use italics (or quotation marks) to identify a word or phrase that is itself the subject of discussion**:

    The term *peer group* is an example of sociological jargon.

4. **Use italics for foreign words or expressions that have not been naturalized in English**:

    She attempted to ascertain the *Sitz im Leben* of the text.

    Her statement was a *cri de coeur*.

    Italics should also be used for words that have been transliterated from another language:

    Philo frequently employed the language of *logos* in his writings.

PARENTHESES [( )]

1. **Use parentheses to enclose an explanation, example, or qualification**. Parentheses show that the enclosed material is of incidental importance to the main idea. They make an interruption that is more subtle than one marked off by dashes but more pronounced than one set off by commas:

    My colleague (the most recent addition to the faculty) is an excellent teacher and writer.

    Remember that punctuation should not precede parentheses but may follow them if required by the sense of the sentence:

    Her idea was influential (in certain circles), but also controversial.

2. **Use parentheses to enclose references**. See Chapter 15 for details.

PERIOD [.]

1. **Use a period at the end of a sentence**. A period indicates a full stop, not just a pause.

2. **Use a period with some abbreviations**. It is still common, although not mandatory, to use periods in abbreviated titles (Mrs., Dr., Rev., etc.), academic degrees (M.S.W., Ph.D., etc.), and expressions of time (6:30 p.m.).

    However, there is a trend away from the use of periods in many abbreviations. Provincial and state abbreviations do not require periods (BC, NT, PE, NY, DC). In addition, most acronyms for organizations do not use periods (AAR, SBL, WCC, UNESCO).

    The same holds true for religious texts, whose titles can be abbreviated with or without a period.

    > Surah 24:42 = Sur. 24:42 or Sur 24:42

    > Romans 1:1 = Rom. 1:1 or Rom 1:1

3. **Use a period at the end of an indirect question**. Do not use a question mark:

    ✗   He asked if I needed an extension?

    ✓   He asked if I needed an extension.

    ✗   I wonder where she went?

    ✓   I wonder where she went.

4. **Use a period for questions that are really polite orders**:

    > Will you please submit your essay by Friday.

QUOTATION MARKS ["""]

1. **Use quotation marks to signify direct discourse (the actual words of a speaker)**:

    > I asked, "What is the matter?"

    > "I am having difficulty understanding this concept," he replied.

2. **Use quotation marks to show that words themselves are the issue**:

> The term "Islam" comes from the word for "submission."

Alternatively, you may italicize the terms in question.

Sometimes quotation marks are used to mark a slang word or inappropriate usage to show that the writer is aware of the difficulty:

> Several of the "experts" did not seem to know anything about the topic.

Use this device only when necessary. In general, it's better to let the context show your attitude or to choose another term.

3. **Use quotation marks to enclose the titles of poems, short stories, songs, and articles in books or journals.** In contrast, titles of books, paintings, films, and CDs are italicized:

> Jeffrey Stout's presidential address was later published as an article entitled "The Folly of Secularism."

4. **Use single quotation marks to enclose quotations within quotations**:

> He said, "Several of the 'experts' did not know anything about the topic."

5. **Do not use quotation marks for indented block quotations (quotations that run more than four lines)**. Block quotations should be indented from the main text by at least half an inch.

Placement of punctuation with quotation marks

- In North America, a comma or period always goes inside the quotation marks (though note European usage often puts the punctuation outside the quotation marks):

  > He said, "I think we can finish it tonight," but I told him, "It's time to go home."

- A semicolon or colon always goes outside the quotation marks:

  > Some call it "a masterpiece"; that's certainly debatable.

- A question mark, dash, or exclamation mark goes inside quotation marks if it is part of the quotation but outside if it is not:

  > She asked, "What is that, Conrad?"

  > Did she really call it "a waste of time"?

  > You could hardly call it "a masterpiece"!

- When a reference is given parenthetically at the end of a quotation, the quotation marks precede the parentheses and the sentence punctuation is at the end:

> His early interest in these issues "led directly to a concern with comparison" (Smith 19).

SEMICOLON [;]

1. **Use a semicolon to join independent clauses (complete sentences) that are closely related**:

   ✓ The first volume is methodological; the final two volumes are the outworking of this method.

   ✓ His lecture was confusing; no one could understand the terminology.

   A semicolon is especially useful when the second independent clause begins with a conjunctive adverb such as *however, moreover, consequently, nevertheless, in addition,* or *therefore* (usually followed by a comma):

   ✓ The text has extremely long sentences; consequently, it was difficult to follow.

   It's usually acceptable to follow a semicolon with a coordinating conjunction if the second clause is complicated by other commas:

   ✓ The Zoroastrian Gathas often appear disjointed; but often, with careful observation, patterns and themes do emerge.

2. **Use a semicolon to mark the divisions in a complicated series when individual items themselves need commas**. Using a comma to mark the subdivisions and a semicolon to mark the main divisions will help to prevent mix-ups:

   ✗ He invited Professor Ludvik, the vice-principal, Christine Li, and Dr. Hector Jimenez.

   Is the vice-principal Professor Ludvik, Christine Li, or a separate person?

   ✓ He invited Professor Ludvik; the vice-principal, Christine Li; and Dr. Hector Jimenez.

   In a case such as this, the elements separated by the semicolon need not be independent clauses.

CHAPTER 18

Misused Words and Phrases

Here are some words and phrases that are often misused. If you're wondering about a particular word or idiom, check here for advice about correct usage.

accept, except. **Accept** is a verb meaning to *receive affirmatively*; **except,** when used as a verb, means to *exclude*:

> I accept your offer.

> The teacher excepted him from the general punishment.

accompanied by, accompanied with. Use **accompanied by** for people; use **accompanied with** for objects:

> He was accompanied by his colleague.

> The package arrived, accompanied with a letter of explanation.

advice, advise. **Advice** is a noun, **advise** a verb:

> He was advised to ignore the advice of others.

affect, effect. **Affect** is a verb meaning to *influence*; however, it also has a specialized meaning in psychology, referring to a person's emotional state. **Effect** can be either a noun meaning *result* or a verb meaning *to bring about*:

> The atmosphere affected his concentration.

The effect of higher tuition is lower enrolment.

Hard work can effect great change.

all ready, **already**. To be **all ready** is simply to be ready for something; **already** means beforehand or earlier:

The students were all ready for the lecture to begin.

The professor had already left her office by the time they arrived.

all right. Write as two separate words: *all right*. This can mean *safe and sound, in good condition, okay*; *correct*; *satisfactory*; or *I agree*:

Are you all right?

The student's answers were all right.

(Note the ambiguity of the second example: does it mean that the answers were all correct or simply satisfactory? In this case, it might be better to use a clearer word.)

all together, **altogether**. **All together** means *in a group*; **altogether** is an adverb meaning *entirely*:

He was altogether certain that the congregants were all together.

allusion, **illusion**. An **allusion** is an indirect reference to something; an **illusion** is a false perception:

The ark image is an *allusion* to the story of Noah.

He thought he had seen Elvis, but it was an *illusion*.

a lot. Write as two separate words: *a lot*.

alternate, **alternative**. **Alternate** means *every other* or *every second* thing in a series; **alternative** refers to a *choice* between options:

The two sections of the class attended discussion groups on alternate days.

The students could do an extra paper as an alternative to writing the exam.

among, between. Use **among** for three or more persons or objects, **between** for two:

> Between you and me, there's trouble among the team members.

amount, number. Amount indicates quantity when units are *not discrete and not absolute*; **number** indicates quantity when units are *discrete and absolute*:

> A large amount of reading.

> A large number of students.

See also **less, fewer.**

analysis. The plural is **analyses.**

anyone, any one. Anyone is written as two words to give numerical emphasis; otherwise it is written as one word:

> Any one of us could do that.

> Anyone could do that.

anyways. Non-standard. Use *anyway.*

as, because. As is a weaker conjunction than **because** and may be confused with **when**:

> ✗   As my leg was injured, I studied in bed.

> ✓   Because my leg was injured, I studied in bed.

as to. A common feature of bureaucratese. Replace it with a single-word preposition such as *about* or *on*:

> ✗   They were concerned as to the range of disagreement.

> ✓   They were concerned about the range of disagreement.

> ✗   They recorded his comments as to the treaty.

> ✓   They recorded his comments on the treaty.

bad, **badly**. **Bad** is an adjective meaning *not good*:

> The presentation was bad.

Badly is an adverb meaning *not well*; when used with the verbs **want** or **need**, it means *very much*:

> She thought he argued against the book's premise badly.

> He badly needs a new approach.

beside, **besides**. **Beside** is a preposition meaning *next to*:

> She worked beside her assistant.

Besides has two uses: as a preposition it means *in addition to*; as a conjunctive adverb it means *moreover*:

> Besides recommending the changes, the consultants are making them.

> It was time for lunch; besides, the students needed a rest.

between. See **among**.

bring, **take**. One **brings** something to a closer place and **takes** it to a farther one:

> Take it with you when you go.

> Next time you come to visit, bring your friend along.

can, **may**. **Can** means to *be able*; **may** means to *have permission*:

> Can you retrieve the books?

> May I borrow that book?

In speech, **can** is used to cover both meanings; in formal writing, however, you should observe the distinction.

can't hardly. A faulty combination of the phrases **can't** and **can hardly**. Use one or the other:

> He can't concentrate.

> He can hardly concentrate.

cite, **sight**, **site**. To **cite** something is to *quote* or *mention* it as an example or authority; **sight** can be used in many ways, all of which relate to the ability to *see*; **site** refers to a specific *location*, a particular place at which something is located:

> You need to cite that source in your essay.
>
> His sight was extremely limited.
>
> That site is perfect for a brewery.

complement, **compliment**. The verb to **complement** means to *complete* or *enhance*; to **compliment** means to *praise*:

> Her ability to analyze data complements her excellent research skills.
>
> I complimented her on her outstanding report.

The same rule applies when these words are used as adjectives. The adjective *complimentary* can also mean *free*:

> Use complementary colours in your presentation.
>
> That was a complimentary comment.
>
> These are complimentary tickets.

compose, **comprise**. Both words mean to *constitute* or *make up*, but **compose** is preferred. **Comprise** is correctly used to mean *include, consist of*, or *be composed of*. Using **comprise** in the passive ("is comprised of")—as you might be tempted to do in the second example below—is usually frowned on in formal writing:

> These students will compose the group which will go overseas.
>
> Each paragraph comprises an introduction, an argument, and a conclusion.

continual, **continuous**. Continual means *repeated over a period of time*; **continuous** means *constant* or *without interruption*:

> The disruptive students caused continual delays in the lectures.
>
> Three days of continuous rain ruined the conference.

could of. This construction is incorrect, as are **might of**, **should of**, and **would of**. Replace *of* with *have*:

    ✗   He <u>could of</u> done it.

    ✓   He <u>could have</u> done it.

    ✓   They <u>might have</u> been there.

    ✓   I <u>should have</u> known.

    ✓   We <u>would have</u> left earlier.

council, counsel. **Council** is a noun meaning an *advisory* or *deliberative assembly*. **Counsel** as a noun means *advice* or *lawyer*; as a verb it means to *give advice*.

> The parish <u>council</u> meets on Tuesday.

> We respect her <u>counsel</u>, since she's seldom wrong.

> As a camp <u>counsellor</u>, you may need to <u>counsel</u> parents as well as children.

criterion, criteria. A **criterion** is a standard for judging something. **Criteria** is the plural of **criterion** and thus requires a plural verb:

> <u>These are</u> my <u>criteria</u> for grading the reports.

> The major <u>criterion was</u> depth of research.

data. The plural of **datum**. The set of information, usually in numerical form, that is used for analysis as the basis for a study. Since **data** often refers to a single mass entity, many writers now accept its use with a singular verb and pronoun:

> <u>These data were</u> gathered in an unsystematic fashion.

> When <u>the data is</u> in we'll have a look at it.

deduce, deduct. To **deduce** something is to *work it out by reasoning*; to **deduct** means to *subtract or take away* from something. The noun form of both words is **deduction**.

> You could <u>deduce</u> from his statement that the examiner was not impressed.

> We will <u>deduct</u> this amount from your fees.

defence, defense. Both spellings are correct: **defence** is standard in Britain and is somewhat more common in Canada; **defense** is standard in the United States.

delusion, illusion. A **delusion** is a belief or perception that is distorted; an **illusion** is a false belief:

> He had <u>delusions</u> about his writing abilities.

> The desert pool she thought she saw was an <u>illusion</u>.

dependent, dependant. Dependent is an adjective meaning *contingent on* or *subject to*; **dependant** is a noun.

> Suriya's graduation is <u>dependent</u> upon her passing Latin.

> Her four young children are her <u>dependants</u>.

device, devise. The word ending in -**ice** is the noun; the word ending in -**ise** is the verb.

different than, different from. Use **different from** to compare two persons or things; use **different than** with a full clause:

> You are <u>different from</u> me.

> This city is <u>different than</u> it used to be.

diminish, minimize. To **diminish** means to *make* or *become smaller*; to **minimize** means to *reduce* something to the smallest possible amount or size.

> His resolve to travel will <u>diminish</u> as he gets older.

> The regulation will <u>minimize</u> the impact of higher tuition.

disinterested, uninterested. Disinterested implies impartiality or neutrality; **uninterested** implies a lack of interest:

> As a <u>disinterested</u> observer, she was in a good position to judge the issue fairly.

> <u>Uninterested</u> in the proceedings, he yawned repeatedly.

due to. Although increasingly used to mean *because of*, **due** is an adjective and therefore needs to modify something:

> ✗   <u>Due to</u> his impatience, we lost the contract. [Due is dangling.]

> ✓   The loss was <u>due to</u> his impatience.

e.g., i.e. E.g. means *for example*; **i.e.** means *that is*. It is incorrect to use them interchangeably.

entomology, etymology. Entomology is the study of insects; **etymology** is the study of the derivation and history of words.

exceptional, exceptionable. Exceptional means *unusual* or *outstanding*, whereas **exceptionable** means *open to objection* and is generally used in negative contexts:

> His accomplishments are exceptional.

> He was dismissed from the group because of his exceptionable behaviour.

farther, further. Farther refers to distance, **further** to extent:

> He journeyed farther than his friends did.

> She explained the concept further.

focus. The plural of the noun may be either **focuses** (also spelled **focusses**) or **foci.** You may choose either form, but be consistent.

good, well. Good is an adjective that modifies a noun; **well** is an adverb that modifies a verb.

> He is a good leader.

> The experiment went well.

hanged, hung. Hanged means *executed by hanging.* **Hung** means *suspended* or *clung to*:

> He was hanged at dawn for the murder.

> She hung the notice on the board.

> She hung on to the boat when it capsized.

hereditary, heredity. Heredity is a noun referring to the biological process whereby characteristics are passed from one generation to the next; **hereditary** is the adjective that describes those characteristics.

> Heredity is a factor in the incidence of this disease.

> Your asthma may be hereditary.

hopefully. Use **hopefully** as an adverb meaning *full of hope*:

> She scanned the crowd <u>hopefully</u>, looking for her mentor.

In formal writing, using **hopefully** to mean *I hope* is still frowned upon, although it is increasingly common; it's better to use *I hope*:

> ✗   <u>Hopefully</u> the argument will be persuasive.

> ✓   <u>I hope</u> the argument will be persuasive.

i.e. This is *not* the same as **e.g.** See **e.g.**

illusion. See **delusion and allusion**.

incite, **insight**. **Incite** is a verb meaning to *stir up*; **insight** is a noun meaning *(often sudden) understanding*.

> His intention was to <u>incite</u> an uprising.

> Her <u>insight</u> into the situation was remarkable.

infer, **imply**. To **infer** means to *deduce* or *conclude by reasoning*. It is often confused with **imply**, which means to *suggest* or *insinuate*.

> We can <u>infer</u> from the poll data that there is a demand for religious services.

> The poll data <u>implies</u> that there is a demand for religious services.

inflammable, flammable, non-flammable. Despite its **in-** prefix, **inflammable** is not the opposite of **flammable**: both words describe things that are *easily set on fire*. The opposite of **flammable** is *non-flammable*. To prevent any possibility of confusion, it's best to avoid **inflammable** altogether.

irregardless. Non-standard. Use *regardless*.

its, **it's**. **Its** is a form of possessive pronoun; **it's** is a contraction of *it is*. Many people mistakenly put an apostrophe in **its** in order to show possession.

> ✗   The community appreciated <u>it's</u> diversity.

> ✓   The community appreciated <u>its</u> diversity.

> ✓   <u>It's</u> time to leave.

less, **fewer**. **Less** is used when units are *not* discrete and *not* absolute (as in "less information"). **Fewer** is used when the units *are* discrete and absolute (as in "fewer details").

lie, **lay**. To **lie** means to *assume a horizontal position*; to **lay** means to *put down*. The changes of tense often cause confusion:

Present	*Past*	*Past participle*	*Present participle*
lie	lay	lain	lying
lay	laid	laid	laying

✗   I was <u>laying</u> on the couch when he came in.

✓   I was <u>lying</u> on the couch when he came in.

✓   I <u>laid</u> the table for dinner.

✓   She needed to <u>lie</u> down for a minute.

✓   The crew was <u>laying</u> the carpet.

like, **as**. **Like** is a preposition, but it is often wrongly used as a conjunction. To join two independent clauses, use the conjunction **as**:

✗   I want to progress <u>like</u> you have this year.

✓   I want to progress <u>as</u> you have this year.

✓   Prof. Dimitriou is <u>like</u> my old high school principal.

Remember also that *like* is not used as an interjection or an estimating word in formal writing:

✗   I'm, <u>like</u>, so happy to see you.

✓   I'm so happy to see you.

✗   There were <u>like</u> thirty people there.

✓   Around thirty people attended the seminar.

might of. Incorrect. See **could of**.

minimize. See **diminish**.

mitigate, militate. To **mitigate** means to *reduce the severity of something*; to **militate** against something means to *oppose* it:

> The report mitigates the previous findings.

> His credentials will militate against the resistance to his appointment.

myself, me. **Myself** is an intensifier of, not a substitute for, *I* or *me*:

> ✗   He gave it to John and myself.

> ✓   He gave it to John and me.

> ✗   Jane and myself are invited.

> ✓   Jane and I are invited.

> ✓   I hesitate to mention myself here.

nor, or. Use **nor** with **neither**; use **or** by itself or with **either**:

> He is neither productive nor ambitious.

> The building is either vacant or neglected.

off of. Remove the unnecessary **of**:

> ✗   The fence kept the children off of the premises.

> ✓   The fence kept the children off the premises.

phenomenon. A singular noun: the plural is **phenomena**.

plaintiff, plaintive. A **plaintiff** is a person who brings a case against someone else in court; **plaintive** is an adjective meaning *sorrowful*.

populace, populous. **Populace** is a noun meaning the *people* of a place; **populous** is an adjective meaning *thickly inhabited*:

> The populace of Indonesia is very religious.

> With so many people in such a small area, Hong Kong is one of the most populous regions in the world.

practice, practise. Both of these spellings have become acceptable for either the noun or the verb. Just be consistent in whatever form you choose.

precede, proceed. To **precede** is to *go before* (earlier) or *in front of* others; to **proceed** is to *go on* or *ahead*:

> The faculty will <u>precede</u> the students into the hall.

> The scholarship winners will <u>proceed</u> to the front of the hall.

prescribe, proscribe. These words are sometimes confused, although they have quite different meanings. **Prescribe** means to *advise the use of* or *impose authoritatively*. **Proscribe** means to *reject, denounce,* or *ban*:

> He <u>prescribed</u> the conditions under which the equipment could be used.

> The student government <u>proscribed</u> the publication of unsigned editorials in the newspaper.

principle, principal. **Principle** is a noun meaning a *general truth* or *law*; **principal** can be used as either a noun, referring to the *head of a school* or a *capital sum of money*, or an adjective, meaning *chief*:

> His lack of <u>principle</u> is a major problem.

> Dr. Smith is the <u>principal</u> of the college.

> The <u>principal</u> reason for refusing is our lack of funds.

rational, rationale. **Rational** is an adjective meaning *logical* or *able to reason*. **Rationale** is a noun meaning *explanation*:

> That was not a <u>rational</u> response.

> The president sent around a memo explaining the <u>rationale</u> for her decision.

real, really. **Real**, an adjective, means *true* or *genuine*; **really**, an adverb, means *actually, truly, very,* or *extremely*:

> The artifact was <u>real</u> gold.

> The artifact was <u>really</u> valuable.

should of. Incorrect. See **could of**.

their, there. **Their** is the possessive form of the third person plural pronoun. **There** is usually an adverb, meaning *at that place* or *at that point*:

> Their instructor gave them all an extension.

> They began the project there.

> There is no point in arguing with you.

tortuous, torturous. The adjective **tortuous** means *full of twists and turns* or *circuitous*. **Torturous**, derived from *torture*, means *involving torture* or *excruciating*:

> To avoid heavy traffic, they took a tortuous route home.

> The concert was a torturous experience for the audience.

translucent, transparent. A **translucent** substance permits light to pass through, but not enough for a person to see through it; a **transparent** substance permits light to pass unobstructed, so that objects can be seen clearly through it.

turbid, turgid. **Turbid**, with respect to a liquid or colour, means *muddy, not clear*, or (with respect to literary style) *confused*. **Turgid** means *swollen, inflated*, or *enlarged*, or (again with reference to literary style) *pompous* or *bombastic*.

unique. This word, which means *of which there is only one* or *unequalled*, is both overused and misused. Since there are no degrees of comparison—one thing cannot be "more unique" than another—expressions such as *very unique* or *quite unique* are incorrect.

while. To avoid misreading, use **while** only when you mean *at the same time that*. Do not use **while** as a substitute for *although*, *whereas*, or *but*:

> ✗   While she's getting fair marks, she'd like to do better.

> ✗   I headed for home, while she decided to stay.

> ✓   He fell asleep while he was reading.

-**wise**. Never use -**wise** as a suffix to form new words when you mean **with regard to**:

    ✗   <u>Enrolment-wise</u>, the university did better last year.

    ✓   The university's enrolment increased last year.

your, **you're**. **Your** is a possessive adjective; **you're** is a contraction of *you are*:

    Be sure to take <u>your</u> student ID with you.

    <u>You're</u> likely to miss your class.

CHAPTER 19

Afterword

Objectives

- Remembering the importance and purpose of your post-secondary education
- Being a life-long learner

The hard work and discipline that you put into your studies will contribute to your grades and, eventually, earn you a degree. A question, however, will inevitably come to mind: *Will I really remember everything I have learned?* Unless you have a photographic memory, it is unlikely that you'll remember everything you have studied. So what's the point? Why spend so much time learning piles of information when you will likely forget a good portion of it? Why put in so much effort when you probably won't directly use what you've learned from large portions of whole courses?

Remember that what you will take away from your post-secondary education is not necessarily details, but rather methods. To put this another way, post-secondary education is as much about *learning to learn* and *learning how to think* as it is about the content of what you are studying. What you learn in university or college, from analytical processing, critical thinking, and persuasive writing, to hard work and perseverance, are all important life skills. These skills will allow you to contribute positively to our societies and will bring you a greater quality of life. Further, your education will afford you the opportunity to learn something about intellectual debate, the importance of thinking creatively, and the value of multiple perspectives—issues which are especially important when engaging with the topic of religion in the contemporary world. *How* you think is often as important as *what* you think, at least in the sense that a wise person is someone who can hold firmly to his or her convictions, even if these need to be modified or adjusted from time to time when faced with challenges or changes in the world.

In your education you will encounter various aspects of religious studies, and these will undoubtedly affect you in some way beyond the classroom. You may begin to understand others with more clarity. You may realize that you have, at times, viewed others through stereotypes or false characterizations that have been unintentionally impressed upon you. In all likelihood, you will come to look at religion and its effects on culture in a different way, in a way that recognizes a much more complex relationship between them than previously thought.

Wherever your educational experience might take you, we invite you to continue in the process of engaged learning beyond the classroom. As you undertake and finish your studies, and then move into further education or begin a career, our hope is that you will take seriously the opportunities that await you to be a life-long learner, in the study of religion and beyond.

Sample Book Review (1,000-Word Assignment)

Fisher, Mary Pat. *Religion in the Twenty-first Century*. Religions of the World. Upper Saddle River, NJ: Prentice Hall, 1999, pp. 128.

Introduction

Mary Pat Fisher has written extensively on religion and the contemporary world. Her books include, among others, *Women in Religion* (London: Longman, 2006) and the widely used textbook *Living Religions* (7th ed.; Upper Saddle River, NJ: Prentice Hall, 2007). The book under review here, *Religion in the Twenty-first Century*, is a relatively brief volume and is part of the "Religions of the World" series edited by Ninian Smart. This series aims to offer "succinct, balanced, and informative guides to the major faiths" (5). In what follows, I offer an explanation of the book's content, followed by an evaluation.

Explanation

Religion in the Twenty-first Century contains four main chapters with various sub-sections. The first chapter is entitled "Global Processes," and it explores various (sometimes contradictory) factors that affect religion in the world today: modernization, globalization, exclusivism, humanism, and postmodernity. Throughout the chapter Fisher gives specific examples of how these factors influence faiths and traditions around the globe. Chapter 2, "Religious Traditions in the Modern World," shifts the discussion away from universal issues and toward individual religious traditions. This chapter outlines indigenous spiritual traditions, Hinduism, Buddhism, Judaism, Christianity, and Islam. Within each of these traditions Fisher offers a breakdown of traditional beliefs and practices, an overview of the current shape of the religion, and a "close-up" picture of a particular stream within that tradition (for example, Lubavitcher Hasidism within Judaism).

In Chapter 3, "New Religious Movements," Fisher explores the blossoming of new religious movements throughout the world in the past two centuries. In this chapter the author investigates the dynamics of these movements by looking at issues such as the founders of new religions and accompanying issues of revelation, syncretism with existing traditions, and group organization. Once again Fisher supplements instances of abstract theory with concrete examples from various movements. Finally, Chapter 4, "Relationships between Religions," returns to more universal issues. Here Fisher begins with the difficult question "Are religions the same or different?" before unpacking some of the common traits among religions. The author then explores two universalist religions, Sikhism and Baha'i, before outlining several recent developments in interfaith relations. Fisher concludes the book in an optimistic fashion, noting that "In the midst of the postmodern religious ferment, there is room for hope that the twenty-first century will contain many forms of religion which will uplift the human condition" (117).

Evaluation

Fisher has provided an engaging and highly readable book. The chapters have depth despite their brevity, and the author has a way of helping the reader feel included in the subject matter. The progression of the book—from universal issues, to particular traditions, and back again to more general subject matter— is logical and easy to follow. The book also has a number of helpful guides, including a glossary, a pronunciation guide, suggestions for further reading, and an index.

As is evident from the quotation in the previous section, Fisher is optimistic about the place of religion—all religions—in today's world. Indeed, this is clear from the preface, where Fisher relates her own journey toward an acceptance of all religions. At the end of the preface she states her aim for the book: "My prayer is that this little book will deepen our understanding of and sensitivities to other people's points of view in our increasingly pluralistic world. May it also deepen our own links with ultimate reality, by whatever path we approach it" (9).

Fisher's openly pluralistic approach is almost certainly the issue that will grab most readers' attention. Some may find her openness and enthusiasm to be contagious. Indeed, when one reaches the end of the book, it is difficult not to agree with Fisher that the religions of the world have much to offer if they could only recognize the collective wisdom they contain. Her understanding of and sympathy for the various religious traditions of the world is to be commended.

Other readers, however, may feel that this openly pluralistic and optimistic viewpoint has drawbacks. First, substantive differences between religions that "go all the way down" are minimized, particularly in the final chapter. While Fisher is aware that study in comparative religion has highlighted differences, sometimes extreme, in the various traditions (100–102), she nevertheless wishes to stress the commonalities between them. This is not wrong in itself. However, one wonders if the publication date of this book, two years before the events of September 11, 2001, might reflect an innocence that has been lost in the past decade. Fisher's argument might be helpfully supplemented by the recent revival of interest in ecumenical and interfaith dialogue that stresses *difference* as a starting point for such discussion. Here the work encountered in our other class readings, particularly that from Catherine Cornille (*The Im-Possibility of Interreligious Dialogue* [New York: Crossroad, 2008]), provides a helpful counterbalance.

Second, there is a tendency throughout the book to praise elements of traditions Fisher finds more universal and thus laudable, while diminishing those groups deemed less tolerant. For example, after highlighting the efforts of ecumenical movements in Christianity, Fisher comments that while "such liberalizing movements are opening doors, conservative Christian movements are trying to close them" (60). Although there may be elements of truth in this statement, it also paints with a broad brush. But, to be fair, the book is very brief, and there is only so much an author can do in such a short space (just over 100 pages).

Conclusion

Although the book never explicitly states its target audience, the foreword does begin by noting that "The informed citizen or student needs a good overall knowledge of our small but complicated world" (5). If this is indeed the intended audience, then the book has done its job well. Notwithstanding the criticisms noted above, the book does a very good job of introducing the reader to religion in the twenty-first century and the various issues that accompany it. While questions remain for this reviewer regarding whether a positive, neutral, or critical vantage point toward religions is most appropriate in such a study, Fisher's introduction helpfully guides readers into these important matters in an engaging way and leaves them hungry for more.

APPENDIX 2

Sample Chapter Summary and Evaluation (500-Word Assignment)

Taylor, Rodney L. "The Sage as Saint: A Study in Religious Categories." In *The Religious Dimensions of Confucianism*. SUNY Series in Religious Studies. Albany: State University of New York Press, 1990. 39–52.

In this third chapter of the book, Taylor continues to build his case that "the Confucian tradition is profoundly religious" even while its religious character is not necessarily explicit (1). Here the topic is holy people or religious figures within religious traditions, and in particular the author seeks to compare the Confucian sage with the Christian saint. The basic premise of the chapter is that although there are key differences, the balance of "imitability and inimitability" of these figures within their respective traditions is what makes the categories of sage and saint most analogous.

Taylor begins by examining the concept of the sage in Confucianism, looking first at the teachings of Confucius himself. Sagehood was not necessarily something Confucius believed could be attained by just anyone, in that he regarded sages to be a select few wise and powerful kings (the "sage kings") of antiquity. This idea changed, according to Taylor, in the teaching of Mencius, who suggested that becoming a sage was possible for others "through rigorous learning and self-cultivation" (43). Mencius' teachings eventually led to "the Neo-Confucian quest for sagehood," where sagehood came to be understood as a state of "the full realization and development of the potential of human nature or mind" (44).

Following this, Taylor moves to analyze the concept of a saint. After discussing various qualities of sainthood, Taylor notes one feature that would appear to separate sages and saints: saints are often known for their character but not necessarily for "intellectual leadership or the exercise of power" (49), whereas ancient sagehood was very much tied to these latter qualities. Ultimately, however, Taylor moves beyond this difficulty by focusing on later Neo-Confucian teaching whereby sagehood could be attained by virtually anyone whether in authority or not. Further, central to all of this is Taylor's idea that there is a "commonality of characteristics between sage and saint clustered primarily around the sense of exemplariness or imitability of the character of each" (51) even while both had a sense of "otherness" and inimitability as well.

By way of evaluation, I note that while this chapter is illuminating, it also raises questions about the nature of comparison. On the one hand, the chapter provides a great deal of insightful information that paints wonderful pictures of both the Confucian sage and the Christian saint. I learn best through specific examples and I found Taylor's explanation of sagehood from Confucius to Mencius to Neo-Confucianism helpful for understanding the development of Confucianism more generally. On the other hand, an issue that came to mind in my reading is something we have been discussing in class: the use of Christian categories to explain aspects of another, at times very foreign, tradition. While the benefits are many, there seem to be serious risks involved in underemphasizing the unique or exotic features of the Confucian sage. For instance, are not the sages remarkable from a Western religious perspective because they are exemplary even though they are not devoted to a supreme being? In this case I think the benefits outweigh the risks, but an awareness of this tension seems paramount.

Glossary

abstract. A summary accompanying a report or paper, briefly outlining the contents.

abstract language. Language that deals with theoretical, intangible concepts or details: e.g., *justice; goodness; truth*. (Compare **concrete language**.)

acronym. A pronounceable word made up of the first letters of the words in a phrase or name: e.g., *NATO* (from *North Atlantic Treaty Organization*). A group of initial letters that are pronounced separately is an **initialism**: e.g., *AAR* (*American Academy of Religion*).

active voice. See **voice**.

adjectival phrase (or **adjectival clause**). A group of words modifying a noun or pronoun: e.g., *the dog that belongs to my brother*.

adjective. A word that modifies or describes a noun or pronoun: e.g., *red; beautiful; solemn*.

adverb. A word that modifies or qualifies a verb, adjective, or adverb, often answering a question such as *how? why? when?* or *where?*: e.g., *slowly; fortunately; early; abroad*. (See also **conjunctive adverb**.)

adverbial phrase (or **adverbial clause**). A group of words modifying a verb, adjective, or adverb: e.g., *The dog ran with great speed*.

agreement. Consistency in tense, number, or person between related parts of a sentence: e.g., between subject and verb, or noun and related pronoun.

ambiguity. Vague or equivocal language; meaning that can be taken two ways.

antecedent (or **referent**). The noun for which a following pronoun stands: e.g., *cats* in *Cats are happiest when they are sleeping*.

appositive. A word or phrase that identifies a preceding noun or pronoun: e.g., *Mrs. Jones, my aunt, is sick*. The second phrase is said to be **in apposition** to the first.

article. See **definite article, indefinite article**.

assertion. A positive statement or claim: e.g., *The data are inconclusive*.

auxiliary verb. A verb used to form the tenses, moods, and voices of other verbs: e.g., *am* in *I am swimming*. The main auxiliary verbs in English are *be, do, have, can, could, may, might, must, shall, should*, and *will*.

bibliography. 1. A list of works used or referred to in writing an essay or report. 2. A reference book listing works available on a particular subject.

case. Any of the inflected forms of a pronoun (see **inflection**).
Subjective case: *I, we, you, he, she, it, they*
Objective case: *me, us, you, him, her, it, them*
Possessive case: *my/mine, your/yours, our/ours, his, her/hers, its, their/theirs*

circumlocution. A roundabout or circuitous expression, often used in a deliberate attempt to be vague or evasive: e.g., *in a family way* for "pregnant"; *at this point in time* for "now."

clause. A group of words containing a subject and predicate. An **independent clause** can stand by itself as a complete sentence: e.g., *I bought a hamburger*. A **subordinate** (or **dependent**) *clause* cannot stand by itself but must be connected to another clause: e.g., *Because I was hungry, I bought a hamburger*.

cliché. A phrase or idea that has lost its impact through overuse and betrays a lack of original thought: e.g., *slept like a log; gave 110 per cent*.

collective noun. A noun that is singular in form but refers to a group: e.g., *family; team; jury*. It may take either a singular or plural verb, depending on whether it refers to individual members or to the group as a whole.

comma splice. See **run-on sentence**.

comparative. An approach commonly used in religious studies to compare religious traditions, texts, myths, and rituals. May also refer to a type of essay that employs this approach.

complement. A completing word or phrase that usually follows a linking verb to form a **subjective complement**: e.g., (1) *He is my father*; (2) *That cigar smells terrible*. If the complement is an adjective it is sometimes called a **predicate adjective**. An **objective complement** completes the direct object rather than the subject: e.g., *We found him honest and trustworthy*.

complex sentence. A sentence containing a dependent clause as well as an independent one: e.g., *I bought the ring, although it was expensive*.

compound sentence. A sentence containing two or more independent clauses: e.g., *I saw the accident and I reported it.* A sentence is called **compound-complex** if it contains a dependent clause as well as two independent ones: e.g., *When the fog lifted, I saw the accident and I reported it.*

conclusion. The part of an essay in which the findings are pulled together or the implications are revealed so that the reader has a sense of closure or completion.

concrete language. Specific language that communicates particular details: e.g., *red corduroy dress*; *three long-stemmed roses.* (Compare **abstract language**.)

conjunction. An uninflected word used to link words, phrases, or clauses. A **coordinating conjunction** (e.g., *and, or, but, for, yet*) links two equal parts of a sentence. A **subordinating conjunction**, placed at the beginning of a subordinate clause, shows the logical dependence of that clause on another: e.g., (1) *Although I am poor, I am happy*; (2) *While others slept, he studied.* **Correlative conjunctions** are pairs of coordinating conjunctions (see **correlatives**).

conjunctive adverb. A type of adverb that shows the logical relation between the phrase or clause that it modifies and a preceding one: e.g., (1) *I sent the letter; it never arrived, however.* (2) *The battery died; therefore, the car wouldn't start.*

connotation. The range of ideas or meanings suggested by a certain word in addition to its literal meaning. Apparent synonyms, such as *poor* and *underprivileged*, may have different connotations. (Compare **denotation**.)

context. The text surrounding a particular passage that helps to establish its meaning.

contraction. A word formed by combining and shortening two words: e.g., *isn't* from "is not"; *we're* from "we are."

coordinate construction. A grammatical construction that uses **correlatives**.

coordinating conjunction. See **conjunction**.

copula verb. See **linking verb**.

correlatives (or **coordinates**). Pairs of correlative conjunctions: e.g., *either/or*; *neither/nor*; *not only/but (also)*.

dangling modifier. A modifying word or phrase (often including a participle) that is not grammatically connected to any part of the sentence: e.g., *Walking to school, the street was slippery.*

definite article. The word *the*, which precedes a noun and implies that it has already been mentioned or is common knowledge. (Compare **indefinite article**.)

demonstrative pronoun. A pronoun that points out something: e.g., (1) *This is his reason*; (2) *That looks like my lost earring*. When used to modify a noun or pronoun, a demonstrative pronoun becomes a **demonstrative adjective**: e.g., *this* hat, *those* people.

denotation. The literal or dictionary meaning of a word. (Compare **connotation**.)

dependent clause. See **clause**.

diction. The choice of words with regard to their tone, degree of formality, or register. Formal diction is the language of orations and serious essays. The informal diction of everyday speech or conversational writing can, at its extreme, become slang.

direct object. See **object**.

discourse. Talk, either oral or written. **Direct discourse** (or **direct speech**) gives the actual words spoken or written: e.g., *As Müller once said, "He who knows one, knows none."* In writing, direct discourse is put in quotation marks. **Indirect discourse** (or **indirect speech**) gives the meaning of the speech rather than the actual words. In writing, indirect discourse is not put in quotation marks: e.g., *He made clear that studying a variety of religions is essential to understanding any one religion in particular.*

ellipsis. Three spaced periods indicating an omission from a quoted passage. At the end of a sentence use four periods.

essay. A literary composition on any subject. Some essays are descriptive or narrative, but in an academic setting most are expository (explanatory) or argumentative.

ethnography. Common in anthropology, the study of particular people, groups, or communities using fieldwork.

euphemism. A word or phrase used to avoid some other word or phrase that might be considered offensive or blunt: e.g., *pass away* for *die*.

exegesis. A word meaning *to draw out*, used to describe the interpretation of a text. An *exegetical paper* is one in which a student studies or interprets a particular passage of a text. Often used interchangeably with *interpretation*.

expletive. 1. A word or phrase used to fill out a sentence without adding to the sense: e.g., *To be sure, it's not an ideal situation.* 2. A swear word.

exploratory writing. The informal writing done to help generate ideas before formal planning begins.

fused sentence. See **run-on sentence**.

gender studies. The exploration of ideas, texts, and traditions from the vantage point of gender; includes *feminist* and *womanist* approaches.

general language. Language that lacks specific details; abstract language.

gerund. A verbal (part-verb) that functions as a noun and is marked by an *-ing* ending: e.g., *Swimming can help you become fit.*

grammar. The study of the forms and relations of words and of the rules governing their use in speech and writing.

hypothesis. A supposition or trial proposition made as a starting point for further investigation.

hypothetical instance. A supposed occurrence, often indicated by a clause beginning with *if*.

indefinite article. The word *a* or *an*, which introduces a noun and suggests that it is non-specific. (Compare **definite article**.)

independent clause. See **clause**.

indirect discourse (or **indirect speech**). See **discourse**.

indirect object. See **object**.

infinitive. A type of verbal not connected to any subject: e.g., *to ask*. The **base infinitive** omits the *to*: e.g., *ask*.

inflection. The change in the form of a word to indicate number, person, case, tense, or degree.

initialism. See **acronym**.

intensifier (or **qualifier**). A word that modifies and adds emphasis to another word or phrase: e.g., *very tired*; *quite happy*; *I myself*.

interjection. An abrupt remark or exclamation, usually accompanied by an exclamation mark: e.g., *Oh dear! Alas!*

interrogative sentence. A sentence that asks a question: e.g., *What is the time?*

intransitive verb. A verb that does not take a direct object: e.g., *fall*; *sleep*; *talk*. (Compare **transitive verb**.)

introduction. A section at the beginning of an essay that tells the reader what is going to be discussed and why.

italics. Slanting type used for emphasis or to indicate the title of a book or journal.

jargon. Technical terms used unnecessarily or in inappropriate places: e.g., *peer-group interaction* for *friendship*.

linking verb (or **copula verb**). A verb such as *be*, *seem*, or *feel*, used to join subject to complement: e.g., *The apples were ripe.*

literal meaning. The primary, or denotative, meaning of a word.

logical indicator. A word or phrase—usually a conjunction or conjunctive adverb—that shows the logical relation between sentences or clauses: e.g., *since*; *furthermore*; *therefore*.

misplaced modifier. A word or group of words that can cause confusion because it is not placed next to the element it should modify: e.g., *I only ate the pie.* [Revised: *I ate only the pie.*]

modifier. A word or group of words that describes or limits another element in the sentence: e.g., *The woman with the black hat donated a million dollars.*

mood. 1. As a grammatical term, the form that shows a verb's function.
Indicative mood: *She is going.*
Imperative mood: *Go!*
Interrogative mood: *Is she going?*
Subjunctive mood: *It is important that she go.*

2. When applied to literature generally, the atmosphere or tone created by the author.

non-restrictive modifier (or **non-restrictive element**). See **restrictive modifier**.

noun. An inflected part of speech marking a person, place, thing, idea, action, or feeling, and usually serving as **subject**, **object**, or **complement**. A **common noun** is a general term: e.g., *dog*; *paper*; *automobile*. A **proper noun** is a specific name: e.g., *Martin*; *Sudbury*.

object. 1. A noun or pronoun that completes the action of a verb is called a **direct object**: e.g., *He passed the puck*. An **indirect object** is the person or thing receiving the direct object: e.g., *He passed Marcus* (indirect object) *the puck* (direct object). 2. The noun or pronoun in a group of words beginning with a preposition: e.g., *at the house*; *about her*; *for me*.

objective complement. See **complement**.

objectivity. A position or stance taken without personal bias or prejudice. (Compare **subjectivity**.)

outline. With regard to an essay or report, a brief sketch of the main parts; a written plan.

paragraph. A unit of sentences arranged logically to explain or describe an idea, event, or object. The start of a paragraph is sometimes marked by indentation of the first line.

parallel wording. Wording in which a series of items has a similar grammatical form: e.g., *At her wedding my grandmother promised to love, to honour, and to obey her husband*.

paraphrase. Restate in different words.

parentheses. Curved lines enclosing and setting off a passage; not to be confused with square brackets.

parenthetical element. A word or phrase inserted as an explanation or after-thought into a passage that is grammatically complete without it: e.g., *My musical career, if it can be called that, consisted of playing the triangle in kindergarten*.

participle. A verbal (part-verb) that functions as an adjective. Participles can be either **present** (e.g., *speaking to the assembly*) or **past** (e.g., *spoken before the jury*).

part of speech. Each of the major categories into which words are placed according to their grammatical function. Traditional grammar classifies words based on eight parts of speech: verbs, nouns, pronouns, adjectives, adverbs, prepositions, conjunctions, and interjections.

passive voice. See **voice**.

past participle. See **participle**.

periodic sentence. A sentence in which the normal order is inverted or in which an essential element is suspended until the very end: e.g., *Out of the house, past the grocery store, through the school yard, and down the railway tracks raced the frightened boy.*

person. In grammar, the three classes of personal pronouns referring to the person speaking (**first person**), the person spoken to (**second person**), and the person spoken about (**third person**). With verbs, only the third-person singular has a distinctive inflected form.

personal pronoun. See **pronoun**.

phrase. A unit of words lacking a subject-predicate combination, typically forming part of a clause. The most common kind is the **prepositional phrase**—a unit consisting of a preposition and an object: e.g., *They are waiting at the house.*

plural. Indicating two or more in number. Nouns, pronouns, and verbs all have plural forms.

possessive case. See **case**.

post-colonialism. The study of texts, traditions, and ideas in light of colonialism and its effects.

prefix. An element placed in front of the root form of a word to make a new word: e.g., *pro-*; *in-*; *sub-*; *anti-*. (Compare **suffix**.)

preposition. The introductory word in a unit of words containing an object, thus forming a **prepositional phrase**: e.g., *under the tree*; *before my time.*

pronoun. A word that stands in for a noun: e.g., *she*, *this.*

punctuation. A conventional system of signs (e.g., comma, period, semicolon) used to indicate stops or divisions in a sentence and to make meaning clearer.

reference works. Sources consulted when preparing an essay or report.

referent. See **antecedent**.

reflexive verb. A verb that has an identical subject and object: e.g., *Isabel taught herself to skate.*

register. The degree of formality in word choice and sentence structure.

relative clause. A clause introduced by a relative pronoun: e.g., *The man* who *came to dinner is my uncle.*

relative pronoun. *Who, which, what, that,* or their compounds, used to introduce an adjective or noun clause: e.g., *the house* that *Jack built;* whatever *you say.*

religious texts. See **sacred texts**.

restrictive modifier (or **restrictive element**). A phrase or clause that identifies or is essential to the meaning of a term: e.g., *The book* that my aunt gave me *is missing.* It should not be set off by commas. A **non-restrictive modifier** is not needed to identify the term and is usually set off by commas: e.g., *This book,* which my aunt gave me, *is one of my favourites.*

rhetorical question. A question both asked and answered by a writer or speaker to draw attention to a point; no response is expected on the part of the audience: e.g., *How significant are these findings? In my opinion, they are extremely significant, for the following reasons. . . .*

run-on sentence. A sentence that goes on beyond the point where it should have stopped. The term covers both the **comma splice** (two sentences incorrectly joined by a comma) and the **fused sentence** (two sentences incorrectly joined without any punctuation).

sacred texts. Texts that are considered authoritative or enlightening to religious movements or faith communities. Also referred to as **religious texts** or **scripture** in some traditions.

scripture, scriptures. Terms meaning *writing* and *writings.* Often used to denote Christian and Jewish religious writings (e.g., their respective Bibles) though the terms can apply more broadly to other religions' texts.

sentence. A grammatical unit that includes both a subject and a verb. The end of a sentence is marked by a period, question mark, or exclamation mark.

sentence fragment. A group of words lacking either a subject or a verb; an incomplete sentence.

simple sentence. A sentence made up of only one clause: e.g., *Joaquim climbed the tree.*

slang. Colloquial speech considered inappropriate for academic writing; it is often used in a special sense by a particular group: e.g., *dope* for "good" or *diss* for "disrespect."

split infinitive. A construction in which a word is placed between *to* and the base verb: e.g., *to completely finish*. Many still object to this kind of construction, but splitting infinitives is sometimes necessary when the alternatives are awkward or ambiguous.

squinting modifier. A kind of misplaced modifier that could be connected to elements on either side, making meaning ambiguous: e.g., *When he wrote the letter finally his boss thanked him*.

standard English. The English currently spoken or written by literate people and widely accepted as the correct and standard form.

subject. In grammar, the noun or noun equivalent with which the verb agrees and about which the rest of the clause is predicated: e.g., *They swim every day when the pool is open*.

subjective complement. See **complement**.

subjectivity. A stance that is based on personal feelings or opinions and is not impartial. (Compare **objectivity**.)

subjunctive. See **mood**.

subordinate clause. See **clause**.

subordinating conjunction. See **conjunction**.

subordination. Making one clause in a sentence dependent on another.

suffix. An element added to the end of a word to form a derivative: e.g., *prepare*, *preparation*; *sing*, *singing*. (Compare **prefix**.)

synonym. A word with the same dictionary meaning as another word: e.g., *begin* and *commence*.

syntax. Sentence construction; the grammatical arrangement of words and phrases.

tense. A set of inflected forms taken by a verb to indicate the time (i.e., past, present, future) of the action.

theme. A recurring or dominant idea.

thesis statement. A one-sentence assertion that gives the central argument of an essay.

topic sentence. The sentence in a paragraph that expresses the main or controlling idea.

transition word. A word that shows the logical relation between sentences or parts of a sentence and thus helps to signal the change from one idea to another: e.g., *therefore; also; however*.

transitive verb. A verb that takes an object: e.g., *hit; bring; cover*. (Compare **intransitive verb**.)

usage. The way in which a word or phrase is normally and correctly used; accepted practice.

verb. That part of a predicate expressing an action, state of being, or condition that tells what a subject is or does. Verbs are inflected to show tense (time). The principal parts of a verb are the three basic forms from which all tenses are made: the base infinitive, the past tense, and the past participle.

verbal. A word that is similar in form to a verb but does not function as one: a participle, a gerund, or an infinitive.

voice. The form of a verb that shows whether the subject acted (**active voice**) or was acted upon (**passive voice**): e.g., *He stole the money* (active). *The money was stolen by him* (passive). Only transitive verbs (verbs taking objects) can be passive.

Bibliography

Alexander, Patrick H., John F. Kutsko, James D. Ernest, Shirley A. Decker-Lucke, and David L. Petersen, eds. *The SBL Handbook of Style*. Peabody, MA: Hendrickson, 1999.

Baker, Sheridan, and Laurence B. Gamache. *The Canadian Practical Stylist*. 4th ed. Don Mills, ON: Addison-Wesley, 1998.

Barnes, Rob. *Successful Study for Degrees*. 2nd ed. London: Routledge, 1995.

Barnet, Sylvan. *A Short Guide to Writing about Art*. 10th ed. Upper Saddle River, NJ: Prentice Hall, 2010.

Beal, Timothy. *Religion in America: A Very Short Introduction*. Oxford: Oxford University Press, 2008.

Bloom, B.S. *Taxonomy of Educational Objectives, Handbook I: The Cognitive Domain*. New York: David McKay, 1956.

Brown, Scott G. *A Guide to Writing Academic Essays in Religious Studies*. London: Continuum, 2008.

Broyles, Craig C., ed. *Interpreting the Old Testament: A Guide for Exegesis*. Grand Rapids, MI: Baker Academic, 2001.

The Chicago Manual of Style, 16th ed. Chicago: University of Chicago Press, 2010.

Cottrell, Stella. *The Study Skills Handbook*. Palgrave Study Guides. 3rd ed. Houndmills: Palgrave, 2008.

Cunningham, Lawrence S., and John Kelsay. *The Sacred Quest: An Invitation to the Study of Religion*. 5th ed. Upper Saddle River, NJ: Prentice Hall, 2010.

Drew, Sue, and Rosie Bingham. *The Student Skills Guide*. 2nd ed. Hampshire: Gower Publishing, 2001.

Ford, David F. *Theology: A Very Short Introduction*. Oxford: Oxford University Press, 1999.

Fromm, E. *To Have or to Be?* 2nd ed. London: Sphere Books, 1979.

James, William. *The Varieties of Religious Experience: A Study in Human Nature* [1902]. New York: Simon & Schuster, 1997.

Light, Richard J. *Making the Most of College: Students Speak Their Minds*. Cambridge: Harvard University Press, 2001.

Madden, Frank. *Exploring Literature: Writing and Arguing about Fiction, Poetry, Drama, and the Essay*. 4th ed. New York: Longman, 2008.

MLA Handbook for Writers of Research Papers, 7th ed. New York: Modern Language Association, 2010.

Phillips, Estelle M., and D.S. Pugh. *How to Get a PhD: A Handbook for Students and Their Supervisors.* 2nd ed. Buckingham: Open University Press, 1994.

Publication Manual of the American Psychological Association. 6th ed. Washington DC: American Psychological Association, 2010.

Race, Phil. *How to Get a Good Degree: Making the Most of Your Time at University.* Buckingham: Open University Press, 1999.

Segal, Robert A., ed. *The Blackwell Companion to the Study of Religion.* Oxford: Blackwell, 2006.

Seinfeld, Jerry. *SeinLanguage.* New York: Bantam, 1993.

Shepherd, James F. *College Study Skills.* 6th ed. Boston: Houghton Mifflin, 2002.

Shepherd, James F. *RSVP: The College Reading, Study, and Vocabulary Program.* 5th ed. Boston: Houghton Mifflin, 1996.

"Taught MA Handbook, 2009–2010," *Durham University, Department of Theology and Religion*; available online at www.dur.ac.uk/resources/theology.religion/postgrad/TaughtMAHandbook.pdf.

Trimmer, Joseph F. *Writing with a Purpose.* 12th ed. Boston: Houghton Mifflin, 1998.

Turabian, Kate. *A Manual for Writers of Term Papers, Theses, and Dissertations.* 6th ed. Chicago: University of Chicago Press, 1996.

Vyhmeister, Nancy J. *Quality Research Papers: For Students of Religion and Theology.* 2nd ed. Grand Rapids, MI: Zondervan, 2008.

Walker, Janice, and Todd Taylor. *The Columbia Guide to Online Style.* 2nd ed. New York: Columbia University Press, 2006.

"What Does My Letter Grade Mean?" *Trinity Western University Academic Pages*, available online at http://twu.ca/academics/resources/faq/lettergrade.html.

Index

THE MAKING SENSE SERIES

Margot Northey with Joan McKibbin
MAKING SENSE
A Student's Guide to Research and Writing
Sixth Edition • *Celebrating 25 years*

Margot Northey, David B. Knight, and Dianne Draper
MAKING SENSE IN GEOGRAPHY AND ENVIRONMENTAL SCIENCES
A Student's Guide to Research and Writing
Fourth Edition

Margot Northey and Judi Jewinski
MAKING SENSE IN ENGINEERING AND THE TECHNICAL SCIENCES
A Student's Guide to Research and Writing
Third Edition

Margot Northey, Lorne Tepperman, and Patrizia Albanese
MAKING SENSE IN THE SOCIAL SCIENCES
A Student's Guide to Research and Writing
Fourth Edition

Margot Northey and Patrick von Aderkas
MAKING SENSE IN THE LIFE SCIENCES
A Student's Guide to Research and Writing

Margot Northey, Bradford A. Anderson, and Joel N. Lohr
MAKING SENSE IN RELIGIOUS STUDIES
A Student's Guide to Research and Writing